GRAY LINES ACROSS TIME

GRAY LINES

ACROSS TIME

The story of Marion Gray in World War I
Originally written in 1925, never published

Marion L. Gray *and* Don Lorenzen, Jr.

© 2021 Don Lorenzen
ISBN 978-0-578-25947-4

2nd Edition, 10-2022
ISBN 978-0-578-25947-5
E-BOOK ISBN 978-0-578-25953-6

Library of Congress Control Number: 2022919333

CONTENTS

1. A High School Senior 1916 *1*
2. An Evening With Eve *8*
3. An Average Week *11*
4. The Basket Social *18*
5. Life After High School *25*
6. On My Own *36*
7. My Path To The Army *47*
8. Camp Kelly — Texas *67*
9. Park Field — Tennessee *76*
10. Moving Toward Overseas *95*
11. Aboard Ship to France *101*
12. Moving Toward The Front *107*
13. My Army Life In France *112*
14. Adventures Passing Time *128*
15. First Taste of Shelling *137*
16. To the Front *154*

17 Verdun *163*

18 Special Mail *177*

19 War's End and Waiting *185*

20 Back To The USA *203*

21 Post-War And Working *208*

22 Visiting Eve *210*

23 Back To Work And The Five And Ten *213*

Marion Gray, image from high school yearbook

1

A HIGH SCHOOL SENIOR 1916

Lucky indeed is the boy who can remember all that he has been taught, and so separate the chaff from the grain, to find the happy medium in life. While it is generally right to do some things, and wrong to do others, under certain circumstances, right becomes wrong. If one could happily separate such instances, to <u>always</u> do the correct thing, life would certainly be one grand time. It takes nerve too, developed in our youth, and I was to gain quite a lot. Nerve, fortitude, it must be developed and takes a lifetime.

I was born in the hills of southwest Wisconsin, and grew up near there. By my teen years I was in nearby Freeport, Illinois. I was thinking along that line, as I sat slumped in my seat of the senior history class. Lafe, the instructor, was so nicknamed because his initials were L.A.F. Larry, some middle name, and the F standing for Fulwider, principal of the Freeport High School. He was teacher extraordinaire in this class on so called Modern History.

Lafe was one of those happy persons with a keen insight into most matters, and with intellect enough to so administrate this and school for the best results. He was short, about forty years old, and a Spanish American War veteran. This was supposed to be a class in Modern History for the last year or senior students in the high school. Today was a fair example of the way Lafe generally conducted class. After three years of cut and dried teaching from the standard text books, this session was taught partly by stories, and made us, the audience for an hour of impromptu life, enjoy the lecture by Lafe.

"Nerve is a mighty fine thing to have", said Lafe, "if you use it wisely. The things that I know about best, of course, are gleaned from my experiences. I'm going to share a few of them with you."

The class settled itself back into our seats, some of them stacking their books, so as to write notes behind them. Others were very plainly disinterested and dozing. Lafe had his own way of waking them up! It was his theory, freely told to the class, that of these seniors seated before him, only a select few would attend college. For the rest, the days of forced study were over. They were preparing to step out into the world of life and business, as the term closed in a few weeks at the end of the school year. So, to all of the class he expounded a measure of responsibility. He would give them things over which to ponder, lessons to review and examples to follow. But it was up to them whether they paid any attention or not. Life itself would be their instructor after graduation, and would mark their scholarship cards entirely on how they applied themselves. So, Lafe would not force this class to study but that was for these seniors alone. To the other classes, he was a martinet; a military disciplinarian, likely stemming from his time in the military.

"When I first came to this school", he began, "I was a cigarette smoking fiend. Perhaps you may have heard some of your older siblings, friends, or parents speak of it. I practically lit one after another. I could hardly resist from smoking in class, and was nearly discharged for it! More than once I was called on the carpet by the school board, but my teaching must have offset my vice for they retained my employ. I did finally quit smoking though, when I saw how it was affecting my health. And when I did quit, I quit cold, right then. It took plenty of nerve, and many a night I walked the floor with my nerves fairly jumping, and aching for a 'coffin nail'. I finally won out, and I was glad that I succeeded."

"Many of you boys that are now playing around with cigarettes in hidden alleys, are going to be challenged in a similar manner. Will you be able to quit when the time comes? Do you have the personal fortitude? And if you think you are lacking nerve, you can build it by studying your weak points and applying yourself to the work of reinforcing them. Any person, of normal mind, by applying himself to any study in which he is weak and become an expert. Persons who are nervous, jumpy to minor noises can practice and find a solution so as to play with dynamite without blinking."

Lafe was leaning back in his heavy oak desk chair, talking almost to himself. Hands behind his head, feet on the desk, looking at the ceiling, paying no attention to the class, drifting into his own thoughts. He took no heed of students tittering, note taking, whispering, giggling unless they became a true distraction. He was in his own world.

"There is another kind of nerve, also," went on Lafe, "for instance, when I was first appointed principal of Freeport high school, there were several boys who were bigger than I was, and they naturally considered them stronger. Perhaps they were, for I am a little shrimp and never had excelled in any sport."

Lafe was a short, slim chap, small, graying hair but neat with the self-satisfied attitude that in other might be called conceit.

"These boys decided that they were not going to be bossed in school or anywhere by a little shrimp that they felt they could beat, so they laid in a trap for me one night. We still have similar boys in the school now, likely, always will have such. In general, students are more respectful toward teachers than a few years back." He continued.

"One afternoon it happened that the chemistry teacher, a short, chubby fellow, about half the size of Mr. Lutes [the present teacher], stayed after school with me, till nearly dark. We were busy in the office and the front window was up a few inches. Now that window is just around the corner, on an offset from the front steps, and perhaps the boys out on the steps did not realize that we could hear them. Perhaps they brazenly didn't care and wanted to scare us with their talk. Anyway, we could hear them planning to give us a beating, and me a good trimming! The chemistry teacher they didn't count. He could've left alone, but chose to stick with me. We discussed it and decided to retreat by dropping out of a rear window and skipping off."

"But when we got to the back of the assembly room, ready to open a window, I happened to realize that such a stunt would only prolong the punishment. It would be showing a white feather, letting these boys know that they had gotten my goat. Running once would lead to repeated ducking and dodging these boys into the future. No sir, I had to settle with this bunch at once. So, I told the chemistry teacher just how I figured my plan. We went back to the office, flashed the office lights on, the hall lights also indicating that we were still present. They must have thought that they had us scared, for they kept waiting. Finally, I put on my coat and hat, and told the chemistry teacher to follow me. We snapped off the lights and went to the front door. After fussing around a moment so that the boys knew we were coming out, I jerked the door open, stepped out, and down the steps right toward one of the biggest boys. He was the gang leader, and the rest waited for him to start something. But before he had a chance to open his mouth, I bumped into him and nearly knocked him off his feet, and I trotted on my way. No apology was given, I was careful to act as though I hadn't even noticed that I had bumped into anything. The chemistry teacher followed me, and by the time that bunch of fellows gathered their wits, we were a block away.

"And do you know, the leader was so upset by the nerve I had shown, that somehow they never attempted to lay for us again. The rest of the boys had been waiting on the leader to initiate action and took no individual action."

"That," concluded Lafe, "is another kind of nerve, but of course it usually takes a little luck to put such stunts over."

I, as usual, was studying some other lesson during this period, but held one ear open listening to Lafe. Nerve, I was hearing more of this. I had felt my self-confidence, nerve, or fortitude growing. Myself, I know that I would never be able to put such a stunt over on any faculty. I was too slow a thinker. Yet, I was good in all my class work. I owed that dedication to my mother, for she was putting me through school, at a time I thought I ought to be working, helping her earn our family livelihood. I had so little spending money that left me more time to focus on gaining knowledge. Yes, I was good in my classes, at figuring problems but any ordinary kid could out speak, or outsmart me in everyday life.

I was no bookworm, for I rarely took a book home to study. I usually got the edge on my classes during the first week or so in the school year and just stayed ahead. My teachers rarely called on me to recite, and I was often studying one lesson while I should have been reciting a previous one. When others were reciting Geometry, I was preparing for the next day's lesson, or even further ahead. But I always knew the problem before the class. A few times I did get caught but the idea is that I was getting good marks, getting my lessons done and keeping ahead of the gang. At anything where I had a chance to study things out, I always was ahead of the rest.

Eve Williams just passed me a note, before Lafe's class started, and during his lecture I answered it. She sat in the seat next to me and we often used this class for our correspondence. Eve was my weakness, and as my girl, was not expensive, for she knew the limited source of my funds. Wednesday, Friday, and Sunday nights were reserved for us by mutual consent.

She had asked in her note, "Are you going to take me to the Junior Class circus tonight?" Just like her, we understand each other, and she was direct, never hinted at her intention. "Yes", I responded, "I will call for you about seven. XX." That was my response, if you know not what the XXs meant, well, I'll not explain.

Usually when school affairs were scheduled, our dates were made several days in advance, if at all, for it was usually taken as a matter of course that we went together, though often Eve could go when I could not. There times, she'd go solo, or with her girlfriends.

Some people say that the course of true love is never smooth, and lately ours had not been. Money, or the normal lack of it, was often the cause. With the little spare change I possessed, I had earned. There were many things to consume the extra funds I had, so often I could not take Eve to places where others would go. Eve felt since this was her final year in high school, that she be able to attend most social affairs than were possible for my means, and she seemed to resent my frugality.

Just now, I was figuring on a white pair of trousers that I would need for graduation exercises, and also a dark serge coat. I could get a complete serge suit for $10. Quite a nice one at that, but the white trousers would be extra and I did not want to ask Mother for help. Better go without first, not that she would refuse me if she deemed it necessary. She was liberal with what she has, but she's already done so much for me already. As an adult, I should increasingly be paying my own way.

My Father had died when I was but nine, while we were living in Grand Rapids, Wisconsin. He had just survived a bad case of blood poisoning the prior year, back in Freeport, Illinois. He then moved us north to Grand Rapids, and bought an acre of land near the fairgrounds, and started as a small contractor building and selling homes. With the first house partially completed, he contracted typhoid from an infected water well. His system weakened after the blood poisoning, he succumbed to typhoid.

The little insurance we had barely paid for the funeral expenses and there was not quite enough left to finish the house. Mother borrowed three hundred dollars, and completed this first home. After trying various businesses for a year, like a small truck farm, we returned to Freeport, where she worked in a restaurant, washing dishes, cooking some, and earning $4 a week. Later she worked as a pastry chef and now as the night short order cook in the Horseshoe café. She worked twelve hours a day, 7 days a week for the princely sum of $16 a week, and with board included, came to about $20 per week. This was about twice what most laboring men earned.

About six months after my father died, my little sister, April, died of influenza. Upon reflection, that must've been very difficult for Mother. This left Mother, Henry, 14, and myself 17. Mother kept us together, put us through school and after three years back in Freeport, she even managed to repay the three hundred dollars she had borrowed in Wisconsin. As oldest, I was keenly aware of how she managed to do all this. I felt partly responsible for her, and had been willing to go to work to support the family, but she was firm that I complete high school. Henry, as lively as I was quiet had been expelled from grade school and was now working at a local garage.

I was thinking over such things when Eve passed me another note, "You look kinda sleepy. Did you work at the restaurant last night?" I answered, "Yes, Walt, who worked there, had taken his wife to a show last night. That was how I earned the money for the Junior Circus tonight".

When I was twelve, I had started working in the kitchen with Mother, washing dishes, for which I earned $8 a week all during summer vacation, I sure earned it! Tall, skinny, yet big boned and strong, it was a man's job I did carrying all the steel boxes with dirty dishes, washing them over the hot tubs of water. That was a start, and each summer I made around $100 to help pay my way thru school and buy clothes.

On Saturdays now, I help the dishwashers at the restaurant, earning $1.50 for that, better than the $8 per week rate! Often, at least once a month, the night head waiter, Walt, took an evening off and I learned to work in his place from 7 until midnight. He was fair, paying me $2 those evenings. And that $2 was my pocket money, under duress of the Junior Circus tonight with Eve!

The Junior class, each year, hosts a banquet for the graduating Seniors, and of course, such an affair costs quite a bit. The Circus tonight was to raise money for the banquet. And we, as Seniors, were excited to expect a great spread of food, and were supportive that the Juniors raised enough money. Therefore, it was necessary that we spend money and set a good example!

I was day-dreaming, meanwhile, Lafe was droning on with a third adventure. "There is still one more example I remember, where my nerve helped me out of a situation. During one summer vacation, I went with another teacher sightseeing up in Canada. We landed in Quebec on a Thursday, and when we got up to the historic fort, on the plains of Abraham, overlooking the city and St Lawrence and Charles rivers, we found that we could not get in until Saturday, when it was opened for sightseers. We did not wish to wait until Saturday for this fort was one of the main reasons we'd traveled to Quebec. The fort covers 40 acres, and is one of the oldest, and strongest forts commanding control over the river traffic, this side of the Atlantic. If any students here ever happen to be in Quebec, be sure to visit it. Even if you have to stay longer to gain entrance. We couldn't get in that day, so we did the next best thing, we walked the outside walls. Along one wall we found some long ladders in place, for stone masons making repairs. As soon as I saw them, I suggested that we go up and view the area from the top. None of the workmen were in sight, neither on the ladders, nor along the wall. It was noon and we might get a good view of the inside and the surrounding area before being chased down! My friend was afraid to try it, so up I went. Lord but those were long ladders, at least forty feet long! I got to the top, and the view was wonderful! With a clear, dry day I could see for miles around, appreciating the view and the importance they provided as a fortress. I don't know how long I would have stayed up there but suddenly some soldier down inside caught sight of me! "Get down from there!", he bellowed. Believe me I got down in a hurry when he pointed his rifle at me!

Lafe smiled, reminiscing. "He forgot to instruct me where to descend, so I climbed down inside, instead of outside. The soldier was peeved but I soon proved that I was but a sightseeing teacher, so he escorted me to the front gates, where I found my friend. He was scared after seeing the soldier escorting me with the rifle in my back! My nerve had allowed me to see more than my share. We returned on Saturday, and visited the fort with the other public visitors."

I believe that Lafe's lectures on nerve that day started me on the road toward improving my own nerve; response to challenges. I knew I was bashful, except with Eve, and I was lacking in nerve confronting other boys. True, I played on the football team, and in my athletic contest I was always on the first squad but I was never the best. I had a place about ten numbers from the top and there I stayed, no matter what game. I was as strong as any of the boys, faster than most, and younger, graduating high school still 17. I did not have that brash nerve that gets one by in tight places. This is where I missed my father. It was the tricks and guidance in development that I missed. In any game, when sober study was needed, I succeeded, but if suave, smooth nerve was needed, I was a loser. It was just that added sureness and punch that I lacked to put over touchdowns and be a leader! Right then I figured that practice and observation would sooner or later make me perfect. This was my weak spot and I could improve myself here. That night I initiated to improve my nerve.

2

AN EVENING WITH EVE

At seven pm, I called at Eve's flat on Galena Street and received a shock. When Eve opened the door, I had been planning the evening's budget during the mile walk down town. I figured we could get by on one dollar. I did have two dollars from the work last night. I had it with me, but anticipated keeping the other dollar toward my suit. "Oh Marion", said Eve, "Wilma Rayburn wanted to stay over tonight for the circus, so Mother asked her to share my room. Will it be alright for her to go with us?". My only possible answer was, "Sure, of course", as I envisioned the other dollar being consumed!

After a recent quarrel, we had just made up and now here was an extra girl to pay for at the circus, which may be cause for another discussion, later. Wilma lived out of town, and always took the interurban car home after school, but tonight she was planning to stay with Eve, and I would spend every cent I had. Any other boy may have gracefully pleaded poverty and stayed on the one dollar, but I could never squirm out of such things. The fact that she couldn't chip in, never came up. Oh well.

Mrs Williams, Eve's mother, had but one daughter at home and no sons, she seemed to take me on as her son. In some way she seemed to sense that I was not anxious for another girl to tag along. She tried to show sympathy in small ways; she offered me a piece of cake that she had been saving for the next day. It was kind, but I was not hungry, and the girls were ready, so we left.

Wilma in school was only a plain dressed, countryfied young gal. Certainly, her dresses always showed poorly done seamstress work, and of gaudy colors, chosen by folks with poor taste. As is usual when a boy has no father, I'd become quite knowledgeable of lady's fashions from Sunday walks with Mother.

My Mother was good at sewing, her dresses and colors reflected good taste and appearance. Like any woman, when she noticed a poor-quality dress, she worked so much and had few friends, I became the receiver for her observations. Tonight, Wilma's look in her best dress somehow offset the slight dress imperfections. Her curly brown hair, made up for once, formed a foil for her brightly colored dress. Wilma's healthy stout frame, contrasted nicely with Eve's slim, lean body. Her soft, easy smile contrasted nicely with Eve's quick, sharp grin.

When we started up the street I walked in the middle, arm-in-arm with both ladies. In a dark section of the street, I practiced my nerve by placing an arm around each of them. Receiving no objections, I continued that walk, maybe part repayment for having to host two girls to the circus. I squeezed Eve's hand, she squeezed back. I did the same on Wilma's side, and she squeezed back also!

The circus was fun, and a financial success, no reason not to. Held in the attic in the high school, the Juniors had been practicing their stunts for weeks with many varied attractions. Admission for each stunt or sideshow, was one to five cents. Some booths sold candy kisses and ice cream, though with reduced portions. Most of the stunts were of the same order, some quite similar but it was a fund raiser, so all good. The monkey booth was placarded on the outside, "WORLD'S GREATEST MONKEY SHOW", "A REAL BABBOON", "ALMOST HUMAN", "DOES EVERYTHING BUT TALK"! I paid fifteen cents for the three of us to peer thru a section of bars only to see a beautifully framed mirror at the back of the cage…five cents apiece, three monkeys! There were many booths of a similar nature.

Later on, we found some booths that were more creative and entertaining, so we had a good time, then headed home. Of a curse, Eve suggested going to the Palace, a local student hangout and confectionary shop. The owner, Jim Dickes, was a high school sports supporter, and hung team pictures on the walls, mine included, as part of the football team. Eve's suggestion left me with 32 cents, tallying an expenditure of $1.68 for the evening.

As so often can occur, a silver lining appeared. Eve's back porch had a swing, which we occupied until midnight, with me planted between two such nice girls. Not to be partial, when I kissed one, I was obligated to pivot and kiss the other. When Eve got a bit cool, I hugged Wilma closer. After that, the cost of the evening was more palatable; I almost got my money's worth!

Wilma had never paid much attention to the boys, and with approaching graduation, it never occurred to me that she might be hunting in earnest for some male. Me, because of my poverty and hardworking upbringing, had been protected from girls. It was here I could use some fatherly guidance. Any smooth-talking girl could twist me around their finger, with me enjoying it for the time being. Not that Wilma was putting anything over, as yet. No, she was merely gaining experience and testing her powers over males in the moonlit evening.

Altogether it was a nice night, and while walking home I decided that I really didn't care how much Eve might kick about the night's performance. I figured that we were even, for she had invited Wilma, while knowing that I could ill afford to pay for two girls and I preferred my regular girl alone.

As for Wilma, she was not a good typist in our stenography class, so was planning to marry after high school, instead of looking for office work. Having no regular fellow to date, since she lived out-of-town, where meeting young guys is increasingly difficult, let alone having them call on her. It appeared she was just starting after one. She could be attractive when she wanted to be, and had just started to try. She seemed a bit too easy for my taste, and I was bashful and inexperienced. A tougher, fast working girl could have put me in her pocket, so for Wilma, that was that.

3

AN AVERAGE WEEK

Sleeping and dreaming, I awoke still very tired the next morning. At six I had to be up, and by six thirty arrive seven blocks away lighting off a furnace fire. That furnace fire job paid me 50 cents per week. I then had to be home by seven, or there about, so I could make breakfast for Henry & I. Mother usually came in on the seven twenty street car which always stopped in front of our house. She was a long-time customer, and only a new motorman would take her to the end of the line, a block further on.

Usually, mother sat for a cup of coffee with me, and told me about the night's happenings in the diner. Henry was always drowsy, slow to awaken, and had to catch the same car on the return trip, but was first to finish his breakfast. I would start the coffee and oatmeal when I got up. Henry would get up, eat and leave. We were all used to the black coffee made strong, like in a restaurant, and oatmeal without milk. If I caught an early bakery wagon, we often had a berry pie. That was our breakfast. Milk was hard to keep and I had not used it since I was a baby. We used it only when making oyster stew, mmm.

Henry was just leaving when mother arrived, "Morning Ma! Bye!". His usual greeting given on a run to the lower corner to catch the street car heading back into town, after turning around at the end of Homer Street. "Morning Ma!", I said. "Wonder if Walt is going to lay off any more this week" Or when is his next lodge meeting night? I had to spend more on the Circus last night than I'd planned, and I need to earn more for my new suit. Any special news last night?"

I don't know about Walt.", mother said as she slipped off her shawl and poured her coffee. "Pretty quiet all night. Shows must be unpopular in the theatres, for the show crowd was smaller than usual, but of course, the usual crowd showed after the saloons closed!".

Mother always had the news of night long before anyone else, for besides being the largest restaurant in town and main night place, the Horseshoe was headquarters for the policemen on their beats. News came in through such channels. Often, I heard some cop, on a cold night, call from the restaurant phone and report in as if calling from another beat! Two or three cops doing this from the same phone to the desk sergeant gave a misleading view of city activities. Coffee was always free to both cops and streetcar motormen. The cop on our beat got his meals free also! That's the stuff that made the Horseshoe so popular! In return, the restaurant got the best of protection, and Mother's streetcar rides were free. Henry rarely paid for his rides also but I was too proud to accept anything not due me. When I was with Mother, her rides were free, but I felt like a freeloader getting it free.

If there were any fires, murders, robberies, or such, Mother was first to hear of them at the restaurant, well ahead of the rest of the city. So, each morning, back home, she relayed the news to me at home over coffee, and would bring some leftovers to share also.

"I do hope we never get mixed in this war business," she said, "There was a little fellow in last night who had been in the Canadian army. The boys had been buying him drinks to get him to talk. He sat there till four o'clock this morning, telling tales about what his experiences and what he'd seen. He claimed to have been wounded thirty times, and he had a wooden leg and lost one arm. After the rush was over, I got the kitchen cleaned up by one thirty, left the door open so I could hear him. He was swearing a lot, telling all, but he didn't know I was listening. I sure hope you boys don't ever have to fight like that!".

Hearing from Mother, I wasn't thinking much about the war. I was too busy with school, and Eve kept my spare thoughts busy. I did hate to have Mother work where she had to listen to the swearing, but I knew such colorful vernacular was part of restaurant clientele, especially late after the saloons closed. However, the moment a customer got too colorful in their language, either Walt or the other front-end man would shut him up in a hurry. They took good care of the 'widder', as they referred to Mother. And likewise, the 'widder' took pretty good care of them too, for Mother not only ruled her kitchen, but as everyone knew, if anything went wrong in the front, she fixed it for she ruled that area too. Walt had found out who was boss when he tried attending a few early morning poker games at one time, leaving the front-end either unattended, or in the hands of a green helper. The 'widder' stopped that quick! Mother was a wonder in a kitchen. Clean as a pin, tall and as strong as me, and not afraid to hurt herself cleaning up. She had a memory like a clock, and would handle thirty or forty short orders all at the same time, working like a flash, never bothered, and never seeming in a hurry. The kitchen had been rebuilt to her suggestions, and was about half the size of most restaurant kitchens, but because of her organization and saved steps, allowed increased efficiency. Other restaurants had food wait times of thirty to forty minutes, and made her wait times of five to ten minutes unbelievable! Many long-time customers, left weekly tips for the 'widder'.

By seven thirty in the morning, I was out of the house, for I had to check on my furnace again, and make sure it was working properly on my way to school. At noon, I again stopped in, on my way home.

Eve was frosty to me this morning. In front of Wilma last night, she had tried to act all right, but now it was obvious she was peeved, and showed it. When we met in Lafe's class, she wouldn't even look at me. When I passed her a note asking her, she responded, "Yes, I'm peeved and why not? If you want to kiss Wilma so badly, go ahead, but don't bother me."

I responded, "You made me take her along. I did not invite her, so blame yourself."

For three days, she didn't speak to me. Wilma, of the other hand, was nice. It was "Marion," this and that till I ducked out of the way when I saw her coming my way. "Marion" may be all right for girl's name, but lord pity the poor fellow who has it wished on him. In a few places, I suppose, several boys may draw that name simultaneously, and over time will recognized as a boy's name. But when one happens to be the only boy in a town the size of Freeport, which was about 20,000, it sure bodes poorly. I had to be either a sissy or a roughneck. In grade school, I was a sissy, until I grew, so that in the seventh grade I came to be called 'skinny' and 'sissy'. Finally in high school, at five-foot, ten inches, and playing as a sub on the football team, my moniker adapted to more of a roughneck image.

Football was strictly a roughneck's game. The boys who had called me Sissy, when I met them on the street, they would edge over to bypass me. One boy, in particular, always crossed the street when he saw me coming. Not that I cared nor even guessed why he crossed at first, until one day I met him in a crowd and overheard his remark to his pal, "Gee, we used to call that big fella 'Sissy', at Saxby school and now he plays on the football team. Now he could wipe up the whole bunch of us with one hand!" Somehow that odd bird so admired the football team, that I could not hold it against him, but then again back then, I had been a sissy! I'd been a bookworm and class scholar, and not a sports fanatic.

I was beginning to realize that "Marion" was a name that was a sweet one for a girl but I was going to need nerve to keep from being kidded by the boys. The correct spelling for the girl's version is "Mariam" but no one seems to realize that.

Friday, June 2nd, I marked on the calendar. It was the last time Eve and I spent a pleasant evening together. That was the night of the annual high school band concert at the Odd Fellows Hall. Each band member was given a free ticket to use on their girl or mother. Mother was working and planned to attend graduation in a couple weeks so skipped the concert. At school that morning in Lafe's class, I had placed my free ticket on the front edge of my desk for all to see. Eve, to my right had not been speaking to me for a few days, said nothing. She caught sight of it after several other girls invitingly held out their hands but she turned away when I waved it around as if suggesting a bidding war. It was valued at fifty cents, but Lafe blew into class before I could close a deal.

In class, Lafe was off on another story telling oration today so we sat back and played around as he described visiting the NY Wall street stock market pits. How the tickers worked, and how the laws of supply and demand controlled the price of various stocks and commodities. "For instance," said Lafe, "If the papers report a bumper crop of cotton one day, prices are apt to go down on all things made from cotton, blankets, sheets, clothing, etc. But if in a few days there were reports of damages on the crop from weather or insects, then the price would increase due to the reduced supply. Here Lafe sat suddenly erect. He had been leaning back, looking at the ceiling as he talked, with his feet on his desk. It was his favorite position for these lectures. Now though, the class had been getting too noisy and as he sat up, he picked out one group in particular, centered about pretty little Blanche Goss.

"Now you girls are always interested in dresses, suppose you, Blanche, tell me what the meaning would be if the newspaper this morning said that dress goods would be increased twenty points". That type of question was one of Lafe's teasers for the one who never paid attention in his lectures. Blanche had no idea as to what the lecture had been about. All that she heard was "dress goods", and "going up twenty points". So, as she stood up to answer Lafe's question, she stammered, "Well, I guess it would mean that dress styles had changed and dresses were to go up by twenty points, or twenty inches". Dress styles were each year getting shorter, but it was a moment before Blanche thought what she had said, and realized what a sensation her shorter dress would make, especially by twenty inches"! She plopped back into her seat, laid her head on her arms on the desk, and cried. Lafe and the rest of the class just howled.

During the five minutes of laughter that followed, Eve managed to push one of her books off of her desk on my side, and pretended not to notice it. I finally bent over to retrieve it, and then she bumped into me while I came up with it. That was one good way of getting together after a fight, and we both considered our fuss as over. By lagging behind when class was over, I managed to earn a half arm hug as we walked up the narrow desk aisle.

Blanche had been one of the girls making the noisiest bids for my band concert ticket, and Eve had especially noticed her bids, as she sat just behind Blanche.

"That was a peach of a joke on Blanche, wasn't it?" I asked.

"Served her right for trying to steal my man for tonight", Eve responded, "But maybe now you will want to take her in one of the new style dresses?".

"Nope, my eyes couldn't stand the shock! I'll be after you at seven. What kind of dress will YOU wear?", I asked.

"A real long one. I'll be ready at seven", she replied and hurried off to her next class.

Freeport royally supports its high school and the high school band responds by supporting every city event. Thus, most of the citizens had often heard the band free-of-charge during the school year but most were willing to pay to hear it this time and so the hall was comfortably filled tonight. After I had seated Mrs. Williams and Eve, I hurried back behind stage and up the stairs to where the boys were assembling.

Finally, the curtain went up, and twenty-seven of us presented a nice Sousa march. Our band usually had nearly forty members but Director Hiatt had cut it down to the best players for this event, and that the stage was too small for all forty of us.

Miss Provoost played two piano selections and Chet Langenstein played a very good trombone solo, but the real feature of the evening was an oration about the "Future of the American Negro", by George Lipscomb. He was a colored boy, our band's percussion snare drum player, and the only colored kid in the high school. He certainly is a wizard! His oration had won one prize already, and he looked like he might have a future as a colored orator.

For some reason a uniform seems to impress the girls. After the concert, and when Mrs. Williams trotted off to bed at 10 o'clock, leaving her door ajar in lieu of a chaperone, it was a bare two minutes before Eve was snuggled in my lap in their big wicker rocker.

Eve asked, "Marion, what are you going to do after you graduate?"

"Honey, I really don't know. I haven't any particular thing that I'd like to do, better than others. I do want to get a good job, and start to save some money. How much do you think we are going to need?" Tacitly it was understood that I had to save some money after I went to work, if we were to have a home. Miss Eve's little black eyes narrowed, and remained firm when she said that I would need at least two thousand. She herself was going to get an office job, typing if possible and save all that she could.

"Gosh, two thousand is a lot!" I replied, "And I'll bet that about the time I get half, some curly headed gink will come along and you'll start out with him. Have your heard from your farmer lately?"

"Yep," she whispered, "He wants me to come down there on my vacation and live with my sister and her hubby, after school is out. Are you jealous?"

"Just a little bit." I answered, "I know he has money, and a farm that you said his dad was going to give to him, while I have got to go easy on the little that I can earn until after graduation. You see that's why when I had to spend so much for the Junior Circus, that night made me mad, because I don't want to borrow from Mother. I still need new clothes for graduation."

"Well, I didn't want Wilma to stay that night, but when she asked me, what could I do?" That was Eve's defense.

"It's past now, so let's forget it," I said, "and we did, till the town clock could be heard striking eleven, and even then, I waited until I could hear Mrs. Williams stirring about in her room, and finally she tossed a slipper out through a crack in the door. THAT meant that she was awake and that eleven o'clock was plenty long enough for us out in the front room with no chaperon. So, I slipped on my cap, buttoned up my coat, with my horn in one hand, the other hand lost somewhere around Eve, we took another ten minutes in the hall before I finally tore myself loose and headed for home. The William's were rather lenient with us in allowing our dates to stretch to eleven! Usually other boys I knew were "shooed" home at ten-thirty!

The next day, Saturday, I worked as usual at the Horseshoe, and then that night Walt laid off again, getting spring fever, I guess, and I worked till 1a.m. covering for him. Sunday morning, I trotted out again to work covering the regular dishwasher's job all day, skipping out for a bare half hour to monitor Mrs. Weiss's furnace. That furnace was hard to manage sometimes, when football or basketball seasons were on. Sometimes Henry had to work it for me. The restaurant always let me off when the games were held on Saturday.

If you wondered, the Horseshoe restaurant was named that because the counter was U-shaped, like a horseshoe.

Monday started the last regular week of school, and was my pay day from Mrs. Weiss. When she gave me my half dollar, she told me that it was getting so warm that she and her daughter would keep a small fire in the grate when necessary, indicating that this job would be ending. She did want me to clean the basement room up, and other odd jobs and paid me another fifty cents for those tasks. They'd taken three afternoons and also tipped me twenty cents!

Wednesday found me with a princely sum of six dollars and twenty cents from the recent few days of labor. Thus, with the few dollars I had saved since the Junior Circus three weeks before, I promptly send to Sears for a three dollar and a half pair of white trousers which were to be part of the uniform to be worn by the senior boys for commencement. After sending that off I had five whole silver cartwheels left, and with luck by mid-month I'd be able to buy me a $9.50 blue serge suit at Walton's or Vaupel's clothing store downtown. I would have liked one of the $15 suits advertised by the tailor shop but it was beyond my means. I figured on the blue serge coat going with the white pants to make the dark coat and white pants outfit that the senior boys had voted on for a uniform. Later the serge would make a good suit, and I needed one.

4

THE BASKET SOCIAL

Eve spoiled my plans, for she had some church meeting to attend Wednesday. Then Thursday she asked me to take her to a basket social at the Embury church. I had been figuring on making all my dates with her at her home for a few weeks to conserve funds printing pictures she'd taken or making sea foam candy, which she was wizard at making! Her fudge was good too. This social was likely to cost me 30 or 40 cents from my small hoard.

"All right," I answered her note detailing the social, "but for love of Mike, don't ring in any other girls, because I need my money badly right now." I was lucky and made over five dollars last week, so I can go tonight. Somehow, she had failed to tell me about the social until the last moment, which was unusual for her, but in the rush of getting her graduation dress ready, I thought that she had probably forgotten it.

The William's flat was on the second floor above a grocery on Galena Street and Eve met me half-way up the stairs. Tears were in her eyes, as she whispered, "Please Marion, don't act mean but Hellen Timms just phoned me at 6 o'clock, asking to go to the church with us tonight because she didn't have anyone to go or come back with. Her Mother did not want her to be on the street alone so late. You won't have to buy her basket, but don't you DARE say anything mean!"

"Oh heck," I said, "And I wanted you all to myself tonight." And then for some reason, Eve got on her high horse, so that while I was waiting for her and Helen to powder their noses and get their coats, she would not even hint as to the color nor makeup of her basket. A word on these baskets, they're filled with food and goodies made by each girl member of the class, nicely decorated, but without names on them. They would put a sealed identifying card inside. Placed on a main table and sold by bid to the highest bidder. The high bidder would then eat with the girl who'd made the basket. The money went to the girl's Sunday school class treasury.

Mrs. Williams mischievously waved a sprig of green leaves at me, a bit of red ribbon, tinsel, and white tissue scraps on the table so I had some idea of the basket identity later. Each girl carried her own basket, concealed by wrapping paper, and when we arrived at the church, opposite the high school. The baskets were all hidden under a cloth on a table. One girl, acting as leader, unwrapped them secretly while everyone was in another room.

The church owned a small moving picture machine and a few films and the entertainment the girls class offered consisted of the showing of these two short films. The movie was dragged out by the operator till we were sick and tired of it, finally the lights were snapped back on and we back to the large room where the baskets awaited. Ready to be auctioned off. After unwrapping, I was unable to tell which basket might be Eve's. She was so tight to her friends leaving me alone, I honestly didn't care if I selected her basket. Only one or two of the boys were high school boys and even these were almost strangers to me. Eve promptly joined one select bunch of girls, leaving me alone to entertain myself.

The Mrs. Jamison, Sunday class teacher acted as the auctioneer, and started off by asking that the boys please start the basket bidding at a quarter. She explained each basket should be worth at least that and I just KNOW you boys want to demonstrate to the girls the great effort that the girls put in, making them, and the good things in them! That quarter specification base made me feel that perhaps the bidding would not go too high, and I would get without spending too much. I noticed that there were eighteen to twenty boys and seven or eight more girls. This meant that several boys would have to bid on more than one basket, hardly fair, but it is a fundraising event. I let the bidding on the first basket go by just to see what these other boys intended to pay.

"Now what am I offered for this one?", said Mrs. Jamison, holding out a beauty. It looked like a large hamper, and was trimmed neatly, decorated well! By looks, it appeared to be one of the best baskets.

"Twenty-five", said a voice weakly.

"Thirty-five," then someone leaped it up, "Seventy-five cents!"

"One dollar!!" Just like that, four bids and over a dollar. My heart flopped, so I held off bidding. That basket went to some drowsy looking odd fellow, who looked rather out of place among all the youngsters.

"Who is that?", whispered a boy in front of me. "Some half drunk, old girl chaser", said his pal, "I don't see what they let him in for, or why they let him bid. Someone said he'd been in jail recently, after getting some girls in trouble." The old drunk certainly pushed up the bidding, for the next five baskets went for over a dollar. The first one held the record at one dollar ninety while the others gradually came down to just above a dollar. Cautiously I watched till a plainer basket let the bidding lag, and I got it for eighty-five cents. It must have belonged to some unattended girl, for each boy was bidding his own girl's basket up until he got it — or else the drunk got it. Twice I saw some earnest bidder withdraw when a basket price traveled above his limit.

I was peeved at Eve and really at all this event, it was plainly a money-making affair with us boys as the goats. Boys attend and spend money, often too high and feel a goat, or those that didn't attend would be goats. The drunk bought five baskets so I suppose that was a better use of his money, but put all prices higher. I expect without his participation, baskets would have sold for fifty or sixty cents.

I was feeling mean again, and spiteful, and at the last I bought another basket. That only cost me forty cents, making a total a dollar and a quarter for the evening. I really ought to have kept quiet but, like several boys, buying two baskets helped, and I wanted to have two girls to spite Eve! I was not sure but I thought her basket probably was not in the two that I purchased since both were plainly trimmed. I recalled from what I'd seen, that Eve did more. I could not be sure until I opened them but they were not the same size as the basket she'd hidden under its wrappings at her home.

Sure enough, I drew two girls, both strangers to me, and I was careful not to look for Eve as these girls came up and introduced themselves. Each girl had their names in their basket and was supposed to eat with the purchaser. So, we three took one end of one table for ourselves and I seated myself, back to the crowd. I didn't want Eve to think I was interested in her, nor the fellow she was eating with, but there I was fooled. For as the girls opened their baskets, acting as hostesses, someone dropped into the seat next to me. It was Eve's friend, Helen Timms, and she had tears streaking down her face. "P-p-p-lease, Marion, go out to the hall and talk to Eve. She's waiting for you." And then Helen laid her face down on her arms, sobbing loudly. I couldn't imagine what was wrong, and I hustled to the hallway, leaving the two girls to care for Helen.

Eve was in one corner, struggling into her coat, also with tears coursing down her cheeks. I slipped one arm about her, and used my clean handkerchief to dry her tears.

"S'matter kid?" I asked.

She laid her head on my shoulder, and sobbed out her story. "Th-th-that old bum bought our baskets. And we-we-were supposed to eat with him. B-b-but I just can't do it, and I WON'T! Why they'd all talk. He has got one girl in trouble, been in jail over it. I don't see why they let him in!" She quit crying for a moment, and continued; "We'll go on home, and just leave him. You eat with your girlfriends and I'll call you up tomorrow, I don't think I'll be in school. I don't feel like going tomorrow."

Just then four boys came out in the hall looking for me. We might be strangers but I played on the football team and so they knew me. It was peculiar at that, for Freeport is one town where the high school sports and activities become front page stuff. We might have been a state college team in the manner that the town and local boys followed us. During the football season, win, lose, or draw, the whole story was a headline item on the front page, and one whole side column was reserved for details. Even the small boys on the street proudly waved at me, and then related it to their dumber comrades, "That's Gray, he plays on the football team." Even my brother Henry's proudest boast was, "That's MY brother. He plays on the football team."

As shy as I am, it always made me feel funny, to have everyone look up to me just because I was on the team. I was not a star player, but that didn't matter. I was 'on the team.' Therefore, these four boys were looking to me as a leader.

"Say, Gray, what'll we do with that old chap?" asked one of them. "He paid for his baskets, so we can't kick him out. Who let him in anyway?" It wasn't difficult to figure out what to do.

"Well then, I guess that we'll have to buy them back and maybe re-auction them. That's all I see to do." That was my suggestion, but it'd mean disaster to my five spot, at least in part!

"How'll we do it, all chip in or how?" chimed one fellow.

"Well,", I answered, "Let's find out how much it will take, and I think I've enough to buy two baskets, if you all can raise enough for the other three baskets."

"All right, you fix it up." They replied in unison, passing the buck to me. Rather, they looked to me to act as a leader and arrange it.

As we went inside, I could see that this incident had almost broken up the party. For the girls were clustered around Helen and the other three unfortunates, while the boys were grouped nearby. The old chap, sitting by himself with only his five baskets for company, with his blinking eyes, trying to figure out what the problem was. Somehow, he sensed that his presence was the cause of the commotion. His continued blinking, bleary eyes revealed he was trying to figure out what to do.

As I walked over to him, I could plainly hear the supportive remarks being made nearby. Their confidence in me put my shoulders back, if that were possible, and made me walk straighter. Heavy lifting in the restaurant had given me rounded shoulders, and I probably looked like a bum myself, instead of the proud hero I fondly envisioned as I walked toward the old sot. The old fellow looked up at me with a rather scared look, for he could also hear the loud whispers from the nearby boys group watching us. In the otherwise quiet room, the whispers carried quite well, "Here comes Dolly Gray",

"He'll take care of the old bum",

"He oughta be kicked out, the darned drunk!",

"Who let such a drunk in, anyway?",

"Gray'll take away his baskets ad kick him out of a window if he gets sassy. He's on the football team!"

Those and other kindred remarks followed me, and clearly the old fellow heard them as well as I did. "Sorry, old chap," I said, leaning across the table toward him, "but you must have forgotten that this is a Sunday School social, and these Sunday School girls don't like the smell of whiskey." "Of course," I continued rather apologetically, "You don't look to me like you've had too many drinks but the girls do mind it, and we'll need to buy back their baskets. How much did you pay for them?" He was eager to please, and started fumbling for his pocketbook to figure what he'd spent. However, by asking the five girls what they'd gotten, and adding it up, we figured it well ahead of the muddled fellow figuring it out. Counting out the money from our group of boys, we repaid him, collected the baskets and went back to our tables. The old chap didn't check our count, he pocketed it and rapidly waddled out.

Eve's basket was a beauty, as was Helen's and to top it all off, I had to chip in all but a nickel on the third basket. After collecting from the other boys, the self-appointed collector had been shy seventy-five cents. I chipped in on that, taking my last cent. The seventy-five-cent basket was the smallest of the five that had caused all the trouble, but it was plenty large for me. Anything that could get my last penny looked like a mountain to me!

It was a quiet group of five girls that sat with me. I felt far from hungry myself, which was unusual, but in decency to the girls, I tasted a bit from each basket. The class did really serve coffee free, and even that tasted terrible to me, as used as I was to my own strong brew and also the black coffee at the restaurant. The girls were profuse with their thanks, all but Eve, and she was quiet. In one way, I felt somewhat like a hero tonight. Really thinking it over, also I felt like a prize boob, and I had but little respect for this class. It was the first social affair that they had given which I had attended and they looked like graduate gold-diggers to me. I was hard pressed to maintain a decent attitude for I felt like snubbing the entire group and walk out.

One peculiar thing, to me, then and later was that of all these working boys, earning a weekly wage, there had been so little change left when it came to paying off the old fellow. I had seen several boys pool funds, or even borrow from one another to get certain baskets. I had not dreamed that these boys were carrying so much less money than was I. It all made me think less of the girls that had engineered the whole affair. Apparently from this little talk I heard several girls had come without escorts, figuring on a small ad in the paper being sufficient to bring in the outside boys but the only uninvited guest had been that old fellow. They generally agreed that it had not been properly planned. Regardless, such speculation couldn't bring back my five dollars.

On the way home, Eve was extremely quiet. High-tempered as usual, she knew all too well that the greatest part of the night's trouble would never have been caused if she had shown me her basket in the first place. Yet she was too proud to admit it, nor show that she realized it. It was rather late notice from Helen, when she planned to attend the social with us. So rather than go on to her home way out on Stephenson Street, she decided to stay with Eve. It was after midnight and I said a short goodbye at the foot of the stairs, not even trying to steal a good night kiss, though Helen was anxiously trying to slip up the stairs, to leave us alone for a minute, if we cared to be.

I was angry. The farther I walked, the worse I felt, so that mile walk home seemed like it was ten times longer than usual. I didn't sleep a wink that night. I slipped off my outer clothes, put on my bathrobe and then sat and tried to read a book. My bathrobe was a beauty, one of the few really nice things that I had. Mother had made it for me, out of the small flags that came with the package of cigarettes. It was certainly a colorful garment, and had been made without cutting a single flag. I was proud of it but that night I was so careless thrashing about, that I tore a small hole in it. Over and over, I reviewed my thoughts about the fine show I had made of myself that night. Spending like a fool, every cent I had saved. All that I had needed to same my money, had been the nerve to tell Eve that I could not go. Oh yes, I blamed myself for going, for buying two baskets instead of one, and also for being the goat for the girls when their baskets went to the old drunk. But I also blamed Eve for her part in the fracas, and especially I find fault with the entire class for the manner in which they had conducted the entire social.

So, all night, I tossed and turned, trying to sleep then getting up, lighting my lamp, trying to read and giving up again. If it had not been for waking the neighbors, I would have gotten out the cheap cornet I had bought last summer or have played my alto. That belonged to the school but I kept it at home. After learning it at school, I had bought the cornet with some extra money I had earned the prior year.

The next day I slipped into my seat in the assembly still feeling blue and peeved and had about decided that Eve was no girl for me. She came by my desk and laid a note on it. She must've written it before leaving home that morning. In it she had nerve enough to try and give me a calling down for not observing the basket hints her mother had provided to identify her basket. If I had watched and bought her basket, it would never have happened so she wrote.

Somehow, I got through the last few days of the school year. Dazed by the effects of the social and the note I had written and heartsick because I had made a mistake and also an apology, I stumbled on thru my last classes, skipping many, keeping strictly away from Eve, even plainly turning away so as not to even pass close to her in the halls.

5

LIFE AFTER HIGH SCHOOL

Lafe called me into his office one morning and said that he was being asked by several businesses and pick out graduates of that year's graduating class for positions in town. He offered me a chance in a lawyer's office but the pay, of four dollars a week, was too small even for me. I had to get out and support myself from now on. So, after explaining to him that I must help Mother, he then picked out another job and sent me down to see the manager of the Five & Ten store. There, after listening to the manager, Mr. Minerd, relate a two-hour oration of the glories of the Woolworth Co., and the prospects for advancement open to beginning employees. Sounded good, so I accepted work there for $8 per week. Thus, with a job cinched, I borrowed six dollars from Mother, to buy my suit. With my other work, I made enough to get past the commencement expenses. I felt so dazed that even the joys of commencement were blurred, and I have but few and sketchy memories of those days. I do remember that the Seniors were called over to the church to practice for the baccalaureate sermon. We had to march in to our seats, to music and after receiving instructions, we held one practice march to be sure that everyone knew what to do. While sitting in my pew, with others, listening to some dry instructions, I remembered I had some letters to get that had been mailed to me through the school. Generally, they were college advertisements, asking each graduate to consider certain colleges, etc. But this time I had received a clothing ad, and since my name was Marion, it was of women's clothing. The boys near me had been snickering about that for such outfits! I can remember the rest of the class were quite scandalized at our behavior in the church even though we were our own audience and only practicing. Trust us, we were solemn enough for the actual occasion.

My work at the Five & Ten store was mostly that of washing windows, sweeping and general porter work. I was officially assistant stock man, an aid to Joe Walls, the head stock man. We took care of the basement and all the incoming stock, while upstairs there were the manager, and the assistant manager, Ralph Gray. It was funny to find a fellow with the same last name but I soon discovered that he was from central Illinois and in no possible way related to me.

My first morning's work made my job look easy. I soon found that there was plenty to do! Usually, we were about three jumps behind ourselves, and there was never such a thing as getting caught up. At seven thirty, we four men were supposed to be at work. My first duty was to sweep off the front walks, and then help Joe fill out the orders left from the night before, by each counter girl. At first, I merely carried these orders up for Joe, and learned my way around the counters, finding out each girl's name, and the way the counters were numbered. Later I helped fill orders.

The rest of the day we had new goods to unpack, check, mark up, send samples of each upstairs, and then pack the balance away in the bins. I was surprised to see that these bins covered an area really greater than the sales floor above. The basement was under the entire store, and consisted of a small open space at the back or alley end, where the new goods came in on a slide, down the basement steps. The rest of the basement was filled with long rows of bins with aisles between. In the front end was small girls cloak room, rest room. Finally, the candy room which was section of boarded off and locked up bins.

There were five long aisles making ten long rows of bins, and more than once I would trot up the wrong aisle looking for an item, like mouse traps, and find myself amongst the bins for the drug aisle, or looking for ladies outsized stockings, and find myself in front of a bin of rolling pins!

Each aisle was lighted by electric lights, hung about ten to fifteen feet apart, and these we turned on only when needed, so that when some article was required, we had to trot up a dim, dark aisle, to a spot near where we thought the goods were, and turn on the nearest light. If I blundered in the dark, knocking over a pile of nicely stacked boxes, then there was hallelujah to pay! Every box or bin was to be lined up flush on the face of the bin. If many packages were to be stacked in one bin, one pile of each must be in front, and these must be trim and neat. Everything in the front of the bin, if possible — that was the Woolworth stock keeping system. It sure made a neat looking stockroom.

I usually had my sidewalks swept before eight o'clock, so then I would go in and start carrying up the stock baskets, that Joe had been finning in the meantime. Every night each counter girl filled out an order blank for the next day's needs and hung it on file. Joe gathered these in the morning, and taking a stock basket, which was a large clothes basket, with a cord tied to one end, to pull it along the aisles. He would trot up and down the aisles placing items the order called for. Once full, he'd place the basket at the base of the stairs for me to carry up. The filled and checked order form Joe placed on the top, for it had the counter number and the girl's name to show where it was to go. Also, it was checked so that she could tell what items were low, and what we did not have. That was so that she would not reorder, thinking we had overlooked an item. After looking the order over, and placing each item on the counter, or in the understock, directly beneath, she placed the blank in the wicket at the manager's desk so that the necessary items could be reordered.

Through these orders and the process, I became acquainted with each girl, in a manner. Phyllis, Ethel, Mabel, Maud, and so on down the line. At first it was hard to remember their names, and the counter numbers but soon I could just glance at the basket, and knew from the stock it contained to which counter it should be delivered. Then, with all the order up, I had to hep unpack the freight and express stock that might have come in by then, and in odd times bale up the waste paper that continuously came down the chute. I had been in the store but about two weeks, when the city fire inspector declared the chute a fire hazard and after that the girls brought down their paper in pails or boxes.

The baler was a big steel box which was in two sections, hinged on one side, with hooks on the other to hold it together and it had a chain and ratchet arranged to a control on a loose cover so that when the bin was filled with loose paper, the cover could be swung over and dropped in, pulled down tight with the ratchet, and a long wooden handle, and bound. Daily, there was over an hour's work at this baler and it was a man's work too in order to result in neat, tight bales. The harder one pressed, the tighter the bale got. Then the cover had to be released, and more paper put in on tope of the pressed section till enough could be in at one time to be tied. Then wires were inserted, the sides unhooked, and swung apart with the top still pressed tight. The wires were pulled tight before loosening the cover. If the bale was not pressed evenly, it might 'explode, wires breaking and flying, paper spilling out. It was a little dangerous. The tighter the pressure, the more could spill.

The paper was sold to a junk dealer and many a time I cussed the baling task for each paper box had to be torn at each corner in order to press it flat. Believe me, it seemed like there hundreds or thousands of boxes daily. The heavy cardboard cartons also had to be torn down and then they were often too large so they had to be cut or torn smaller. My hands would be tired, worn out daily but there was one blessing, as earnestly as I worked, my wrists, hands became so strong that when introduced to anyone, I had to be careful not to crush their handshake. Hard work certainly develops one's muscles. It also helps one forget, for work kept my mind completely off of Eve. True, I did dream of her, and think and plan of the wonderful things I would like to do. One dream I hopefully reviewed was that perhaps their flat may catch fire, and that I might rescue her single handedly, then leave her on her knees begging me to forgive her. Yes, then I magnanimously respond, "Certainly", and then walk off and leave her. Perhaps. Such is the life of a dreamer. And the dreamer who isn't working to keep his hands and thoughts at least partly busy, is apt to even try to carry-out his dreams. One might try but seldom succeed.

Monday and Friday nights were window trimming nights at the Five and Ten. We came back at seven, and the three of us, Mr. Gray, Joe and I worked at one or two of the big windows. Often Joe would trim one window, and Mr. Gray the other, while supervising both. I brought out vases, glass shelves, and stock up for them to display, or cut crepe paper to fit on the shelves. We would pin sheet music to hang above, serving as a valance for the upper half of the window. On window trimming nights we drew a quarter each as extra money, or supper money but since I went home, that was extra pay. Sometimes we would be through by ten o'clock thou usually it was eleven and often one or two in the morning. No matter how late we worked, the windows had to be finished and we had to be back at work on time the next day.

Saturday nights the store was open until nine-thirty, so of course, I had at least 3 nights a week that I was busy, and in a way, I was glad for it. Also, on Saturday nights, Joe dressed up and acted as assistant floor walker, while I stayed downstairs to sprinkle water through each dusty aisle and sweep up. That was a regular Saturday night job, giving the basement its weekly cleaning. But also, I had to answer the whistle, and fill orders that the girls sent down. There was a speaking tube at the back of the store, besides the little office, with a whistle in the end of the tube. The girls would blow into the tube upstairs, causing the whistle to sound. I would respond back, "Hello?" into the lower tube, and they could then convey their rush order item.

For a couple of weeks, and often thereafter, Joe had to spend half of his Saturday nights helping me find the needed stock. With the thousands of small items we had, many of these tube rush orders were for items few use, most of which I had never heard of. One girl asked for some "Takanobee candle sticks", and after finding Joe, he showed me their location. They were a green pottery candle stick, so called because they were imported from Japan or China, and called "Takanobee" on the invoice.

It was surprising to me to find so many items in the Five and Ten store that were from foreign countries. At first, I resented this, that we should stock and sell products from other countries when it seemed possible to me that our own products ought to be so much better! The newspapers constantly spoke of machinery we have in the US, and therefore we ought to be able to produce products better and cheaper than these other countries, no matter how cheap their labor was. The first time we unpacked an imported case of chinaware, from Japan, I changed my mind. I had seen the thick, heavy American ware, cheaply produced but plainly coarse and heavy. Cheap in looks and price, whilst the products from Japan were elaborately wrapped, packed and beautiful in comparison. And at half the price of American ware! I never could understand how the Japs or Chinks did it. Such fine, delicate ware, decorated ornately, and glazed. Such fine thin ware! A cup and saucer together costing only 6-½ cents! Being lighter, the freight and steamship charges from the Orient were lower; sometimes less than the freight from our home ware from Virginia.

The light, foreign wood used in their packing cases always interested me, and when the boxes were opened, the light matting of odd rush packing had to be removed. Then came bundle after bundle of the same matting. When I started to open one, I found that just the outside was matting and underneath came a half dozen each of either cups or saucers. Each wrapped up in a twist of those same odd rushes. When these were peeled off, out came the dish, wrapped lastly in newspaper.

They were foreign newspapers, and whether the words were in Chinese or Japanese, I never knew but many of those first papers I saved to review later and try to decipher the advertisements. Many illustrations, especially one for fountainpens, had the name of an American company shown in English as stamped on the barrel of the pen. I could understand that, but the cartoon and comics were Greek to me! Without being able to read the written material, I could not understand much about the comics but I studied over them just the same. Such stuff I found fascinating.

We were always careful in removing the covers on all cases, for we sold all of the wooden boxes to local firms to be reused for their packing & shipping for 3 to 10 cents each. There was a joker in these cases of China ware. Since the matting and rushes were of no value to us, and hard to dispose of, we usually repacked that back in the box before nailing them closed for resale. That is, we tried to. The problem was that by the time we unpacked and unwrapped the China ware, the packing material was fluffed up and difficult to fit into the box. Sometimes we'd reopen a nailed box to pack more waste rushes into it.

The American pottery was different. That came in barrels and hogsheads, mostly the latter. Starting with the cups and saucers on the top layers, it contained all the table ware in one hogshead. I had to learn how to unpack that stuff too. Packed in loose straw or hay, they were not even individually wrapped in paper. I was surprised that when the first hogshead arrived, Joe told me to open it on its side, not standing up. "But Joe, if we do that the blamed dishes will fall out on this cement floor when we take the lid off."

"Yes," he answered, "They will if you pull the whole cover off. Just loosen one board, and remove it, then start pulling the cups and saucers that will be on top, out through that opening. When you get all you can, reach at the top edge, remove another board and so on, till you get a start far enough in at the top so that they won't spill out. You see, that way you can crawl in to retrieve the bottom layers and by keeping a bed of straw always in front of you, any dishes that slide down, land in the straw." "Of course," he continued, "it's easier to start one of these things standing up, but then figure out how to get to the lower layers, that's the challenge!"

True enough. In order to get the bottom layers out, one would have to get right in and stand on some of the dishes, and that wouldn't do without breaking dishes. It'd also require a table next to the hogshead upon which to stack dishes. A large table at that, since the hogshead weighed seven to nine hundred pounds, sometimes up to twelve hundred pounds, requiring two men to handle it

Meanwhile, the weeks and months rolled along. With so many evenings taken up, girls bothered me but little. Sometimes on a Sunday out at Krapes Park I would meet a girl I knew slightly in high school, and perhaps walked her home.

One summer night I met Bertha Morris at the band concert by the ball park, which was being fixed up in a very fine manner. It had been the old fairgrounds, and baseball park. Now one section was laid out with shrubbery and a new bandstand, making it an ideal spot.

Bertha was a tall, robust girl, dark eyed, with frizzy black air that danced on a light breeze. Not handsome, nor pretty but still attractive, she certainly was. After talking about old school affairs for a time while listening to the band, I found that she was alone, so I naturally offered to walk her home after the concert. She readily agreed, and since the street car ride up town didn't hurt my pocket book much, we dropped into the "Palace" confectionery for sodas. In return for my trouble, I got one small kiss when I left her at her home. I'd hoped for two, and would have felt cheated in comparing them to those Eve had given. After the way Eve and I spooned by the hour, that kiss was pretty droll. Certainly, it didn't feel like those of Eve's. Eve's kisses always had more feeling behind them. I guess, having just met Bertha, I couldn't expect too much.

The next Wednesday, I tried for a return engagement and phoned Bertha for a date at the movies. We went to the Lyric theatre and after had sodas, then headed for her boarding house, where she lived with a married cousin. Bertha was interesting, describing her work in the office at the Rawleigh Medical plant, and the jokes that were pulled there often. That was nice and we arrived at her boarding house about ten o'clock, and then the joke was on us. For the cousin had gone out for the evening with her hubby, and locked the door. I didn't mind that, with such nice company, we trotted around to the side porch and an inviting porch swing, only to find it was already occupied by one of Bertha's sisters and her beau. Bertha had four sisters living there also, and each sister had a fellow. Wednesday being a popular date night, the whole blamed gang was soon in evidence, occupying every space to be found! No one had a key, so Bertha and I enjoyed the privacy of the porch railing, since there were not enough swings, chairs and rockers outside to go around.

That was the last night I called there, and I didn't even get a kiss goodbye. Five single sisters rooming with a married cousin was too much for me!

Somehow, as a rule, none of the girls at the store appealed to me. Then too, there was a store rule, prohibiting a male employee from going with any of the girls. Joe, however, was in his third year there, got away with going out with Ethyl. I could have easily gotten interested in several girls, but somehow the girls that were most attractive to me were engaged, or already had a steady fellow. Eve sometimes came in the store and several times when I happened to be upstairs, I saw her at some counter but I always avoided her vicinity. I had heard that she was in some office as a stenographer but I didn't know nor care much about it. Or I thought that I didn't.

One fine morning though, I was filling the candy order, and carrying up buckets of candy upstairs. The heaviest of these, I had to empty in the bins for the girls, and while doing so, I heard someone say, "Good morning Marion." I knew that voice and surprised as I was, I managed to stutter out "Mornin", before I rushed away. Eve's eyes were pleading in a half smile, for me to say more, but I didn't dare to. I had promised myself not to even speak to her, and tried to lie to myself that I didn't want to. I did not have the nerve to admit, even to myself, that I was still in love with her.

I knew I was lacking in fortitude, in some ways, and with steady effort, and analyzing every emotion, I was getting so that few sounds even caused me to blink. Often, we boys in the basement, being by ourselves a great part of the time, working in the darkened basement would come up suddenly on one another. I was hardly startled, even if someone played a trick and tried to shock another. I easily steeled my nerves by practice that such stunts could not make me blink.

I was paying five dollars a week board at home, and using the rest for clothes, and pleasures. After 3 months, I got a pay raise to $9 a week, and was happy! Mother, having gotten us children through school at last, relaxed enough to enjoy life a little and suddenly surprised me by marrying a little baker named Mr. Heiny Wolf. Certainly, I knew that she had received many proposals, mostly from ambitious cops or easy-going loafers who wanted a wife to support or help them. They looked with envy on her weekly income. Others from men who appreciated her for her keen mind and self, rather than from a financial standpoint. Mother, the "Widder", used to approaches, laughed them away, and I had hardly heard of this baker until they were married. It was almost a secret, for Mother kept on working for a time, got married one afternoon and few of us knew about it.

All this made me feel older. I was eighteen that August in 1916, supporting myself and unless accidents prevented me, I would in time, be a store manager, making a good salary. I didn't know what salary the managers drew but it must be a lot, for everyone seemed to think so. Too many fool kids, like myself, rush into a business and start out as an apprentice, right at the bottom of the ladder without the slightest idea of what is paid at the top. Such is life.

Outside events occupied my mind but little. True, there was a war going on somewhere in Europe, and occasionally accounts reached me of tales of daring, but I was so wrapped up in the Five and Ten store that I never thought of anything else.

Work was getting harder and harder as Fall crept along. October came and we had daily sales, often giving away articles that cost from ten to thirty cents each. Some as a "special", for a dime. I had to help upstairs often now, and one day during October I was tickled pink as a sight. We were having a granite ware sale, and one window was piled high with pots and pans, centered around large dishpans. They were really seconds, with minor blemishes, but would have cost nearly a dollar at any store. The sales always started a nine am, so as to draw in customers during the slow morning hours. At 9 o'clock Mr. Gray started off by pulling out a bunch of the smaller pans from under one counter, where they had been hidden.

Customers were waiting all over the store, not knowing what counter to go to, as all the special items were hidden below various counters. Mr. Gray let out a yell, "Here we are folks, right this way!", and then a crowd jammed in tight around that counter. In five minutes, those pans were gone and Joe yelled from another counter, and the crowd pushed his way. This method spilled the customers back and forth, giving the outside ones at one counter the best chance to get to the next counter first!

The smaller articles we sold first, and the larger held back so a good many people were waiting for the dishpans, of which we had only about three dozen, and when Joe yelled for those, he was almost mobbed! There was only one way to sell these, He would grab one up, hold it out with one hand, get the dime in the other, and then release the pan. Sometimes there was confusion, with two persons claiming a pan, and fights were to surely be avoided. We were too darn busy to settle arguments. Mr. Gray and Joe were doing the selling, for with these items, the poor sales girls would have been mobbed and jerked to pieces. The manager and I were trotting about, helping where ever necessary, and watching the other counters for shoplifters.

Finally, everything was gone except that stack in the window, and I climbed in to remove it. Mr. Gray stood at the doorway, barring it from the customers, so that they could not crush in, and passed each piece out, getting each dime as he did so. The mob was howling for the rest of the dishpans, for there were ten customers for every pan, and they knew by now that these were all that was to be had. Poor Mr. Gray had to brace himself to keep from being shut in the window, and Joe had to jam in from behind the counter, even having to walk on top of some merchandise, in order to get in there and help us hold off the crowd! It was the side window that saved us, or we'd have been in real fix! With the side counter helping, there were few customers that could reach our spot and yet these few with the crowd pressing from behind, caused Mr. Gray to slip and land in the pile of pans in the window. Luckily these were just stacked on one another, not on the glass shelves or a large, costly window may have gotten smashed, and someone hurt! I caught him, though and braced myself in the opening until he got on his feet and recommenced selling. He used his pockets as a cash register, and made no change. If the customer didn't have a dime, he passed the item to a customer who did. The girls at other counters were busy changing money, so as to give out dimes to those in need.

Finally, the last pan was sold, and we stepped out of the window display, while disappointed customers stormed around, wanting more pans. We though the fun was over, but it wasn't for out on the sidewalk an old man and a heavy woman each had one handle of one of the large dishpans, and they were in a whirling dance, each trying to shake off the other! A free fight always draws a crowd and this comic fight soon was lost in a mob of curious persons. I did want to see the end of it, but the crowd moved on up the street, carrying the human merry-go-round with it. I never did find out who won. Some chaps would have followed that fight for an hour, but it would've taken an earthquake to make me forget my duty. I was paid for working in the store, so there I remained.

The sales lasted through October, and I was glad when they were over and done. While the sales continued, we had nightly windows to trim out., often during the day too, and work piled up on every hand. Christmas goods were rolling in too, till our aisles down stairs were packed with goods and it was a puzzle where to put the new deliveries. Some of the Christmas tree ornaments had to be piled on the ledge of the main floor, atop the side wall shelves. They didn't look nice, stacked up there is odd cardboard boxes but we had to sue that space.

Joe was promoted to assistant manager, for Mr. Gray was sent to another store, and that made me head stock man, and I began to have a succession of helpers for a few weeks. One day short, squat Ed Davis came in, and since he had been in the store two years before, he was made a stockman, until the Christmas rush was over. Then he was to be sent on to another store. I didn't like that setback, but Ed had more experience that I had and so it was only fair to him. Then in January, he went to the Rock Island store, and I took charge of the stock again. Then the manager was promoted, and big tall, dark complexioned fellow came in, named Mr. Heilmann and he was as bluff and noisy as Mr. Minerd had been quiet.

One of his first tricks on me was to send me to fill an order while I busy unpacking a shipment of ribbon. When I returned, I checked over the shipment, only to find one big, ten-yard spool of 400 width was missing! I was not a dumbbell, though, for I promptly suspected that some girl had lifted it while it was lying there on the checking counter. But to make sure I repacked the shipment in the boxes they came in, and found that that showed me still one spool shy. For if that spool had never been shipped, then when repacked in their boxes, there would have been no empty space. So upstairs I trotted.

"Mr. Heilmann," I said, "Someone has taken a spool of ribbon off the checking counter, before I was checked and marked. Do you know of any samples being taken in?" I had asked Joe first, but he had not been downstairs, so he'd sent me to the manager.

"Nope," answered Heilmann, "Are you dead certain that you know how to check in that ribbon? Better go down and recheck that invoice. You know that the ribbon invoices can be rather confusing." "I've rechecked it twice, and repacked the box, so I know it's gone." I knew someone had taken it, so I stood my ground.

Heilmann, being the overbearing chap he was, said, "Dammit, I didn't ask you what you knew. Go down and recheck that invoice, and let me know when you're done."

"I'm through with it now," I said, throwing the invoice over in front of him. "I checked that stuff over twice, and I know more about it that you do!" I was angry, for his demeanor would have gotten anybody's goat, and I don't know how I found the spunk to answer him back as I did. If he had not be so coarse about it, I would have knuckled under but I flew off the handle for once, and told him who was wrong.

I expected him to come out of the office after me, and I was so mad I was ready to quit. Mr. Minerd had been such a quiet manager, always preaching and demonstrating how to do things, that I had become used to doing my work thoroughly, with great care for every little item. To have this new man questioning my ability made me boil. Especially because of the bullying manner in which he did it. But, instead of jumping on me, he laughed, "By God, Gray, if you know your business that well all the time, we're going to get on fine! I was just trying to see if I could bluff you." Then, as he came out of the office, he patted me on the back, and pulled out the missing ribbon from where he'd hidden it! "Here you are," he said, "and don't ever be afraid to talk back to me when you're sure you're correct. That's one thing I like in a chap. There are so many chances in a Five and Ten store for you to be wrong, and so many things that have to be carefully checked, that I'm damn glad to find a stockman who knows when he is right and ain't afraid to say so! You and me are going to along just fine!" And we did. For a while.

Now I had to help trim windows, and train a new assistant, and with Heilmann to bluster about, there plenty of men hired but they lasted only a few days each. Finally, I got my brother to help a bit. Henry and I ran the basement for quite a while. It was great!

6

ON MY OWN

Mother, now Mrs. Wolf, moved to Forreston, a town about 10 miles away, where her new husband, Heiny had bought a poolroom. I had to shift styles, and care for myself. At the old home on Homer Street, Henry and myself had our own rooms, and claimed the furniture in them as our own. Mother let us take that bedroom furniture and also enough other stuff to make a home of our own. Henry and I rented a four-room house up near the first ward elementary school.

That was an odd experience for me. The two us, Henry, now fifteen, and me at eighteen to have our own home. The rent was only four dollars a month, and we did our own cooking for the times when we ate there. For cleaning, an old lady next door came in every morning to sweep, make beds, etc. Work was easier now with my brother in the basement stock area, for he was unafraid to work a bit. After we had moved, I had a little more time to spare, at least I called it that. For now, whenever there was no work at the store, in the evenings I had to find something to keep me occupied.

Those lonesome evenings, with no one at home to keep me company, I began to once more think of Eve. Somehow, I could not forget her. Three times I had met her in passing, and each time she spoke, unless she happened to be with her parents. Then she would pass me by without looking nor saying a word. Then, one evening while killing time on a street corner, wondering what to do, I saw her coming down Stephenson Street.

She stopped when she saw me, and spoke, "Good evening Marion. Isn't this war going to make things awful? So many boys will have to fight, and I expect you'll be going too, won't you?" I hadn't been thinking much about any war, for though the papers were full of war news, the sinking of the *Lusitania*, and the Declaration of war by so many countries, it remained distant and impersonal to me. War had been going on in Europe for years now, but busy with high school and now my job, it meant little to me. The idea of fighting was something strange, akin to a deadly football game, I suppose.

"Well," I said, "I haven't been thinking much about it but I suppose I'll probably go after a while." She seemed willing to talk, but I moved on. I felt that I had given my word to avoid her, and as much as I wanted to talk, I feared old man Adam might see us, and know that I had broken my word to him. Somehow, my word meant more to me than anything else and I feared to break it more than I feared any beating he'd give me. I had been taught to keep your word, and it'd been drilled into my morals. The thing was Eve had planted an idea in my head, the army.

Then, after Eve was gone, I realized just what I done, and I kicked myself for not having the nerve to stop and talk. I had been forgetting my resolution to practice nervy stunts, and here my lack of nerve had cost me a fine opportunity. Then too, I realized that she had been giving me a hint, that I would be in favor if I appeared in a uniform. I knew that Adam cherished family heirlooms of the Civil war, and it was a safe bet that he was a strong Patriot, and would be proud of a soldier boy, especially one going with his daughter. He had but the two daughters, Eve and her sister, Erma, who was married and lived in southern Indiana. It appeared that Eve had intended to ask me to enlist, make up with her, and with me in uniform, she could quell her family's arguments against me. I suspected that they favored a farm boy in Indiana who would receive a nice big farm from his dad when he married. He'd jokingly mentioned it before at the William's flat but maybe he was half serious. At that, given a few more weeks, I may have made up with Eve, but the very next day I started off on another track. Rather, I was pushed for I could hardly claim that I had initiated it solely myself.

Joe was out to dinner when the basement bell rang for me. The old whistle had gone out of service, as too unsanitary and had been replaced with a modern push button bell, which was far louder, and cleaner. So, upstairs I trotted, to find that the regular music girl was ill and some tall blonde was working in her place. This new sales girl had a call for some piece of sheet music that was on the rack above the piano, but she couldn't find any copies in the understock, so she asked me to climb up and remove a packet for her. The piano was in one rear corner, and above it we had built a rack of thin poles, on which we tacked sheets and strings of the more popular numbers of the sheet music. It was a neck breaking stunt to get the old step ladder out, and teeter on it trying to reach and remove or replace any of those music play sheets. "Thanks, cutey," said the blonde when I got through, giving me a smile to boot!

"Welcome," I snapped. I was not used to having any of the girls trying to flirt with me. Generally, they treated me as just one of the servants, ordering stock from me, and howling when it wasn't delivered up quick enough. So, "Thanks" was a new word to me for such. The blonde must have asked one of the other girls for my name, for as I went out the door on my way to lunch, she was going my way also, and hailed me.

"Come on, Marion," she mocked at me with a sweet smile, drawing out and emphasizing the Marion. "Hurry up if you're going my way, and say, you've got to change your name, since Marion belongs to me!"

"What do you mean," I asked, as we both started up the street together.

"Why, exactly what I said, my first name is Marion also," she answered. "What's the matter, did you look so much like a girl that they named you that? You look like a sweet looking kid at that though. Maybe you don't taste so sweet though. I'll have to ask the girls at the store how sweet you are when you meet them in the dark aisles of the basement."

Phew! She was a fast worker! I had never been gone at by a girl in such a manner, it was all new to me, as she chattered on in the same manner all the way up the street. I couldn't get in a word edgewise. She lived but a half block below me and so it was right on my way home, to go with her.

"Gosh," I finally said, "You sure are a fast worker, such a little shrimp. I don't remember ever seeing you at school, but you talk like a high school girl."

"Nope," she cooed, "I'm from a little town in Minnesota, and I graduated from a music school in South Dakota. But you know, you're really the only good-looking boy I've seen in the two months I've been in this town. You're too cute to be let loose. I'll bet the sales girls fight over your brown eyes. How many have you got on the string, anyway?"

"You,.w-w-why you little shrimp!", I stammered. That was all I could think to call her, though she was as tall as I was, though a bit thin. She had me so buffaloed that I couldn't think straight.

"Aw, please, Marion," she chided, "Won't you at least tell me who your best girl is? I'd kinda like to fix up and beat her time."

"Well, you can't do that," I managed to say. "For you know it's a store rule for us boys not to go with the girls in the store."

She had a ready answer. "Yes, but I'm not a regular girl. I'm just working for fun, while Gertie is sick. When she comes back, I'll be so lonely, I won't know what to do. Here I am in a strange town, and I don't know a soul. That work is just fun for me, and gets me away from home for a while."

By the time we got to her house, she knew I was a recent high school graduate, and that my brother and I had a house just beyond theirs. And that must have tickled her imagination, for she waited for me on the way back to work. I'd thought on her, and managed to feel sorry for her poor, lonesome self, that I suggested a date later that week. She was not hesitant in accepting it. I was so dumb I thought I had made the date, not her! That night she would have waited for me, but since I had to sweep the store after closing, it would have been a half hour wait for her.

The next noon she was right on tap. It was raining, and we had our awnings down, making a dry spot along the store front. Here she stood, without an umbrella. She did have a light rain coat and cap, however, but waited till I came up and offered her to share my umbrella on the walk home.

"Oh!" she trilled, "Aren't you afraid to get wet?"

"Why?" I asked, as we started off walking. "I don't mind a little water, once in a while. Really, if I had all day, I'd like to play in the rain."

"But," she responded, "aren't you the least afraid of getting wet? Really?"

"Nope." I responded. "Why should I be afraid?"

"Why kid," she said sweetly, as she snuggled up against me, under my umbrella, "Don't you know sugar melts?" It was the first time I had ever heard that line, and especially directed at me, and it caught me totally off guard!

"Gwan," I answered, "You blame little teaser, I'm not sweet."

"Hmm, how do I know," she grinned up at me, "I ain't never tasted."

We were continued up Exchange Street, and turning down past the county jail, in a deserted spot, and so, what in the heck could I do, there under the tight, little umbrella, with her pair of hazel eyes asking me such a question? Did I kiss her? Ask me, yeh, go ahead. As if I'd ever tell. And what's more, blamed if I care who saw. That was the other side of Stephenson Street, the main street from where Eve lived, so it was a safe bet that she wouldn't see us. And no one else mattered. After the date the next night, I forgot to think so much about Eve. I was more interested in the present than the past, and I figured Eve as part of the past.

Mr. Heilmann kept me busy every day. Marion Goldman kept me busy the nights. Most Sundays I didn't travel to Forreston to see Mother. Those few times, I'd leave very early only to have to return that day very late. Most Sundays, Miss Marion took me out in her old touring car. It was only three years old and could travel twenty miles on one filling, and if you ran it over thirty minutes at a stretch, it got hot, and had to be stopped to cool. But it was a car, and almost the first one I had ridden in.

The war was influencing the nation, and the town. Freeport High School organized an army cadet corps, and one hundred boys bought neat gray uniforms with black trim. The band also got new uniforms to match, but trimmed with black and orange braid, the school colors. The army stationed a Lieutenant at the school, as part of the enlistment service, and also to train the new cadet corps. Where upon the alumni also promptly organized a training company under his supervision, to learn proper drilling maneuvers on Monday and Thursday nights. As an alum, and beginning to think about the war, and duty to country, I managed to be there the first Thursday night, and learned to line up by height, count off, do right and left face, and even squad formation marching left and right. That was fun, in a way, with a competent instructor, and the group all fast learners. In three Thursdays, I was quite well versed in the ordinary marching drill. Mondays remained windows night at the so could not attend. I think all this impressed Miss Marion, to some degree, but less so since it took time with me away.

But then Mr. Heilmann heard of it, and promptly changed Thursday night to window night. He suggested the reason to Joe, or rather Joe got on the reason because of Heilmann's questions, and tipped me off. Heilmann was afraid that I would enlist, and would delay or prevent that if he could. So, I nailed him after Joe passed me the news and said, "Mr. Heilmann, I want Thursday nights off. At least till nine or nine-thirty."

He looked at me kinda queer, and then asked, "What the hell for?"

"To practice army drill at the high school." I answered. "I'd like both Monday and Thursday nights off, but Thursday will suffice."

I was getting wise as to how to deal with him. By asking right smack out for two nights, and suggesting one would do, I figured I would get it. Monday nights we really had to trim windows, to clean up after each Saturday mess. Each window was old or a bit mussed up from pulling out special patterns each Saturday. Some customers are that way, especially women, you know. They want "not just a pan, that one in the window" and no other one will suffice, and so we'd drag that one out, unless it was very impossible at that moment.

Well, I expected Heilmann to give me a night off. Instead, he gave me a lecture, and brother, could he lecture! One day Joe had called me up, to stick near the office, where Mr. Heilmann had taken a shoplifter; a tramp who had been caught filling his pockets without paying. Joe was afraid the guy might start a fight and somehow every chap since football, that I'd known always figured me in, in case of a scrap. As quiet as I was, having had only two fist fights to my name in eighteen years, it seemed funny. But up I trotted, and I never did hear a such a flow of oratory any better than Heilmann turned loose on the guy! Hard-boiled, as also was the tramp, Heilmann snapped out his questions in a roar that could be heard clear out to the front sidewalk! Gradually the tramp answered, and he kept asking questions, evolving the discussion to more conversational tones, until at last there were whispering, and I couldn't hear them. And, I'll be blamed, but that tramp fellow wasn't actually crying when he left the office!

Afterward, Heilmann came out and grinned at us. "Boys," he said, wiping his sweaty forehead, "Now, THAT, was work. I knew I wouldn't get a cent out of him, but I wanted to try and see if I could make him cry. He was bawling like a baby, thinking of his old home, his mother, but he'll forget it when he gets a drink or two in him."

Now it was my turn to receive the full force of this same powerful, persuasive tongue that Mr. Heilmann directed at me. Down in a deserted aisle in the basement he took me and boy did he talk! I knew by now just how forceful he was, and steeled myself to proceed carefully listening.

"It's this damn war business," he began, "that has gotten under your hide, Gray, like it has so many other young fools Enlist! Enlist! Go win a medal! Be a hero! That's all of which you're thinking. You don't see me, or any of the older, wiser men going crazy over getting shot! And what girls going to kiss and hug a maimed young man, let alone a dead man? Sure, you may be a hero for a short time, but while the wise guy is staying home, loving up the girls, and making headway, you poor dupes want to go get killed!"

"And if you do come back, after the war is over? Think anyone will give you a fortune then? Or that you will find a wide open, easy street? Just look at the old vets from the Civil or Spanish-American wars. Sure, you can't find that any of them are millionaires, can you? At least not due to them being a soldier, anyway."

He continued, "This is a business man's war. It's a Wall Street war. Those bankers who lent money to France and England, and other countries, figuring they would win, see that they may lose, after all, so we've got to hop over and help them or those poor bankers will lose all the money they invested. But do you think the bankers are going to fight? Not on your tintype! They'll let you poor kids go and get shot up and become 'HEROES'. And you can win all the medals you want. THEY are the guys that get paid for it." "Yes," he ranted, "it'll be the farm boys, and damn fools that march away, while these bankers from Wall Street cheer them on! And when they win and come back, those same wise guys will roll around in big cars, throw ceremonial parades, and pat them on the back.

If there are any good-looking girls you think will be waiting for you when you return, just be damn sure one of those wise banker guys don't get her while you're gone."

And so on. Heilmann could talk. His keen mind picked out the points on which I could least argue. I didn't give in even for an hour. It was three hours before I said I'd wait a while, then enlist. He patted me on the back. "Good," he said, "I knew you might be young and hot-headed, but you're not a damn fool. If the war does go bad, let these other guys go first, that WANT to fight, and if you're needed later, then this draft law will go through, and you can report when the bankers and the others go. Go when you're needed, not before."

I'll always put those three hours of lecture down as a master piece. It took me a long while to pick through the faults in his arguments. Really, Heilmann was self-serving. He wanted his pet stockman kept right here. He knew I could do the work of two men. His talk was almost pro-German, giving reasons to keep me out of the war. So, I stayed on at the store, and he worked me on Monday and Thursday nights. For now.

Springtime, May 1917, and I continued with a girl named Miss Marion. That's an awful dose to take in at one wallop, especially if she's a cute blonde! You've got no idea what those three things together can do a young man of eighteen, especially after Heilmann's lecture!

I'll relate what they did to me. Among other things, we had had several assistants in the stock room. All of them were bad, or worse. One especially, Roy Selton, was a relative of some store manager, a cousin of Mr. Minerd's, I think. He was quite the pippin. We had the front furnace [there were two], torn down for repairs and since it was a pipe-less furnace, it left an opening in the floor above that was quite large, and seen down through. It was a dirt collector, and in a little used aisle so I seldom went under it. It was not until the sales girls started asking me if Roy liked the way they were dressed, that I began to get wise. Sure enough, he was spending half his time, peeking up through the floor opening to see the people, especially girls as they walked over it. I didn't think much of that behavior at all!

"Say, Roy!" I asked when I caught him, "What the devil do you think you're doing, sky gazing? Come on and do some work. If there's anything those girls wear that you really want to see, just ask them, and they'll show you. They've been telling me about this, and they said you're too bashful to ask." One of the girls must have been near the opening, for I could hear her laugh! Roy, was shame-faced.

The weird thing about it, to me, was that those girls almost seemed to like it! Blamed if they wouldn't pick on Roy for orders when they could, and follow him up dark aisles on any provocation. Girls sure can be funny, like they were inviting him on!

Things like that got on my nerves, and besides, it was spring, and I had been working hard. It takes a blonde to put the cap on anyone at such a time. One night going home, I met Miss Marion outside her home. She was crying, and I sat on the porch steps while she had her cry out.

So, all she would say is that she was afraid for the war, that so many are being swept up into the war frenzy.

Posters were appearing:

"HELP WIN BY SAVING AND SERVING! BUY LIBERTY BONDS"
"THERE'S ROOM FOR YOU! ENLIST TODAY!"

I think the war talk was all beginning to scare Miss Marion, and that I may leave. Funny, Eve wanted me to join, and Miss Marion, no. We sat and talked, she seemed calmer. I did not relate to her my discussion with Mr. Heilmann. I still wanted to join the local cadet corps, and train on either Monday or Thursdays. This I did share with her, but that I'd likely have to quit the Five and Ten, since the ultimate goal of Heilmann is to keep his store staff stable, and I suspect he'd let me go now and train a new stockman, rather than let me leave on short notice. Maybe that had Miss Marion afraid too, she was getting very attached to me, with "the cute brown eyes", as she said.

I could not figure it, but after Roy Selton arrived, everyone I knew about me seemed to be getting more and more reckless. Even before I left the Five and Ten store, I could see it, for girls that used to smile shyly and blush at a suggestive remark were beginning to use 'rough' language and give flirtatious smiles. Even before I was married, some of these quiet girls had begun to get careless as to whether they'd go up the steep basement stairs first. Now it might be the influence of the war, and dangerous times or something but they certainly were getting wilder daily!

So were the men. Even I used to practice reckless stunts such as during the unpacking of glassware, I'd set two of them on the checking table and then opened the next case. Instead of returning to the table to lay down my hammer, I'd toss back toward the table potentially breaking glass.

The next day I related my decision to attend the drill training to Mr. Heilmann, and sure enough he wanted to sack me, but I quit. Maybe that was why he'd brought in Roy Selton. Hmmm. I guess we are all disposable to management. It made me happy in reflection, that I was moving on in life, having the nerve to face such a decision. I had four dollars to my name, and would have to resolve where to go. Stay in town and maybe marry Miss Marion, or move toward Forreston with Mother. I mean, Henry, at fifteen would have to move too. Miss Marion and I had spoken of marriage.

I bumped into Eve walking from the Five and Ten. I think she almost was trying to 'bump' into me through her plan. She said she still had feelings for me and us to be together. It shook me some, as I'd become quite attached to Miss Marion. My thoughts of Eve had long faded way, and I related so and said that I was dating Miss Marion. I also expressed my interest in still enlisting in the army, of which Eve now did not think of highly. She reminded me of the opinions from Mr. Heilmann. We parted our ways kindly, always as friends. The encounter did solidify my relation to Miss Marion, and compelled my desire toward getting married, if she'd agree.

It was touching but simple with Miss Marion. I went by her house, I related the conversation with Eve, and she said she was relieved to hear that was over and no longer a competition. I then asked her if we should marry, and she was drop jawed, and excited! I spoke to her father briefly. He was understandably concerned about how this would happen, me with no job now. I related our plan for me to temporarily move to Dixon for work. He ultimately approved, and understood he'd help if I'd agree to send home money also. It was then agreed we'd go to the Justice of the Peace, and have a quiet ceremony. Her parents were not expecting to host, nor pay for any expensive event. Our ceremony was quiet, touching just her family and Henry were present, as Mother could not travel under short notice. After several days with Miss Marion, it was time to get work and begin planning, whatever would happen.

After, Henry and I packed our necessaries, and headed toward Forreston to be with Mother and stepfather Heiny. Funny, I had quit the Five and Ten to do military training on two evenings, and thus leaving town, I'd lost both! Such are the loony decisions that we make in our youth.

It was nice to see Mother and learn more of Heiny. They were congratulatory about my marriage. Mother related her first wedding was similar, nothing fancy. Her wedding to Heiny certainly was similar. Henry and I had hardly heard about that! Their business was going well, so they happily supported us, at least for me in the short term. Mother mentioned a job southwest from Forreston, in the town of Dixon. I took my four dollars and struck west by bus only to find that the position had been filled. Thus, faced with defeat, having to turn back to Mother's, probably to borrow money from Mother or Heiny, I pulled a trick I became proud of. I had walked about town in Dixon, looking for jobs when I thought of it. I promptly went to the best restaurant I could find, ordered a fine meal, and after dispatching it, I bought two boxes of cigarettes. They were the last I would have for months, for when I stepped out of the door of that restaurant, I discovered I had twenty cents less than the fare back to Forreston! So now I was compelled to either find a job, and get credit of room and board, or bum my way back to Forreston. I had never bummed rides, nor hopped rides on a freight train, and had no intention of doing so now. I was convinced to get me a job, and stay in Dixon until I did.

Yep, that was at two o'clock, and by four-thirty, I had a job in the Borden condensed milk factory! Then, with a job for sure, I managed to get credit for room and board until payday. I was proud of my 'nerve' that night. It took strong character to do what I'd done. I grew a lot that day.

My work was supposed to be as a laborer in the Borden stockroom, but the old head foreman took one look at me, asked a few questions on my ability to think and figure things out, and instead started using me as a handyman. Whenever a special man in any part of the factory was off, I filled his job until he returned. That's what he called a 'handyman'. I liked it. It was more challenging and interesting, promised more job security too. That old foreman, Mr. Gregor, must have thought I was a wizard, from the jobs he stuck me on. One day it was a caramel slicing machine, in the candy room. It was an opportunity to see how they made candy. That lasted two days, till the regular slicer returned. He found a mess, for after getting along fine for two days, I forgot to watch the wheels a moment too long, or I didn't apply enough confectioner dust on the slab of candy being run through the slicer, and it got tangled up in the slicing wheels. Oh boy, what a gooey mess! I was glad when the whistle blew while I was just beginning to clean it out.

The next day I was running a nailing machine making boxes by nailing the sides to the ends. Flip! bang! flop! bang! flip! bang! Flop! Bang! All day that same rhythm, each flip a turn of the boards, each bang as I pressed my foot down, and sent three nails into the wood. Another man was nailing bottoms on the boxes, while two of us made the sides. After filling, the tops were nailed on after the cases. The day after that, I was on a gang of four carton machines, pasting the bottoms of knocked down cartons together, prepped for filling. That type of semi-automatic machinery, like the nailer and carton sealer, never appealed to me. Sure, a guy only had a certain set of motions to memorize, then repeat all day. It would become very monotonous rapidly.

So, time passed for me into late summer 1917, in Dixon at the Borden milk factory. Every few days I was performing another position for one to several days. Some interesting, some not, making the day drag by. I lived in a rooming house nearby, took most meals there. I met other roomers from across Iowa and Illinois, a few from other states. It was interesting to hear of their lives, and why they found themselves in western Illinois. Life poses challenges to us all, and in the US, we have almost unlimited opportunity. My Mother used to say, 'life is what you make of it'. Sound advice for anyone.

In my spare time, I'd write a letter to my wife, Miss Marion or Mother. Miss Marion would write more than I, but I think most guys are poor letter writers. I'd visit the local park, walk downtown, and even tried the new movie house. It was showing the new films from New York studios, and recently a new source from Los Angeles, from a place they called Hollywoodland. They were interesting, cost 2 cents to view a sixty-minute show of three to four films. Some were accompanied by music from a piano or an organ. Such a new diversion.

I considered organizing an army drilling troop but I had so little experience from back in Freeport, not sure it'd work well. Besides, I didn't want to get too stuck to this town, nor job.

Even here in Dixon, everyone seemed to be getting wild and careless. One day I heard several girls talking in the factory tin can room, kidding a young fellow about a girl he had been going with, and about a disease he had caught. Imagine it! It seemed incredible to me but that was one instance of several. Daily papers reported often of 'kissing bees' staged on the railway station platforms by gangs of girls, where they kissed every soldier on a train passing thru. Not that these girls knew the soldiers, but that they were on a troop train passing through on their way to France. It was a regular custom of these girls at that station, most seemed to be on the east coast but then other towns took up the hint. I never saw it in Dixon, but I suppose it could in bigger cities, like Rockford, or better, Chicago.

7

MY PATH TO THE ARMY

Me, I had decided that I was going to enlist, somehow. I had no idea, but a stop at a recruiting station set up in many post offices would resolve that. I wrote to Miss Marion to explain my desires, and a week later I got a letter from her with an assemblance of a permit to join, but she sounded angry too. I did not understand why. It sounded as if she didn't care if I did get shot, so the next payday I drew all my money, paid my bills, and headed for Forreston to bid goodbye to Henry, Mother and Heiny.

Monday, November 5th 1917 I was in Forreston for a nice visit, short and tearful with family. Mother, of course, worried that I'd be maimed or worse killed. I looked on it as patriotic, and an adventure. She supportively wrote me a required approval letter from my mother. On Tuesday, I took a train back to Freeport, stayed with Miss Marion. She'd made an appointment with a doctor because she'd been feeling odd for a while. It turns out the doctor was unsure why. He said it could be she was with child, or some sort of allergy from the area, it was different from her life in Minnesota. The doctor was unsure, and we didn't think she could be with child, we'd been together rather little. We decided she'd return to Minnesota in a few days, and see if it was allergies.

She also wrote a supporting letter. At the main post office to enlist, I met a short, sour Army Sergeant who told me to come back on Wednesday to process, so Wednesday I returned. The same Sergeant gave me an examination, accepted the letters from my wife, and Mother as sufficient permissions, and told me I was accepted into the Army, then instructed me I had two days to pack up, and report for duty from Freeport. That would give me time with Miss Marion too!

CHAPTER 7

It seemed like a long time since I'd left. Shoot, it'd been almost 7 months since I had graduated high school. But it was long after I should have enlisted, though I'd had some good adventures. Time with Miss Marion was short, and special. I had concerns that maybe she'd been seeing someone while I was in Dixon, and we argued some. It seemed she was still devoted to us but willing to part for the war duration. We enjoyed walks and some kissing time. I'd missed that more than I had expected. I promised to write often, at least better than I had from Dixon. We finalized her plans to head back home to her native Minnesota. She'd arranged to stay with an aunt and cousins. We said our final goodbyes, and packed a small, old suitcase for the trip.

Months before, the Freeport alumni militia group, had traveled to a camp somewhere in the south, and each day's newspaper carried reports of their training. I'd had no desire to join the militia, albeit Army infantry. Several years before, I had seen pilot Rene Simon, in a Moisant aircraft from Queens NY, give an exhibition flight at Freeport and I had never forgotten it. I wanted to be an aviator. But the sour Sergeant said the Aviation corps was filled. At best, I would have to go into the Quartermaster's Corps, and possibly transfer over later. So, I planned to try. Anything was better than staying back. Daily I was accusing myself of being a slacker, and I was unsure that Eve thought me one. To the point that I wondered if she would have married me, if I'd asked before getting tangled with Miss Marion. Perhaps her answer would have been in the affirmative. If I had put the question to her while dressed in army khaki. Perhaps not. Regardless, I was past the chance to find out.

I was hoping that the Sergeant would march me down Stephenson, the main street, to the station, but no such luck. I had been dreaming that Eve might see me go, at last, but when we finally left the post office room, one other volunteer and I made the march down a back street. The other boy said his name was Elly, Eli, or something. I didn't catch what it was, and didn't much care. No fanfare at all. At the station I did not recognize a single person, and at 1:15p.m., we were off on a train. Chicago was our first stop, and after that, God alone would know. The trip away from away from home, starting at last, my great adventure was a lonely trip. True, I was nineteen now, and had been since August, felt myself a man, but I had never before been very far from home and now I was leaving, perhaps to never return. Right now, sitting in a smokey, dirty train coach the war had no glamour at all! The fond dreams I had made included a wonderful send-off, had been like bubbles and now they were burst. Instead of starting to war in a parade, with a band and flags waving, I had gone sneaking down a back street, with not even a "Good luck!" cry behind me, and only the Sergeant's handshake to remember.

Then too, that afternoon, there was another thing that made me lonely. I was born in the hills of southwest Wisconsin. Even Freeport, Illinois was hilly. Now though, past Rockford, and on our way to Chicago the dull afternoon sun shined on a limitless plain. The edges were lost in haze, and if anything makes a hill boy lonesome, it is the sight of big friendless, empty plain. True, there were always houses in sight, but that big expanse of land, almost treeless, looked bare and lonely. I would rather have seen the rocky, brush covered hillsides of the desert.

Chicago was a dream to me. I had never been there before, but from the Milwaukee Road RR station, Elly led the way over to the Army recruiting station on South State Street. There we reported in, our papers were taken by some private and after waiting what seemed like many hours, we were told to stick around and be handy when supper time came. We roamed the street for a block north and south till finally about 6pm., fifteen to twenty volunteers were assembled and marched to a nearby restaurant for our evening meal. Afterward, we were led to a gloomy old hotel, up a long flight of stairs and given a room, two to a bed, so Elly bunked with me.

I had no money to spend, so that evening I went right to bed, but with all the changes, I slept little. I was wondering if I was doing the right thing going into the Army. Lately, I had been hearing that men who had only a saw and hammer had been getting jobs in the government camps, like Camp Grant, as carpenters and drawing 80 cents to one dollar an hour! Imagine it, a ten-hour day would pay about fifty-five dollars in a week. If they worked on Saturday afternoons, as they might, it would be sixty dollars! Way more than my nine dollars a week at the Five and Ten store, or fourteen a week at Borden's dairy! I'd heard such several times and put it down as rumor, but hearing it on the train made it more real sounding. But I had enlisted, so why worry such things anymore, even if true.

Elly came into the room about midnight, and we tossed and talked the rest of the night. Our principal worry was where we were going next. Not much else to think on. Some army posts like Fort Riley might be our next stop, or Camp Grant. We didn't know where, but assumed any trail would lead us to Europe in time. The next day we worried some more. We reported to the recruiting station for meals, and every hour or more between.

It was after supper that evening that we were taken to the basement room below the recruiting station, and lined up. A blustery Sergeant was in charge, and he had a mass of our enlistment papers in his hands, trying to call roll off of them. Finally, he gave it up.

"Oh hell," he bellowed, "how do these damn recruiting stations ever figure a man to make head or tail of things the way they muss the forms up. Here, Youse Guys! Everybody that's enlisting in the infantry line up here!", and he pointed to a spot along one side wall.

"Corporal," he commanded one of his followers, "Take their names down for me!"

"Coast artillery, come over here!", he yelled forming another line, some guys trotting over to it, and he assigned another guy to gather names. I began to get wise to the system. I was recorded as Q.M. for quartermaster, but when he said Aviation, that was where I went. And no one objected, and so there I stayed! That was the only official transfer I made, from the quartermaster's corps over to the Aviation branch of the US Army Signal Corps. I was never called down for the transfer either, and doubt if anyone ever knew it, nor cared if they did.

So there my name went down on the lists as an aviation rookie. After listing the whole bunch of us, there were nearly one hundred of us by then and we were lined up and marched down to the Dearborn RR station and put on the evening passenger train bound to St. Louis and Jefferson Barracks. Elly and I stuck together and got a seat between us. Several of the rookies on our train were from Chicago, and had friends at the station to see them off, and more than one hugging and kissing scene made me feel odd and somewhat jealous. Whiskey was also in evidence and one poor chap, Walter Parker, as someone related his name, got excited while kissing his sweety goodbye and forgot all about leaving till the train started moving. He was still on the platform, and in trying to catch the moving steps, fell on the icy platform. From where I was, it looked like he rolled clear under the train! The train did not stop, for no one on it noticed him. We went rolling on, leaving him somewhere behind. At a later stop the conductor must have gotten a wire about the accident, for one of the boys said Parker lost both legs, and might die. What a way to start for war. Pity the chap. The accident was past, and I could do nothing either way, so I did not try to stop the conductor to verify the story. It was none of my business, so why worry. But I did worry, enough at least to start writing a memo notebook, to keep a record of the happenings during my term in the army.

On through the night we rumbled, and while trying to doze in a lounge seat, I was thinking of how lucky, or unlucky Parker might have been. His accident might be worse than many yet better than others things that may have happened to him had he gotten to France. Perhaps I should have asked about Parker, but I didn't, and never heard about him again. Such is life.

Next, I began to wonder how long I would be in Jefferson Barracks, and what might happen from there. At least, I would probably get my Army uniform there, and send my civilian suit home. Morning arrived and we rode into the smoky St. Louis station, about nine-thirty a.m., then we pulled into the Jefferson Barracks. Again, we were lined up, and I figured this would be the last time to be stood in line in civvies. As usual, I was way off. We were marched first to one brick building, headquarters, I suppose, and after waiting there for about an hour, off to another. After fifteen minutes, we were off again to another where we finally left our suitcases stacked in the basement of a brick barracks building.

We were queued again, this time to march to the mess hall, where it seemed to me and the entire city could be fed at one time. That mess hall was an immense affair, and must have seated close to five thousand men at a time! There were several doors, and at each some mess officer presided. The soldiers lined up outside, in column of squads and when at some signal, a whistle sounded, each door was thrown open simultaneously and the soldiers marched in, single file. Every table held ten men on a side, with a non-com directing each line. Ten men were counted off in a hurry, at each opening before the line passed to the next row. Plates, cutlery, and cups were on the table, so no mess kits were used. All the food was in dishes, family style, lined out along the table's end. The first man seated had the first grab for what he fancied, then passed it on down the table.

Attendants in blue denim overalls with aprons were present to refill dishes as they were emptied. Coffee and milk in pitchers, were present on the tables. A person in blue denims, hollered, "Help yourself, but do it in a hurry or you may get left out." For the supply of food was not unlimited, and often dishes were refilled but once. It was wholesome food, however, and well cooked, so that part of one's worries were ended; for a time. The regular soldiers wandered out whenever they were through, and did not have to wait and file out in a column, but our non-com took care of us, and we filed out together.

We waited around till about one o'clock and then were lined up and marched out in front of a big, new, unpainted building, and looked like an immense dancing pavilion. Here we were sat and lounged in the afternoon sun, and nearly an hour later we were called in.

"You birds are lucky!" said our non-com, "It was a dull day today, or you would have had to wait till tomorrow to go through."

Inside the construction of the place still resembled a remodeled dance hall for a number of desks occupied the inner space where the dance floor would have been located. A railing separated this space, allowing a twenty-foot aisle around the outside. This aisle seemed to be divided into rooms or sections by painted lines and cloth drapes. Some of the rooms were enclosed completely with drapery, cloth walls. All about the entire room, going from small 'room" to another was an ever-moving line of completely naked men. Apparently, this was another examination, making our third thus far. I'd already had similar ones in Freeport and Chicago. I did have much time to scan things over, for we were hustled into a room on the right, rear corner, and told to strip to our hides. Our clothes were to be placed in another the empty cubbyholes along the side wall, and then we were rushed out to be examined.

Our enlistment papers were assembled at the first desk to our right, and as each man came up to that desk, his records were verified, making him answer the same questions over and over. Then as fast as each man was through, he moved on to the next section, and carried his papers along with him. There was a desk just inside the railing, at the side of each room, and as we passed from one examination to the next, our papers were stamped at each desk and passed on.

We had our eyes checked, heart, lungs, hearing, teeth and even muscular control of each important part of our bodies. Those were some of the examinations we had to pass. The former examinations in Freeport and Chicago had been fairly thorough, but these were right down to rock bottom. I was worried about Miss Marion, had promised to send her part of my pay, as I had in Dixon. I'd lived on the bare minimum, sending her my pay, which had lowered my weight down. My normal 140 to 145 lbs at five feet-ten inches was down to 128 lbs, pretty light. I must have gotten stretched in the processing. I'd thought I was 5-10", but here they measured me at 5-11", nearly six feet! If I had been heavier, I would have thought myself a big man!

At the heart test there was trouble. Again, and again the medical officer put his stethoscope to my chest, and listened. "Ever have any heart trouble?", the doctor asked.

"No sir", I answered, puzzled. How could I have a weak heart, having run a lot and played football?

"My heart isn't weak, is it?" I asked. "Why I have always done hard work, and it never troubled me. I played football in high school, and ran the mile and two-mile on the track team too."

After saying that, I felt kinda cheap. Probably this doctor had gone to college, and associated football with a college team. He might be thinking I was a braggart, slim, light and young as I was.

"No," he smiled, "It's far from weak. It's the other way! Too strong for a chap your size. But that running and hard work explains it. The heart muscle in your case is almost too well developed." Then he waved me on. I was greatly relieved and quickly forgot my angst from moments earlier.

One test seemed odd merely twenty hops forward on one foot, turn, switch feet and return; then walking the same and back. This was probably to find out if our walking muscles were working properly. Hmm, pretty short test if we were to hike any distance, though it was here that I received my first chalk mark. My right leg had been twisted when I was a freshman in school, while I was trying to tackle Johney Hart in football practice. Since it worked as good as ever, my right knee was still twisted a bit so that it seemed like I was bow-legged. I am, but the knee is the worst of it. That blamed inspector had eyes like a cat, for he not only noticed the bow legs, but he noticed that the right one was worse. I then had to do a lot of extra hopping, kicking and bending to prove that it was still all right. But as he finished testing me, and I went on, he drew a red chalk mark along my knee. Hmm. Not likely a good thing.

The next test was for hearing using a watch. I was nervous so that the first time I couldn't hear a watch held behind my head. Maybe I was nervous, because on the next trial I could hear a pin drop five feet behind me.

Finally, we had covered two sides of the room and were half way down the third side, and the last desk was before me. True, there were several other booths on the fourth side, but no moving line could be seen there, so not sure why it was there. A number of naked chaps waited at several of booths and others were trotting back and forth, though not in the line.

The office in charge of this last desk must have been out getting a bit of fresh air, and certainly he took his time but at last he did come in and I noticed from his collar and shoulder insignia that he was a major. The other officers had been lieutenants and one or two Captains but his was a real honest-to-goodness major. I was paying little attention to the test he was giving, for there were about thirty chaps ahead of me at this point. I was watching the line behind me, and booths along the last side. This test was a short one, and soon I glanced ahead to find myself about eighth in line. I noticed that a Sergeant was keeping the line back at a mark on the floor. As each man was called, he was pointed to a spot in front of the desk, and turned clear around for the Major to inspect him, answer a few questions and then was waved on. One man stepped out who was marked with several little red chalk marks on his body, and when he passed on, I noticed the Sergeant step in and mark in red chalk, "REJ" on his back. Only then did I notice that the line in front of us was splitting into two directions.

Some were going on to one booth, and few were in sight, seeming to go, like this lad with the "REJ", back to the dressing room.

I began to watch, to see what was going on and why. The seventh man moved ahead, and then the sixth; both to the right line. Number five moved in front of the Major, and after a hesitation, this man moved to the left, his back marked with the "REJ". It was now that I noticed a whisper begin to enlighten me, "Lots of rejections, ain't there!". I began to shiver, and my throat tightened as I caught the meaning. I'd been assuming I was in the Army already, and here these boys were being tossed out. Big, strong, husky looking chaps, being sent home. Unacceptable, No Good, Forced Slackers. God, what thoughts raced through my mind, as I stood there shivering. Not from the cold, from being a failure in the eyes of the Army. To leave Freeport for the Army, and then return due to being rejected, would be horrible! What would mothers, wives, or sweethearts of these men say upon their return? How could they face their friends? In my mind, to start and return was worse than never starting.

Two men went to the right, while I was clearing my head after this shock. Here I had been thinking I was already in the Army, accepted with nothing but an assignment somewhere for training. And now, with the stops thru this inspection process for my heart, hearing, and my leg; I understood the use of the red chalk. Lord, I was worried.

One man ahead of me. I was next, and while waiting my turn, it took great effort choking back tears of rejection fear. Here I had been almost dodging the service for months, getting married, making a fool of myself before Eve in doing so, and now at last, finally I'd enlisted only to be rejected? At least I was convincing myself I would be. The man ahead of me, with but one or two chalk marks on him moved forward, and turned left, marked with the fatal "REJ" on him. Head up, I stumbled to the spot, with the Sergeant steering me some. I was glad to see the Major glancing aside, talking to an aide. I squared my shoulders, and struggled to calm myself, as he focused on me. He glanced at me as the Sergeant swiveled me around.

"Humph," snorted the Major. "What knee?"

"Right knee, sir,"

"What's wrong with it?"

"Nothing sir. It was twisted in a football game, three years ago, but it's been fine and I served as the kicker in my senior year." I was not the first kicker, but I felt that a lie would help. Truth was, my knee did not hurt a bit.

The Major glanced back at the papers, muttered something about high school, and then asked me a few questions about my education.

At last, with a snort, he waved me on, and I blindly marched forward, to the left. The Sergeant's hand shot out, felt like a chalk mark was stamped, but after a couple steps I realized he was directing me. "Not that way, this way!" he snapped, and he shoved me to the right!

Tears were running from my eyes in earnest. I had to stop in a corner, under pretense of rubbing something from my eye. I was so relieved not to be rejected, a forced slacker. Lord, what a scare that had been! Somehow, probably because of my education, the Major had passed me. Sounded like so many of the men had never finished high school. I hated to think of what I would have done had he set me aside. I certainly would not have gone home, even for Miss Marion. At least that was my immediate thought.

The officer in charge of the next booth took several men at a time, and I was just in time to for the next bunch. He started talking as I entered.

"Well men," he began, "you have volunteered to fight for, and serve, your country. You men assembled here have passed all the tests, both physical and mental, but you are not yet soldiers. Now though, in a few minutes, it will be too late to turn back. If there are any of you that want to quit, now is the last chance you will have. Once the oath is given, there is no return. Soldiering is one job you cannot quit, until your time is served. It is one job with no chance from which to back out. Death alone takes you out of the service, except in special cases, until your enlistment is up. So, think it over carefully, before you are sworn in, and if you have reservations, now is the time to do so."

No one left. We stood, raised our right hands and took our oath allegiance. "Sworn in." Those words had a magic sound to me then, for now I was at last a soldier, US Army. But then it seemed to me for several days afterward that I was a kind of slacker, for having waited so long to enlist. I kept wondering what had held back the boys around me also. Some of them had probably been in a similar fix as myself, some may have been too young, and perhaps to some, the war had not been of a serious nature until now.

There was one more ordeal to go through. That was the vaccinations, typhoid inoculation, and these army doctors were certainly rough administering them! We were sent through in a rush, lined up like cattle for slaughter. Marched single file through an aisle between two high desks, containing a dreadful array of bottle and instruments, most of them syringes! A soldier on one side handled the vaccination, which was easy, the other was awful. A swab of iodine touched me, and a moment later the doctor in charge jabbed his hypodermic needle into my shoulder, a quick shove on the plunger, a tug to jerk it out, and then shoved me on. "Treat'em rough and make'em like it!" would appear to have been his motto.

One big man marched up with his chest out, and a moment later fainted! He had to be carried off while a little shrimp of a guy behind him, shivered and struggled, was held by two attendants, but then walked off laughing! "Golly, I thought that was going to kill me, but it's a cinch," he said. If a chance had been offered these men to quit here, many would likely never move to become trained soldiers.

Next, they took our fingerprints, and identification marks had to be recorded, and then that was it, no more tests, nor exams. Everything had been such a rush, now it was over. We had to sit around and wait for our shoulders to dry where we'd been jabbed, so that when we dressed there would be no danger of infection to an open wound. Finally, we dressed again our civvies and then were marched to one of the brick barracks where we were measured for our army clothing. By then it was too late for anything else in such a large group, and we spent the rest of the day in our civvies. After mess I was so tired! Blankets were furnished and we were bunked in the basement of that brick barrack, I went right to sleep. We were cautioned to stay right around there after supper, since some guard might mistake us for unauthorized visitors in our civvies. It was easy, since I'd slept little in Chicago, and a bit on the train last night, so I was very tired out. My worries climaxing with almost being rejected caused me to be tired also. I finally got a solid sleep, even in this strange place.

I'd been beset for months with worry over my wife, and even Eve. How Henry was faring, and feeling like a slacker, that this night's rest gave me some peaceful, needed rest. Most men marry to settle down, I was married in June, this made five months since I'd been unsettled.

As one of the boys in that basement said to a married friend that night, "When a guy has gotta join the army to get away from his wife, she sure must be awful!" I had to agree with him. Not that Miss Marion was awful, I'd just felt tied down at such a young age.

In the morning we put on our civvies for the last time, and right after mess we were lined up and marched to the long line of [QM] quartermaster's windows. At each window we were handed some article of clothing or equipment, and we continued trooping past all of them. We were issued blue denim barrack sacks in which to keep extra clothing, and many fellows had to load these up to not drop gear enroute. By the end, we were each staggering under our individual loads, and marched to our barracks. There we changed and began stowing gear.

It was a queer sight, seeing all the lads staggering to the barracks, dropping gear, picking it up without spilling another item. From the QM to our barracks was a couple blocks, though with our loads, it seemed far longer! Most had filled their denim sacks, but some poor dumb bells tried to carry everything just as it was piled on. Here is what we were given:

>Denim barracks bag,
>one belt,
>two pair of cotton breeches, or khaki as we called them,
>one blue denim work overalls,
>one pair woolen ditto,
>two army blankets,
>one woolen coat,
>three suits of summer underwear,
>two pieces to the suit,
>three suits of winter ditto,
>one pair of woolen gloves,
>one pair leggings,
>one service hat with cords, [which most of us placed on our heads immediately]
>two flannel or OD shirts,
>two pair of shoes,
>four of stockings,
>one slicker,
>and in our pockets, our collar ornaments, ID tape, and tags.

Lord, what a load, and I had to stop and laugh, watching some of those dumb guys carrying everything in a large stack! They would take two steps, fiddle for ten minutes trying to pick up something they dropped. Others partnered up, guarding their stash while the other made two trips to carry it. By watching the others, I caught on to the use of the barracks bag and I loaded mine up, carrying a few odd items, and it was a large load!

The fun had only started, for when we got to the barracks, a corporal rounded us up, had us gather our gear in two upper rooms where we at last discarded our civvies, and sent the stuff we didn't want home. My suitcase had been all this time in the basement where I'd spent the night. I retrieved it before starting to undress. Most of the boys had luggage, though a few had worn only the clothes on their backs. After we had all got out our luggage and stripped off our civvies, the fun commenced watching some of us trying to get into an army suit / uniform. For some, it was like they never had their measurements taken! Pretty funny, just not me, I was lucky. It seems natural for some chaps to do everything backward the first time, even dressing in new clothes. Some put on their breeches and then grabbed underwear, trying to figure out how to get it on under. What? Maybe they weren't used to wearing underwear? Crazy backwoodsmen? Yes, they were as dumb as that; some worse yet. More than one laced his breeches leg up tight before trying to get into them. The biggest joke was exposed with the leggings. Very few seemed to be able to get them on straight. As it was, they were rotten fits, and looked like the very devil even when done right! Only a few fitted the calves of the soldiers at all.

I pulled one dumb trick. I had been wearing garter bands on my civilian socks. And used them on my army socks. With the leggings on, the rubber garter buttons rubbed the inside of my calve, inside those tight leggings. One day was all I could take, skin rubbed raw. The leggings held the socks fine, so I tossed my old garter bands.

There was a mailing desk in the corner, and an express office station in the other room for us to use in sending home our suitcases, or bundles of civvies for some. Also, a Jewish clothes man stood at the door, offering one, two, or sometimes "tree" dollars for our suits. He'd get many suits worth a good twenty or thirty dollars, for a couple dollars. The soldiers needed the money, not their old clothes, besides those old clothes may never get used again back home. Sadly, some of these boys may not return, but no one mentioned that. At last, a line of odd-looking soldiers was out on the parade ground each with a blue denim barracks bag holding all their army possessions. None of us was allowed to keep a suitcase, nor traveling bag. We could keep small items such as razors, memos, toothbrushes, etc. but no bulky packages or articles.

The signal corps rookies were put in one group, and turned over to a corporal who was to deliver us to our barracks. Up till now we were newcomers, unassigned but this corporal delivered us to the 16th company, way up at the east end of the parade grounds. The 16th was the last of the companies forming. The 15th company was composed of mostly colored men. Another corporal took charge of us on the parade grounds and gave us a going over; first of all, telling each man what was wrong with their clothing and how to correct it. Most of all, to take all articles except flat pictures or such that could bulge out of our pockets. Those pockets must at all times be buttoned tight, as must every visible button on our uniforms. Then he lined us up into a semblance of a military line and told us a few things.

"Now lissen, yuh damn rookies. Yuh're in the army now, and don't you forget it! Yuh done signed up, been sworn in, and accepted. An get this through yuh're damn think skulls for once an all time! Yuh got one job now, yuh can't quit when yuh want to. Yuh can howl all yuh want to if yuh don't think yuh're getting treated right, but it's little good it'll do yuh.

The only time yuh can quit is when yuh're times served. An, not till then! So yuh better make the best of it, and get these orders we give yuh through yuh're damn thick skulls and like it while yuh're doin it! If yuh don't like it, just say so, an we'll damn soon make yuh like it! Clear?! The sooner yuh learn to soldier, the better for yuh. Yuh can make things easy on yuhself by keepin yuh eyes open, and mindin orders, or yuh can make'em damn hard, by getting gay and tryin things yuh're own way. They's one nice thing about this army, either you do as yuh're told or yuh don't. If yuh don't follow orders, yuh may git your head busted, an, we got an awful nice guardhouse, and lots of cigarette butts lying around that need picking up. An there's more, don't follow orders and you could get nice K.P. fatiguing jobs to teach you! So, remember, if yuh don't like the way we do things, just say so, and we'll DAMN SOON MAKE YUH LIKE IT!"

And more of the same, so began our army lives. Finally, when we looked a little more like soldiers, he trotted off, and a colonel come back with him and inspected us. Then we were assigned to bunks, or cots in a new wooden barracks building, back down the hill behind the brick company HQ building for the 16th. This little old brick barrack was originally the company barrack, I guess, but now there were so many men that it was mostly office. Some few men did sleep upstairs in it but behind it, there was string of new or almost new, wooden buildings called cantonments.

This was Saturday, the 10th of November, and there was no drill for us that day, but we did get a lecture from the corporal on several topics. How to keep our cots in order, how to fold our blankets with the "U.S." coming out on top, and where to place our barrack bag, and even how our extra shoes must always be shined. They are to be placed with the toes showing at the foot of our cots.

All this was new to me. Yet by keeping my eyes open, I got along all right. Saturday evening, I went around with some new friends, one of them, Clinton Shattuck from Grand Rapids, Michigan. We went to a shooting gallery, watched it a while and walked back to the post.

Jefferson Barracks sure is a pretty army post or so it seems to me with its immense parade ground at its center, the HQ building on the east side overlooking the Mississippi, and the Officers row on the north. With all the homes, it looked somewhat like a misplaced respectable, residential street placed there. On the west the canteen, street car station, and odd buildings. The large brick company barracks or HQ on the south side. Farther back on the south and west sides, the mess hall, many wooden barracks, QM supply sheds and other miscellaneous buildings. The guard house jutted out into the parade ground about in the center of the west side. A small attached station to it, under a big old tree the bugle calls were blown. They'd hung a large megaphone from a branch and each call was blown four times, once to each direction. Aided with the megaphone, it sure did carry their calls, for miles I expect!

I learned to watch out for the black and gold hat cord worn by the officers, and to watch their shoulder straps but it was quite a while before I could distinguish between the field clerks, the officers. Those blamed clerks dressed almost like officers, and their hat cords were very similar but they were really civilians and yet usually they answered a salute, as though they were officers. It could be confusing at first.

Sunday was another easy day. I wrote letters home, and began to get acquainted with other soldiers. Somehow, most of these boys were like me, for they seemed to have been kept out of the service until now for one reason or another. Many of them seemed to have just figured it out that there was a war going on, that might need them. Perhaps, I was not as bad a slacker, as I had feared.

Monday was my first day of drills, and I thanked my lucky stars for those few evenings in the high school alumni drill corps with the Lieutenant. His explanations of the simple maneuvers in drill helped a lot. Some of these boys around me had never thought of such a thing as trying to keep step while marching. Band practice had helped there as well, timed by the drums. Here, of course, we had nothing to keep time by, except the incessant "HWUN, TWO, HREE, HORE!" as it sounded from the corporal shouting. That trick of keeping in step was easy for me, yet a challenge for the less coordinated boys. The corporal had nothing to do but teach and focus on that he did. It helped that he was an expert at plain cussing! His commands were just given in breaks between his cuss words! Listening to the chatter of the other boys, I began to believe that many a fond mother was sure going to be surprised when her darling son came home, capable of cussing up a storm! Most practiced cussing assiduously, believing that practice makes perfect.

I'd heard that there was a lot of gambling in the army, but the rookies were pretty controlled, and dice were kept out of sight. Cards games were taboo also, especially with money in sight.

Monday at 2:30p.m., I started on my first K.P. duty, working in the big mess hall. Here we were checked in at a desk, and assigned different jobs. Mine happened to be cleaning out some of the giant steam pots. They stood shoulder high, in which the foods were cooked by steam. That kitchen was sure a sight, used as I was to the restaurant work. It dwarfed a small restaurant though. Ovens stood in rows, alongside the large steam pots. At mess time my job was at one of these pots, handling a big dipper, filling the boilers in the rolling wagons. These little wagons, had a steel box on wheels, held a pan filled with hot water on which food pans were set, to keep food warm until served. Each wagon held three pans, each filled with a vegetable, potatoes, etc. When filled they were rolled out to the center aisle of the main mess hall. Here the table men brought up platters and big dishes from their table, which were then filled from these wagons. In this manner, two wagons holding six items, would serve several tables, and there would be but two men to go into the kitchen for replacement pans as they emptied. I could easily see what a mess there would be with one man at each table if that man had to chase to the kitchen in order to refill every dish on his table, and seconds called for. It'd be a madhouse of colliding men, pans, and messes.

At the table, when any soldier wanted more of any dish, such as potatoes, and the dish was empty, he would hold it above his head. The table K.P. would take it, trot to the aisle, and refill it. Believe me, there were plenty of extra calls but whomever was in charge gauged things about right so that one of two extra calls from each table would about clean things out, reducing waste. One did have to eat fast to get any seconds, for if they were slow or shy, they'd find things "All out!" Work in the army was seldom hard, and the hardest part of the K.P. job was that we worked till about six-thirty or seven at nights and then had to roll out at four-thirty a.m., an hour and a half before regular reveille.

Tuesday at 2:30p.m., I was off duty and went back to my barracks. For a few days it was incessant drill, drill, every morning with a long hike starting at one p.m. It lasted till three or three-thirty. With lectures in the spare times on health, cleanliness, and even on sex. Yes, especially sex, for these army doctors seemed to fear women and sexual diseases as if they were the plague! In ordinary life, sex was taboo as a subject of discussion but here it was an almost daily subject.

Jefferson Barracks was merely an assembly place for the different branches of the army. Here new enlistees were taught the rudiments of army drill and discipline, and held till orders were forthcoming to ship them on to other forts, posts or fields. There they would be assigned to regular companies and given special training. As it was, the brick barracks facing the parade ground were each designated at company headquarters, and there, a few non-coms were kept as heads of these companies. The non-coms, [corporals and sergeants] acted as instructors, etc. to teach new rookies army life basics. So it was that we rookies were divided into squads, as in regular army discipline. When the bugle was blown from the guard house for reveille, mess, retreat, and all order formations, we were rushed out of bunkhouses by these non-coms and lined up by height on the parade ground, opposite the company HQ. The tallest men fell in line to the right, and the shorter men on down the line, without regard to any other special places. The 16th company was the first one at our end of the field. The 15th company was the only one that formed behind us, and most of the southerners in our company said that we were the first company, since the darkies could not be counted with the white men, and the 15th company was composed of coons. As for me, I was used to seeing the well-educated negroes of the north, and if not well educated, they were at least well-behaved but were usually well-educated. These southern darkies were a treat. Whomever had issued them their clothing had taken advantage of them with their traditional liking for colors and they had been given all the available dress uniforms. Since many were in khaki, they looked like anything but soldiers when they lined up. The had apparently no idea of what drill was. The colored Sergeant in charge of them was a corker. He would run up and down the lines, trying his best to get some semblance of order, and it was fun to listen to him tell some ignorant rookie where to head in at. Many of these coons could not remember an order for a minute, or chose not to, and often some little chap would see a tall friend at the other end of the line. He would try to squeeze in beside him, thinking it didn't matter. And then the sergeant would rave!

"Lissen, you black baboons," he would roar in a voice that could be heard for blocks, "Line up there by height, and make it in a hurry. Line up, LINE UP! Dammit it all! Cain't you tell what I mean! Don't stand in front of one another, STAND ONE BEHIND THE OTHER! Gee Roosalem crimeny Jackson, you black-faced tar baby! What-in-the-hell you doin way down there? You sawed off hunk of coal! You ain't no six feet tall! Get back there with them other monkeys yore own size!"

And then he would trot up to one end of his line, trying to get it straight, and yell to some offender, "PULL YOUR NECK IN!" you baby buzzard, "You, I mean, No, No, No. I mean that that guy there!" The one with the buck teeth! No, no, not you. You with the big feet! Oh hell, Colombia! Now you're all out of line!" And they were, for the moment one moved, trying to straighten his chest to where he thought it ought to be, then the guy next to him would move. Many of these boys could not stand still, even for a minute. It was fun too, to see some of the boys try to stand with their shoulders back, like a soldier. Round shouldered as most of them were, when they tried to stand stiff and straight, some chap would get the idea that his chin should be higher. In raising his chin, his stomach would stick out like a drum. The guy next to him focused on his feet were correct so he bent down a bit checking but trying to remain standing straight.

Most of the colored boys were enlisted as stevedores, to shovel coal, or just in labor companies. Their reward was the bright uniform. The poor fellows that had to take the khaki were out of luck. Uneducated they were mostly, as could be told from listening to them for a few minutes. From the snatches of conversation, I heard, I'll bet they gave their non-com plenty of trouble with extra training needs. They had extra challenges since the army had assumed folks knew some things. For example, some of them had never owned shoes before enlisting. They could be seen coming to assembly carrying their shoes. They didn't know how to put them on, let alone tie them! Some arrived dressed, appearing all lumpy; they must've had on all or most of their clothes in layers. I don't know why, no one would take it from their cot area. The 15th company did not always stand formation behind us. I guess their work or maybe extra training basics kept them from passing in review. I expect a hardboiled old trooper would have died if he had seen them calling "Eyes right!", in what they considered to be a straight line.

Evenings, I usually spent talking to the boys, or walking up and down the sidewalk along the parade grounds. Sometimes, I went over to the canteen but I was almost broke, so had little use for that place. I did get a three-dollar canteen book with coupons to be used for payment, and bought some necessary articles with it. These could be handy to buy items and charged against our next pay. I was in little need of items while I was at Jefferson Barracks. I did pay to have three photos of myself taken to send home. I was thinking that Mother and Miss Marion, would like to see their boy in khaki but after getting them I was far from proud of the appearance I'd recorded in the baggy, ill-fitting clothing. I certainly looked far from being the neat, erect soldier that I fondly imagined myself to be.

Thursday the 15th of November, I had occasion to give my better half, if she might so be called, another cussing. When we lined up for mess at noon, the Sergeant called my name, as one on a list that had to assemble in the afternoon at two pm, at our regular assembly place. At two o'clock we were lined up, and marched to a room in the HQ building, where some captain sat us down like a school class, and began examining us. There were perhaps forty boys in that room and he picked on me first. Perhaps my education caused that, expecting more from me as a high school graduate. "Now boys," the Captain began, "I will tell you why you have been called here. This post is to be allowed to nominate at least two men, maybe more, to attend West Point sometime in the Spring, to attend officer training there. This will be an opportunity that few boys ever receive. As you probably know, a boy has to have great scholastic standing, and then be appointed by the President, your state senator, or congressman. Usually, only one to three boys are allowed to enter West Point each year from any one state, and so you see this appointment is going to be a tremendous opportunity for the boys that we, or I select. The Jefferson Barracks post commandant has placed this task in my hands. Now you young men have been selected from your records because you have each stated that you have a high school education, or better. Now, how many of you have attended or graduated from college? No one answered, or held up their hands, so he continued.

"None? Well then, how many have attended a prep school, or accredited high school?" I raised my hand, for I knew that Freeport was an accredited high school.

"Fine," he said, "Did you graduate and what was the name of your school?"

"Freeport, Illinois high school in 1916, sir." I answered, "It is accredited."

"Your name, soldier?"

"Marion L Gray, sir"

"Age?"

"Nineteen, sir."

"Where were you born?"

"Big Flats, Wisconsin, sir."

"Single, of course?"

"No sir, married."

"What married? Too bad." he responded, "That spoils your chances. Only single men are allowed. It is taken as a matter of course that all men admitted to West Point will spend the rest of their active life in the Army service. With the four years of college training required, only single men are allowed. This would be a wonderful opportunity and if orders are changed to permit your taking the admittance examination, I want you to report."

He continued, "Young men your age, make the finest material to develop, and after passing the application exam, it would make for an exceptional opportunity indeed!"

After a few more minutes, he dismissed us, with only one boy seriously being considered. Of course, there were to be several months to pass before the examination, so he may find other candidates, but my chance was out. It made me mad. Here I, by foolishly, getting married on a whim, had lost my chance to be a West Point cadet. Somehow though, with the aviation service in the back of my mind, I did not care so much, but at the moment I was blaming Miss Marion for the pickle I was in. I needed to take responsibility for my actions though. This marriage business had many little entanglements in the army.

I was in the awkward squad one week, and then our corporal, just dismissing us from drill, assigned us to the regular company for drill, maneuvers and continued training.

"Boys," he said, wiping his sweaty face while we were at ease. Many of us were wondering why he was sweating, while we had been exercising! "I gotta hand it to this bunch. I been drilling a lot of damn rookies for five months now, and it's a hell of a job! Yeh, I didn't have to teach any of this squad the difference between left and right feet but this squad is the fastest damn learning bunch I had, since I been here! We train once a week and here you are ready to join a regular company. That's a week sooner than any other squad with who I have worked. You damned birds sure set a good record! I wish to hell the rest were as good. After this you guys are to line up with the regular company on all formations. You're out of the awkward squad now."

I gotta say, we all felt very pleased with ourselves at that!

Each morning at eleven, the whole available company cleaned up, shined our shoes, and lined up for the "passing in review", a sight to remember. First would come the colors, and the band, and then the companies, marching in line by squad. They would come past our station, company after company, until in turn, we fell in line and followed after. They turned at the corner, marched down the east side of the parade grounds, and then at the far corner, swung out in platoon or company fronts. Then with the band playing, at its station on the left, where it had swung out and stopped, opposite the H.Q. reviewing station. We would pass line after line, past the C.O., doing "eyes right", as we went by. That immense body of men, all marching in step made for a grand, impressive sight.

Once dressed in khaki, a man loses his identity. He becomes a mere part of a great machine. No matter how stiff and straight he may stand in civvies, his clothing distinguishes him from the rest, but one of a mob. But put that mob in khaki, and at once they become like a marching machine, and I know of no more impressive a sight. In column of squads, now by platoon, then company, and passing across the parade ground, it certainly is an impressive sight. When I had my photo taken at the canteen to send home, I also bought a postal card showing that daily march to send with it. The postal card showed a review with men carrying arms. We had yet to receive any weapon issuance, nor training. That didn't matter for I sent that postal card, it still gave them the illustration of "passing in review", and would impress them, as I had been.

For a few days my right shoulder had been sore, after my first inoculation in the arm. The next Friday, the 16th, I got one more, then three shots, a week apart, completed the schedule. So, on the 23rd, I'd be done. I'll be glad of that, hopefully the soreness will dissipate after I get the last shot.

Saturday I was unlucky for I was assigned to the 48-hour mess hall list, and was due to spend Sunday and Monday there till 2:30 daily. but Monday at 10a.m., we were called out of the mess hall with orders to get ready to leave Jefferson Barracks. That is the army way, for during the afternoon, we had a minor physical examination, and then got our clothes in order, and waited.

Tuesday, we had an equipment inspection, lining up on the parade ground with all our clothing spread out just so, on our blankets. A Colonel tread by gloomily by looking over each man's equipment and raising cane if anything looked a bit dirty.

Tuesday afternoon I got my first army mess kit; knife, fork and spoon, canteen with cup, which fitted around the bottom of the canteen. That stuff was called ordnance, which I'd thought was weapons. When the Colonel lined us up and said we would march over to the ordnance warehouse, I thought we'd be getting guns, or pistols. In the army, those aluminum mess kits were, "ordnance."

8

CAMP KELLY — TEXAS

It was Wednesday at 3:30p.m., when we finally were packed in a day coach, as part of a train load of enlisted volunteers in the aviation section, and started on our way to Camp Kelly, Texas. On the way, I was taught to pronounce the name of San Antonio, as "San Antone", for Camp Kelly is located just outside that dusty little town. We were to learn the art of army waiting.

Our baggage car was fitted as a mess kitchen, and that evening I got my first lesson on how to balance a mess kit, cover, and coffee cup all in one hand! This was the first time I had been outside of Jefferson Barracks in uniform. I half-expected a cheering crowd at each station when we stopped, or maybe benefit from some nice group of girls dispensing kisses! But usually there were only old men or kids selling candies, cookies, or sandwiches. At the town of Hoxie, Arkansas, though, several girls came alongside the train and since we were not allowed outside the cars, we had to lean out windows to talk to them as they trotted down the line, reaching up and shaking hands with each passing soldier. One girl gave out slips of paper with her name and address, inviting a few boys to write to her. Out of many slips, I figured it would cost her a fortune to pay postage, let alone answer each of many letters. I refrained taking one, as I was a married man. For somehow, in the rush of life at Jefferson Barracks, I had forgotten my petty troubles, wrote little, and enjoyed my army work.

Those day coaches were nothing wonderful in which to ride and get any rest. By the time we arrived at Texarkana, Texas, early the next morning, we were all glad for a chance to get out and stretch our legs. Thomas O'Hara, Clinton Shattuck, and I were buddies for the trip and stuck together in one double seat, allowing us to stretch out a bit.

I enjoyed the chance to walk about the town of Texarkana, but I envied the boys who still had money in their pockets with which to buy candy and sandwiches. I had just seven cents, and five of that would have bought a candy bar, but since I could not treat each of the other boys in my seat, I kept it all in my pocket. Later on, I would have bought anything I wanted, from a pack of gum to an apple, and split it three ways. I was yet too proud, to offer any of my buddies anything less than a standard portion.

Texas was huge. With our train rumbling slowly across the northern part of the state, chugging along like a local, stopping, it seemed, at every station. We must have been running as the third section on some local passenger schedule, with the other trainload of soldiers ahead of us as the second section. We continued to stop at every station, sometimes in between too. That was certainly a dreary day's ride, with nothing to look at but the cut over land, stumps and small trees. Some lumber company had taken out all the larger trees. Occasionally a poor negro shack showed up but in that all day ride, I seldom saw any place that looked like white man's home.

Near Dallas, the land got better, and wide farms began to appear. South of Dallas, in the dusk of the evening, large areas of cultivated land showed up, with houses dotted along the landscape at intervals.

We arrived at Camp Kelly early the next morning, Friday the 23rd of November, at 830a.m., we detrained. Then came one long day of marching here, and there, for one purpose or another. We stopped at one tent for a quick examination, probably to make sure that none of us had contracted any deadly disease that would necessitate quarantining our outfit. Finally, about noon I was sorted out with 208 others as part of an immediate shipment to nearby Santiago. My buddies, Clinton, and O'Hara disappeared and I was among a group of perfect strangers again. Waiting, waiting, with seemingly nothing to do but stand, lie down, or sit. No place to go either, wondering most of the time if whomever was in charge of us might not have trotted off, and forgotten us. We could walk around where ever we happened to be but with only wooden sheds to stare at, we either looked up, or occupied as offices and we knew better not to try to inspect them.

There was one treat. Airplanes! We spent most of our time stretching our necks, looking up at the planes overhead. Most of them just flew in long circles, or swooped in easy banking curves. They were flying, that was all, but to us it was such a treat! We were like people at a circus, watching acrobats high in the air, not so much interested in the feats as in knowing that we were watching something dangerous, and wondering just when there was going to be an accident. Sometimes, however, a plane would do some stunts, and I soon got to be able to pick a stunt plane out, by the way it was maneuvered, even before the pilot tried a stunt.

Most stunts depended on speed for their execution, so the stunting plane would rise for altitude, and then finally swing forward in a short dive to gain speed. Of course, at any height at all we could not tell whether they were climbing or diving except by the speed at which they moved forward. Even from a steep angle, an airplane when viewed from the ground, could appear on an even keel. The absence of any stationary object near them and their distance far above the horizon, made it difficult to determine if the plane was level.

I observed that a climbing plane, was traveling slower than a leveled off plane. A diving plane slipped across the sky faster. Most stunts started with a climb, followed by a dive to gain speed, then stunted into a loop. By watching the dive begin, I could call out to the other soldiers around me in time for them to witness the loop. One plane pulled a beautiful trick, one that I had never heard of prior. It climbed, and then dived and started nosing up as though entering a loop, but instead of looping, the pilot kept it boring straight up, until the motor could not pull it further, and then it would drop, straight down on its tail, sliding backward, for what seemed a long distance. Then suddenly the tail would catch the air and the aircraft would flop over, making a short hook, leaving the tail on top, nose down. Then it would dive straight down, in a spin, rotating in a circle, much as those paper-winged darts we used to make. Down, down, down that slow spinning plane would drop till, when it seemed as if it must be out of control, it would suddenly swing out in a short curve forward, level off and go on its way, as if nothing unusual had happened. To us, those stunts spoiled our liking for the ordinary flying, and it got so that only the most vigilant would watch the planes overhead. Like anything new, it was a treat for a while, but soon got tiresome, except to those few who will always find enough novelty in something to keep watching. Me, I kept watching out of fascination, and searching for subtle differences between pilots, which appeared more skilled.

Late in the afternoon, the Santiago trip was called off, for now at least, and I was marched with the others, to a long tent city. Street after street of tents. These tent rows were numbered and we started up the main street past rows one, and two, going on up and dropping off a few men at each row. Apparently, we were being shoved in wherever there was room for us. I finally landed in line 51, toward the back. The main street was between the mess tents and the tent city proper, for there was one mess tent opposite each double row of tents. A short street, at right angles to the main tent street, came between each double row of tents. The first two tents in each row were the oblong, ridge tents with a pole at each end, and were used as the headquarters and for the line Sergeants. The rest of the tents were the round top kind, requiring but one pole in the center.

I landed in with six other boys, named Dennis, Fletcher, Luce, Ely, Nash, and Overton. We had canvas army cots, and I soon had my bag opened and my blankets out. After mess, during the long, dusky evening hours, before taps sounded, I heard plenty of news about Kelly field. Most of these boys in my tent had been there for months, and were still awaiting transfer. Camp Kelly to them, was an immense prison. They were not in the flying program. Sand and windstorms were frequent, and it was common talk that clerks in the offices had for a time been careless with the service records in their possession, and had allowed sudden gusts to blow them off their desks, and out windows, many lost entirely! So, these men here could not know whether their service records were still in the camp, or not. Sooner or later, perhaps, the army red tape would connect up their registry in the lines with an absent service record, and then they'd get their back pay, and a transfer. I felt bad for them, and forewarned what could happen to us new rookies.

With pay and occasional letter from home, it would not have been so bad. Kelly Field was just the opposite of Jefferson Barracks. Jefferson Barracks, manned by regular army officers, and with personnel used to the routine of taking in new men, was run quite orderly. Kelly Field, entirely new, even being a new branch of the Signal Corps, was a mess. Everything was mixed up and only just now was beginning to get into a semblance of order. Pay was only a tradition to this tent city. Some of the boys drew some money, but seldom if ever. Mostly inconsistent. Mail was pathetic. Every once in a while, some boy wanting news from home, poked his head into our tent and asked if any of the new men were from his home town, or area. Sure, he might send out letters, if he still had money for stamps, or could borrow some, but the incoming mail system was in a mess and few letters were received and delivered. Tent lines were shifted almost daily, and several of these men had been in as high as ten rows of tents in almost that number of days. Because of this shifting, mail if delivered, seldom moved to find its owner. In the army mail system used here, apparently no efforts were made to trace any man when he moved, and so it was that several of these men were practically severed from connection to their home for months at a time.

Fortunately for me, at our arrival to Camp Kelly, the Y.M.C.A. secretary in San Antonio, volunteered to handle the mail. By establishing the YMCA as a post office in a hut in camp, where all misdirected or uncalled mail was left, thousands of letters could be redirected. Soldiers could register their location, and mail finally began to get to the destined owner. One corner of the YMCA hut had a room with a couple windows. This was used to call out mail. Promptly at seven p.m., these windows opened, one man appeared at each and began calling names off the envelopes; each window, alphabetically, A-L, the next M-Z. It was a pathetic sight, a sea of faces in the semi-darkness, turned up toward the readers, each standing quietly to be able to hear, all anticipating a letter! Men trickled out of the sea, as the called passed their last name alphabetic letter, or with a letter in hand. Some smarter boys had a list of names to listen for, maintaining a forward position and gathering mail.

As the boys in my tent had told me, many of these boys had not heard from home in months, and I was interested while watching the sea of faces. Hard-boiled faces, softened, became eager and pathetic, anticipating to hear their name.

"BA Dryer" was called, "BA Dryer", was repeated. A young chap suddenly stiffened, then jumped up shouting, "Here! Here!". He pushed forward to retrieve his letter, as others in front, passed it back to him. Tears were in his eyes, as he took the letter, examined the address and post mark date. Another held a match to allow him to read it.

"First damn letter in seven weeks!" he exclaimed. He bent his eyes closer on the letter, "Oh damn! It's BA Dryer, not BJ Dryer. I thought he called BJ Dryer. I don't know anyone from Missouri. Tain't mine". He passed it back forward, and walk away dejectedly.

Others patted him on his back in sympathy. You had to feel bad for the guy. Spirits soaring one moment, and dashed the next. Not all the others shared in his luck. Because of this better YMCA location system, it worked better. I saw several that received letters, and many were outspoken in favor of this new plan for handling mail.

One evening, I went over with Overton and Nash to the YMCA hut, back amongst the wooden buildings, just to listen to the mail being called out, I lucked out and got a letter that had been forwarded from Jefferson Barracks. It was from Mother, and had a dollar bill in it! I sure appreciated that dollar! I was darn glad to get a letter myself, though I had been in the army, at this time, only a little more than two weeks and had now received two letters already.

I stayed most of the time in the tent city, for I saw that from the way the buildings and tents were scattered about, I was going to need a guide every time I went over to the section where the offices, etc. were located. I did go over once, with Nash, to see if I could get into the army band at Kelly Field. I was not optimistic, since I did not have my cornet with me, and had no hopes of Miss Marion sending it from her home in Minnesota. The band, at present, required each player had to furnish their own instruments. I did glance at a score one chap was practicing, and was surprised to see that it was a C or D class material, that I could play on sight. I decided that the band was sour grapes for me at present. Besides, if this was the best music they could handle, I was not anxious to be in it. I was proud of my old high school band, and the music Mr. Hyatt, had taught us. We used the class C material, and a few, class B pieces for concerts.

The only thing I appreciated at our tent city, was the mess tents, for I had learned how to get my share and some extra. Each mess tent served two tent rows. The men in the lines were supposed to eat at the mess tent opposite the end of each double line. With so many men moving to various tents, the servers & cooks could never know who was to be in their tent line. So, Overton had figured it out, and taught me to check what each mess line was serving. He & I would then choose which line to go through, or repeat in another tent. I hate tomatoes and cabbage, so I was able to avoid those dishes. We had little to do, so we'd wait an hour or two, in the front of a mess line. Upon opening, we went through, ate, washed and dried our mess kits, and then moved to another line for their food. The servers were supposed to offer seconds, but by us acting as first serves in the line, we got two meals if we wanted them. It was a wise trick, and not exactly fair, but it worked. Overton and I both liked to eat. The army taught us to be opportunistic.

I had been in line 51 one day, when the Sergeant stopped me as I was passing the H.Q. tent.

"Come in, Gray," he said. I went in, he pointed to a chair, taking one himself.

"Sit down, and tell me how you like the name of Marion", he asked.

"It's a hell of a name," I responded, "It's alright for girl, a dog or a cow, but damn poor for a guy. You gotta either be a sissy, or else a roughneck. It's made me more of a roughneck. What makes you ask that, Sergeant? Do you know someone else with that name? You must see some queer names!"

"Yep", he chuckled, "My name is Marion Coy, and every time anyone sees it on a letter, I am mistaken for a girl. When they find out I'm not, they think I must be a sucker, with such a name. I never have met but two other guys with the name, and you're one of them."

The Sergeant and I went on telling anecdotes for an hour. To look at that hard-boiled old bird, you would never guess that he had also been called "sissy", as I had. I told him of the old Saxby school bunch, at five feet and weighing eighty pounds, used to call me "Sissy" in the seventh grade. Then, two years later, at five-nine, and a hundred-forty pounds, they crossed the street to avoid me. Not that I was dangerous, but I was also playing football, so that was enough.

Maybe that talk fest helped. I was never put on K.P. while in that line, nor given to the "fatique" parties for cleaning the grounds. The Sergeant, perhaps, thought carrying the moniker "Marion" had been enough in life. As it was, the only time my name popped up on K.P., was the day that I was scheduled for my third inoculation shot in the arm. Mine didn't bother me, but, Lordy, what a time some other boys had.

At Jefferson Barracks, we had been given a small card, showing the date of our first inoculation, and then it was also stamped with the 2nd shot also. This card was my only record of the shots. I was lucky that I'd kept it, because many other boys had lost theirs. Guess what? Yep, they had to start over! Lordy, what a bunch of cussing was heard around that medical tent! Some chaps taking their fourth or fifth shot, as some claimed. Some guys will lose anything, but in the army, excuses don't carry. Each card when completed, had to reflect the dates of all three shots. I could see from the way these boys talked that the Medical Corps was not in their favor. As I saw then, and later on, the regular outfits may detest the Q.M. Corps but it is positive hate that they reserved for the "pill rollers", as the medical men were called. "Pill Rollers" was used due to the fact that the average army doctor's prescription called for pills of one sort or another. Pills, pills, pills. A civilian doctor prescribed bottles of something or others, but in the army, its pills, pills, pills.

Drill was one word not in good usage for me in the tent city life. My regular procedure was to arise by 6a.m., wash, and off to eat breakfast, wash up my mess kit, perhaps lie on my cot for an hour or so. Then get called to fall out for a couple hours of yard policing, or street cleanup when the whistle blew. After, it was time to line up for mess again by 10a.m., as it was not unusual to line up two hours before the noon mess call.

One thing that I hated at Camp Kelly was the sand storms. The wind was always blowing, and some food tasted like they had ground glass in them from all the sand that had blown into it! At mess, we had to march past the cook's table in a long line, each man balancing his mess kit, cover, and coffee cup, as best he could, as the cooks and servers dished out food. If it was stew, it would be a cup of stew into the mess kit, maybe a couple boiled potatoes tossed in also, and two slices of bread. A cup of coffee, looking like mud, and half as sweet as I preferred. Often, I had to throw the bread into a coat pocket, slam the cover on the mess kit, while I rushed for a quiet spot to eat where the sand was not blowing in so bad. It was impossible to eat out in the open on many days, unless one preferred adding two or three spoonsful of sand to their meal!

CHAPTER 8

Thanksgiving Day arrived and we got a generous helping of steak and even cranberries for once. Yes, and wonder of wonders, a tiny dish of real ice cream, and an apple or orange. We made up for it, as our Thanksgiving dinner was served about two p.m., instead of the usual noon, and 6p.m. Due to the large meal, we got no supper.

I must have been lucky at Kelly Field, or I arrived just at a time when things started to get organized and move. On Saturday, December 1st, I was hauled out of my tent by Sergeant Coy, and told to pack up, for I had been transferred to the 160th Aero Squadron, a new outfit! The boys in my tent were happy for me, but I felt bad for the boys left, some had been waiting there ahead of me. Nash and Overton shared my luck too, for they were transferred also and according to Sergeant Coy, Kelly Field was getting cleaned up. With my barrack bag on my shoulder, I and six others, were marched over to line 22 by Sergeant Coy. That was the last time I saw of him.

New tent lines were being put up opposite the old ones, starting opposite line 1 and 2. Lines 21 and 22, where the 160th was assembling, were in the new set. That new squadron was a mess. In the middle of the street stood a pile of folding cots. A hard-boiled Sergeant, tanned so darkly that he looked like an Indian, had us sort them out, open them up, and place them in our tents. He then lined us up, counted us off into squads, one squad to a tent.

As near as I could make out, the Kelly Field system of handling service records was to put each man's record into their files according to the occupation he was listed under. Many, like myself, were put in as chauffeurs, truck drivers, or clerks, while a select few were listed as cooks or bakers. So, when a new squadron was organized, just so many of each trade were needed. If there was a shortage in a given field, others were reassigned to fill the need. Thus, we had one cook, and when our Sergeant asked for a couple volunteers, no one stepped up. Cooking was a job no one wanted, certainly not me, after working in the restaurant back home. Promptly, the Sergeant picked out several likely looking men, and made them cooks. The army always fills its needs, and you can't quit!

We had drawn three regulars, former infantry men, each on their second hitch or better, as the nucleus of our squadron. One had been a corporal, the other two privates in the Hawaiian Islands, before shipping back. Now they were all listed as Sergeants. The corporal became Top Sergeant, and the other two became QM and Mess Sergeants. Knowing the army game, as they did, they soon whipped our medley into something resembling a squadron. Sergeant Veach was the Top and one of his first requests that first morning, was for someone who could run a typewriter, and do some office work.

"It's a damn good job for some of you birds, if you handle it right, and a chance to be Sergeant Major of this outfit", he said.

I wanted no office job, and was inclined to figure that I could not believe all we were being told. Some chap nearby knew I had a high school education and pointed this out to Sergeant Veach, whereupon Veach started moving toward me. We were in a mob and by the time he got near me, I had my eye on a chap who had spoken about typing, so I pointed to him.

"I'm a poor typist, Sergeant, but this guy says he's pretty good at it."

So, Sergeant Veach, picked on Private Wright. Over time, Veach proved right, as Private Wright made Corporal, Sergeant, Sergeant First Class, eventually, Sergeant Major, as predicted. I kept kicking myself for passing on the best job in the squadron! For my purposes, I was still focused on becoming a flyer, and that typist job would've gotten me exposure to officers, who later, could've given me a recommendation to flying when the time came. I had certainly made a larger error that day!

9

PARK FIELD – TENNESSEE

It took three more days to get us fitted out, partly settled, and on Dec 4th, were loaded into a string of sleeper cars and headed for a new aviation field, near Memphis, Tennessee. That was a fairly nice trip in those sleeper cars. Three men being assigned to a double berth, two on the lower, one in the upper. We drew straws, and I got an upper berth, all to myself.

In Texarkana, we stopped for a half hour, and many of the boys went up town. When we were ready to leave, the Sergeant was having a fit, waiting for some troops to return. He trotted out a new bugle and needed some ex-cornet player to use it. I was that guy, and having recalled the notes from my blue drill manual, that I had gotten at Jefferson Barracks, I became a bugler right then. I did use the manual for my initial calls. I admit that recall certainly didn't sound like the old army calls but at least I made enough noise that the boys came trooping back.

Someone told me that in the regular army, the bugler acted as a messenger for the officers, and so I thought that I had a good job as bugler, and I might get acquainted with the officers, permitting me to plead my interest in aviation. When I enlisted, I was under the impression that an officer was much the same as a boss in a factory, and easily approached. By now I saw my mistake. The Top Sergeant and the office sergeant are practically the only ones to know the officers in a squadron, and maybe a few other sergeants. Again, turning down the office job at Kelly Field had eclipsed my best chance.

The train pulled into Park Field, Millington, Tennessee, about 3a.m. on Dec 7th, and after one peek out thru the frosty window, I rolled over and went back to sleep. We were not turned out till 7a.m., and then we had a barren, cold barrack to move into. Even the furnace was not in working order yet, and we shivered and froze for a day until it was working.

There were about a hundred and sixty men in our squadron, and our barracks were arranged in two sections, each accommodating eighty men. It was a really long building, maybe three hundred feet or so. At the east end, were two small rooms, one for the Top Sergeant, the other served as an office, then came one long room, holding eight cots and another small sergeant's room against a dividing partition. There was a door leading into the washroom and bath house, and by making a run thru the washroom, one got into the other half of the barrack, laid out in mirror fashion of the front end. For heat there were two open top, or pipe-less furnaces, one for each half, and when operating the men near them roasted, while twenty feet away, one would freeze. It took me one night to learn to use paper under my blankets, for we had no straw ticks and it was bitter cold. After that, every newspaper I got ahold of went to thicken my mattress. One of the boys said the newspaper trick was known by every railroad tramp.

I was surprised to find that one man in our squadron had been in the army six months, and was still in civvies! His service record had been lost, and he could draw no clothing, nor pay. He was used to that by now, and past the kicking stage, so he did as best he could. Sergeant Veach put him to work as a fireman, so he could keep warm. One day he burned his pants, and one of the guys with an extra pair, passed them along. It was sometime in January before he finally got fitted out.

One squadron was already at the field, the 140th, and they were just marking time, doing guard duty, general work, waiting for contractors to finish up the hangars, and for the weather to warm, so that flying could start. I was still the bugler, and on a 7:30a.m., Sunday, and when the guard was changed, I filled in as bugler, relieving a chap named O'Connor, the only bugler in the 140th. That night it was bitter cold, and since there were 20 guards, two prisoners, plus myself, in the guardhouse. There were only fourteen cots for us all, I did not sleep. I left the cots empty for the tired-out guards, who had to walk post on a cold night. With 10 posts, and three shifts of men for each post, that made each man on two hours, and off for four hours. The usual plan was four hours on, and off eight, but with it so cold, the officer of the day [OOD], revised it to two-hour shifts, sometimes only one. Clothing was barely useful, many a chap went out to a two-hour stint with towels or extra underwear wrapped about his head, or under his hat to try to keep their ears warm. A few of us were lucky enough to have received knit caps or ear pads from home, and I lent mine out to one of the guards each shift. As bugler, I was lucky, in that I had only to step outside of the guardhouse, blow my calls and come back in. Even at that, I had to heat my bugle's mouthpiece so that it did not stick to my lips! More than once, at five below zero F, it was so cold, that I left a call partly finished because my lips stuck to the mouthpiece!

The guard carried automatic shotguns, for we had not been issued any army rifles, nor pistols. Only a few of the boys even knew how to handle any weapon at all. More than once they let one go off accidently, while loading or unloading it!

Park Field was about twenty miles from Memphis, and three miles from Millington, our nearest US Post Office. A work train came out from Memphis each week day morning, when it was not too cold to work. I was surprised to see that most of the workers were slow moving darkies, but somehow at that, the camp sprang to life, day by day, and building after building was finished. And simultaneously, officers, men, cadets, and others kept arriving in a seemingly endless succession.

I got a letter from Mother, after we had been at the field a week. She said she was going to write my wife, Miss Marion, and I had said it was fine. She would likely enjoy it. Somehow, she seemed to consider our fight as something which might happen to any young couple, and acted as if it might be patched up. I didn't think so, but she seemed to like Marion as well as ever. I certainly did not.

Talk of variety, our squadron had it. We had a representative from every state and territory in the Union, except one. Several men had been born in other countries. A big, dark foreign looking chap bunked next to me, Msellem Msellem. Say it if you can, both names the same. He was born twenty miles north of Jerusalem, was quiet, inoffensive, and nearly thirty years old. I wondered what had brought him into this branch of the service.

Then there was a short, dried-up farmer from Iowa, nearly forty years old, Bill Godiksen. Later on, I found that he was a retired college professor, turned farmer. Another guy was a famous comedian from New York city. There were two other Grays in the squadron; Pinkney, tall, quiet, dark-complexioned with a shock of black hair, and Montello, a short, heavy set, noisy chap with a lock of his hair always hanging over his left eye. We got along, not especially friendly, though we shared the same last name. My two best pals were Smith and Betts. Leroy Betts was a heavyset guy with dark hair, shorter than me from Rockford, Ill. Benjamin Smith was tall, skinny, red-haired, freckle-faced cowboy from Roswell, New Mexico. Good guys, and quite the pair!

Such was the 160th, made up of tramps to college professors and all proud to be regular army men, not militia, nor draftees. A fine bunch all around.

Ben Smith's chief diversion was to catch either Betts or I lying on a cot. When we weren't looking, he would come with a run and jump, and dive over two cots, and land on top! It didn't matter whether the cot withstood the punishment or not. We treated Smith likewise, when we caught him dozing. After we wrecked six cots, Sergeant Veach came out of the office and being unable to find out who was wrecking the cots, gave an ultimatum to the effect that the next man breaking a cot will be on K.P. for a long week! Surprisingly, the cot destruction ended....

On the 13th of December, Monty Gray went on as the other squadron bugler, and the 140th added another also. So, the three of us that were off duty each, had to find something to do to keep off the K.P. and the fatigue cleanup crews. That is one funny thing about the army, even a good, hard-working chap as a civilian would learn to be an expert duty dodger in the army. Certainly, Monty and I, the two Grays, buglers for the 160th, did not overdo ourselves.

Alarm bells were installed in each barrack and each sergeant had a whistle, so that there was no actual need for a bugler, aside from the army tradition, blowing reveille, retreat, and taps on occasion. When first call was blown in the morning, the Top Sergeant, who had already awakened by the guard on that post, would ring the bell so that really the bugle was of little use. The men at the guardhouse had to keep their clothing on at all time, during their 24-hour duty stint. When not on post, they could lie down and sleep, but could not remove any clothing, nor boots. Being at the center of the post, these guards formed the fire brigade, and had to haul the heavy hose cart around whenever there was a fire, or a drill. Usually, all fires were reported to the guards, or by them, so that gave the guard house crew a head start. The bugler acted as the fire alarm, calling every available man to help squelch the fire.

Capt. Zimmerman, in charge of the garage at the field was named as the field Fire Marshall, and since he had been a bugler in the infantry prior to getting his commission, he also took charge of us buglers. The calls we blew must have sounded awful to anyone who had heard a real bugler, and Capt. Zimmerman ordered us to practice calls for four hours daily. That meant no K.P., nor cleanups, so it suited us fine. We would trot off to one of the end hangars, usually No. 1, at the far east end. There, we'd practice for 30 minutes of the four hours. The second or third day that we were at it, the captain found us. He told us all about his previous service as a bugler, and then picked up a bugle to illustrate how it should be done.

"A real bugler" he said, "will crack a bugle about every three months. I have known men who could not use one over month, but that is exceptionally hard. By 'crack', I mean not to really break the bugle, but they will blow it so hard that the tone will be damaged, though sometimes a real crack will be found. I suspect that there is always a crack somewhere in the bell because the tone is shattered. Then he blew a call on the bugle and Lord how he did make it roar! It snapped out on the air like a command from a gigantic machine. It was a genuine army bugle call with snap and crack of an officer's command. It came to me then that while we had been blowing calls by note, and copying our timing from my drill manual, these experienced buglers, just did it according to their own notions, whether they used the correct notes or not. They could certainly make their bugles talk!

Capt. Zimmerman handed the bugle back, and said, "I can see right now that you boys are not going to make buglers while using that issued bugle. You ought to buy your own bugle, if you ever want to blow a decent call. We used to always buy those long cavalry bugles, and though they are not to be used in the infantry, we were never called down for using them. Certainly, you boys are not going to crack one of these stiff issued bugles. Damn poor stuff to issue.

That was common for a lot of the army material. Some manufacturers were making a pile of money selling junk to the army. Those bugles were not so bad as a lot of other material but they gave me something to think about. There was no reason why the army could not have had thin-belled, better toned instruments. Certainly, the cost for such would not have been much, even in war time. If I had planned on staying very long as a bugler, I may have bought my own horn with my first pay but I was awaiting a chance to get into, or around planes and learn to fly. This army discipline and the red tape seemed to be to be confining me where I was. Certainly, I would've had a better chance to get in as a cadet while a civilian than I was going to have at this field.

Wed, December 19th was a rainy day, and we practiced our bugle call in #1 again. I got wet feet both coming and going so when I was back in the barrack, I removed my wet shoes and not taking time to put on dry stockings, went down the aisle and stood on the furnace grating drying my wet stockings on my feet. Not a good idea. That was about 4p.m. and I remember dreaming something that night about flying with angels in a closed box, which reminded me of an ambulance.

It must have been about noon the next day, when I was awake, and clear-headed enough to see that I was in a big bed in a square, white room with windows on three sides, and open to the winter breeze. Around one arm was what looked like a tire tube, with some sort of gauge on it. All about the room were army medical officers. There must have been five or six. One of them had a clinical thermometer in his hand, and somehow my ears caught a sound, "temperature 106". If that was correct, then it appeared these doctors were on hand to watch me die. The gauge and tube on my arm were there to measure my blood pressure, and the old Major beside me had one hell of a time trying to make it work. He couldn't get it to show pressure at all. He tried another gauge and still no result. The rest of the officers began to crowd around as if I had no blood pressure at all. I heard one say, "he must have some pressure, his heart is still beating."

I began to get interested myself, and the gauge must have registered a little, for I heard a satisfied, "Ahhh" from someone. Then I got woozy, and dropped off while trying to clean a speck off one window, from twenty feet away! Somehow, I knew that I was out of my head, delusional, trying to reach that far with one arm, but heck, the window looked like it was right on my nose, and the speck bothered me!

Later that day, or maybe it was the next, I recall several waking moments when I knew that either the old medical Major or some other doctor was always in the room. Present also, was a tall chap, with brown hair, and light-colored eyes, a private, or some enlisted man. About noon, this private tried to get me to drink prune juice and a small cup of cold coffee. I must have dozed off after the prune juice, and awoke later that afternoon, somewhat improved, for only the private remained in the room. I tried to ask questions, but he shut me up, and told me what he knew of my case. I had pneumonia, and had been very bad, but was improving. I was the second case in this new hospital, having arrived by ambulance on Thursday morning. Some chap named Walter Knight had been the first patient. He'd been on guard duty, became ill, and tried to unload a shotgun. I cost him a big toe, and that shoe. Perhaps he gained knowledge of how to operate a shotgun but I'd bet he was delusional, like myself. The hospital was so new that the furnace had not been in operation yet, and might be in a day or so. Faber, my male nurse, had carried my prune juice and coffee over a mile from the temporary hospital and mess at the far west end of the field.

The next day Faber had brought me a bowl of milk, a slice of bread, and coffee. I drank the coffee and refused the milk. It might be good for me but I'd never liked cold milk since I was little. From then on, I got better in a hurry, and in a few days was allowed to sit up and stagger out to the kitchen and eat with the hospital corps there. There were no female nurses here yet, and these boys had to handle all the cases.

Red Smith and Betts came to visit me one afternoon and relate the news. The hardest thing for them to do was speak without cussing.

"Hello kid, how the hell are you?" stuttered Red.

"Damned glad to see you Gray!" said Betts.

This hospital atmosphere put these boys on better behavior, and they had to stop cussing. In the barracks they were used to slipping in one or more "damns", or "hells" in their sentences, often more. It made me wonder what their fond mothers would think of their darling boys. Especially if they arrived shouting, "Hells bells, folks, I'm damned glad to be home and see y'all!", or maybe worse!

My Christmas at the hospital had consisted of prune juice and coffee, and a few days later, Faber showed me the present that some Memphis organization had sent out for the soldiers. It was a Red Cross kit bag, duck cloth with several pockets for various articles, and in it a pack of smoking tobacco, two packages of cigarettes, and two chocolate bars. I did smoke cigarettes but not while in the hospital. I packed the chocolate bars away, and slyly nibbled one up several days later. The other, Faber and I shared when he said I might be able to eat it. I told him I had given the other bar to one of the squadron boys that had stopped in to visit. He would have given me heck, if he'd known that I had already consumed it. If pneumonia couldn't kill me, then surely chocolate wouldn't either. I hadn't written home until I was able to sit up for over an hour, even then, I told Mother, I'd been sick a few days but was okay. Weeks later in another letter, I told her how sick I had actually been and had pneumonia. I also wrote Miss Marion, told her of my pneumonia, but down played it. Not sure she'd really care anyway.

By New Year's I was able to enjoy quite a dinner, and was perking up in a hurry. Four other boys from the 160th came to visit; Stone, Sandbo, Doyle, and Sergeant Wright. The rumor was that the 160th was about to move again. They group had the same issue as Smith and Betts had — trying to refrain from bad language. I was better and they were less reserved swearing than prior visitors, figuring I was almost normal again.

By the 12th of January, I was able to get around in fine shape, and was released to my squadron, which had not moved yet. That long walk down the hill was an awful effort for me, and for a few days I was pretty weak. By the 16th, I was assigned to guard duty with the 214th squadron, a new group that had shipped in. Red Smith was bugling in my place, so I was on regular duty again, but it lasted only a few days, because another new squadron had been formed, the 161st. It was organized with recruits from Memphis and local towns. Monty and several others were transferred into it from the 160th, so that put me back on duty as a bugler along with Red.

Mother sent me two express packages that had newspapers from Freeport in them, along with six big cans of home fruit preserves! Boy, did those cans look good to me! The news was good to hear too! Our mess cooks, were none too expert, and I was still recuperating, so I was hungry. I still divided my hoard with Smith, Betts, and others. With five cans, sharing across five meals, it was a treat. I did conserve one can to enjoy myself, they'd lasted three days.

Tuesday, Jan 22nd was our first payday, and I got pay up to Jan 1st, $53 in total. I felt wealthy! They did withhold $3 for my canteen book at Jefferson, and $6 from canteen books from Park field. I sent $25 home, and proceeded to lose most of the rest playing craps and poker. Up till now we had many little card games, and a few crap games for nickels and pennies, but boy did I get my eyes opened! That night craps, poker, blackjack, hearts, and other games flourished! The big crap game was in the bathroom, on the cement floor, and after losing most of my money there. I watched the excitement. Most of the 'sharks' at craps slipped the dice sideways out of their hands, with a twisting, spinning motion. Later I found that a die, when spun so, tended to act like a top and either the upper or lower number would show. None of these boys could roll any number they wanted every time but certainly from the way some won, they sure could control it sometimes. When someone was evidently too much of a 'shark', that roller was compelled to roll the dice against a board and thus reducing their control of the results. With everyone doing their best to cheat their neighbor, it became a fair game, since all the cheating equalized. Come to think of it, most games of chance are like that. Really games of skill, not chance. Poker and other card games required more skill and bluffing, with a dash of luck thrown in.

Two nights later I saw a new face in the bathroom at the crap game. It was the colored shoe-shine chap, from the canteen. Black as coal, short and tubby, with a round, chubby face, he was a little angel to look at. His easy-going attitude and jovial smile made a likeable fellow. Wisely, he was not rolling for high stakes. Somehow, he knew he could make far more off these boys by keeping their good will, than by winning all their money. He played to keep even, and it was a treat to watch him. He handled nothing but dollar bills, in shooting or in fading. He played even by fading only one or two dollars at a time, and shooting with a dollar a shot. He never doubled, when he passed. When I first saw him taking the dice, I got a shock. On each of his chubby hands, his fingers were all damaged. He had one good finger out of ten, the others were all missing one or two joints. I felt bad, and by sticking around, another boy asked him how it was so.

"Jess reachin for de dice", he said. "You know dais big nigger boys carries some big razors, and when dey don't like da way yo roll de dice, dey jess chops away at anything in sight. An I'se allus unlucky enuff to git my paws right in de road. Glory be dey hain't never got no moah den a finger!"

So that was it. Certainly, this little bird must have done some crap shooting to have lost all those fingers. They had not all come off at one time, let alone two or three slices. I wondered how he handled the dice, and so I watched. At his turn, he'd not reach out for the dice. He held his hand out and one of the boys would drop them in his palm. Without even glancing at them, he would rattle them back and forth, and shove them out on the cement, meanwhile keeping his eyes on the rest of the boys. He never once even glanced at the dice, and when he said, "Come on foah, baby needs shoes, make me two deuces, dice". Sure enough, up rolled two twos! When he was even, he missed, and lost the dice. Sometimes he pretended to be trying to make his point, but by careful watching it was evident that he was just having a good time, not trying to win money from the white boys.

When it wasn't freezing, it rained. January was a real mud month for us. One afternoon just after guard duty, I was put on one of Lieutenant Borden's 'mud details', prior known as a "fatigue party'. This round we were called to help dig out trucks stuck in the mud. We worked until 2a.m. that night. The main road at first ran up the hill near the hospital, but later on a better road was built along the hill, leading down to the valley and the regular field west entrance. Before the good road was built, in one day I saw three army trucks get stuck on the hill road at the same time. We, the "mud detail", were busy digging out a fourth truck at the bottom between the barracks and hangars. It was muddy!

Army life certainly did agree with me, in spite of, or maybe because of the pneumonia and mud. In November, I had enlisted weighing 128 lbs. After the hospital, I'd lost weight down to 110, but on Feb 5th, I was in the Aero supply room. A scale there I used, showed I was over 160 lbs.!

Park Field was getting bigger day by day, and every day the weather permitted, planes roared overhead. Dipping, twisting, turning, and even looping. I was so used to seeing them that I seldom watched. I think the stunts I'd seen at Kelly Field in Texas, were more impressive, but then that was a more advanced training field. We had civilian instructors here, and they did little stunting, probably because army regs prevented them.

Close to two hundred cadets were now at the field, and eight squadrons of enlisted men. The 65th, 140th, 161st, 193rd, 214th, 281st, 282nd, and mine, the 160th. Two squadrons were camped in tents because there were only barracks for 6 squadrons. Officers were changing almost daily, with rumors flying that one squadron or another was shipping out.

I wrote a short letter home, to the Freeport Daily Journal Standard. Mabel Goddard, my English teacher from high school, saw it and wrote me a dandy letter back. It sure seemed good to get a letter from back home, other than the regular letters from Miss Marion, and Mother, which came from Forreston.

On Saturday, the 16th of February I got my first leave, a 36-hour permit, commencing after retreat Saturday, and ending Monday morning at reveille, so Betts and I headed for Memphis. He had been lucky enough to get a pass also, and with $5 I borrowed from Corporal Haley, we left to spend it. We caught the 6:30pm train to Memphis, and after wandering around half the night, spent the rest sleeping at the "Y". The next morning, we rushed out at 8am and began seeing the sights. We were interested at one place in watching squirrels as they played in a park off main street. The whole square block was devoted to this park and the squirrels owned it. A peanut stand on one corner did a record business, and with a little trouble I could coax one of the squirrels to eat from my hand. I had to be careful, since the squirrels weren't careful how they bit, and I was fond of my fingers!

Betts and I spent the day trotting around, vainly imagining that some beauties would take us to be aviators, and fall for our splendid selves. It appeared by now, that the girls could tell the difference between an officer's neat and natty uniform, and the hit and miss fit of our army issue stuff. Undoubtedly, they were also aware of the difference in spending money of the various uniforms too. There were so many soldiers and cadets in Memphis, that maybe all the beauties had been captured.

We inspected all of the Memphis business district during the day and envied all the khaki clad soldiers we saw that hosted fair companions. Finally, about 5p.m., as we were crossing one busy street, Betts nudged me, and though I gazed at his direction, I missed what he was seeing.

"Say, pipe those chickens we just passed", he said, "I winked at the black-eyed baby, and she winked back. Let's go back across the street and see if we can pick them up."

We had passed them in the crush at the crossing, but by watching a moment we could see them when they reached the other side. They walked a few feet down the street, to a quiet spot, and then stopped and seemed to be looking back at us. We didn't wait for any other invitation, and in a moment, we were over by them. One was a dark-eyed, olive complexioned little brunette, and the other a tall blonde. The little girl looked as if she was about 18, while the tall blonde must have been twenty-four, or five.

"Hello kid," said Betts to the smaller girl, "I've been look all over for you."

"Yes, you have," she laughed, "And whatcha goin to do now-sha found me?"

"If we stand here, we'll be blocking traffic," I said, "So I suppose we better take you up the street, till he figures out what he ought to do. Ain't that right?" and I turned to the blonde beside me.

"Sure," she answered, "Let's go. Are you boys from the flying field at Millington? Do you know a boy there named Harold Parker?"

"Nope," I answered, "I'm not interested in boys. What's your names?"

The blonde spoke up, "I'm Blanche, and this is Edna."

"I'm Gray, and this is Betts", I responded, using my last name, avoiding a discussion about Marion.

That was the kind of pick-up it was, and since Betts decided that we were all hungry, the girls led the way to a little lunch room, about ten blocks away. There we spent a whole dollar and thirty cents in an hour and a half. Then a show took nearly two hours. It was 9:15p.m. when we delivered the girls to their door.

"Here's our flat on the second floor," said Blanche, my blonde guest, as we stopped at the address, she called her own. It was a narrow door between two shops on a side street. Inside the door was short hallway and stairs up to the second floor. We took the girls up, and Blanche opened the door and turned on the lights, then held the door expecting us to come in.

"Come on in, make yourselves at home, boys," she invited.

"Gosh, we'd like to," said I, "but we have to catch the 9:45p.m. train back to the field, and we can't stop."

"Oh, the devil with that train!" said little Edna, Bett's girl. "Can't you take the morning train back?"

"We'd get court-martialed if we did." Answered Betts, "and besides all our kale is gone, so where would we stay?"

"Huh," snorted Blanche, "why worry over that? I guess this can hold four of us without breaking down," and she shook the corner post of a dingy, sloppy looking bed she was standing beside.

"It might," I said, "But if we get in bad this trip to town, we'll never get in again, so we better wait till next time. So long till we come in again, it was fun meeting you both!" I said, and Betts and I left right then.

I'd heard other soldiers just back from leave tell rather hot stories of how easy going these town girls were, and I put it down as hot air. Now I began to wonder a little myself. I wasn't disappointed myself, since I am married. Certainly, Betts and I had commented all day on the free and easy manner in which all the girls were with soldiers. There was no mistaking the invitation that we had received. These girls were easy issuing invitations, but I for one was rather afraid of such girls. We had heard too many lectures from the army about the diseases one could catch. I'd decided that I had rather be good and careful, than careless and sorry. Betts wasn't saying anything, as we hurried to catch our train, but he was holding his nose, very expressively.

Tuesday, the 26th of February, I got a surprise. A questionnaire had been passed around a week or so before, asking how many soldiers could play musical instruments. I had entered, "alto and cornet." Now I was called up to an empty building near the officer's mess. I discovered that some Memphis band had loaned out excess old instruments, so Park Field was going to have a band. Each man as he filed in, picked out an instrument, and took a seat. I was nearly the last one in, and found only two cornets left; both battered old Conns. There wasn't much choice, so I grabbed the one w/ two mouthpieces and seated myself. Presently, the director, after some instructions, started us off on a very simple class "D" piece, and old march that I could read on sight, and nearly go to sleep on. Since I had been the last cornet player to arrive, he put me to playing the 3rd and 4th cornet part. In the entire piece, I had but one little snappy four note run. I tongued it so neatly that each time we played it, the director came over till he finally found out what seemed to be wrong, and he moved me to solo cornet. There I remained being put ahead of even one of his own cornet players from the 161st.

As I found out, a cheap mail order cornet is worth what you pay. My fifteen-dollar cornet could not compare with the old Conn. I had learned on a hard to blow cornet, but this old battered horn would reach high "C" with almost no effort. Light lip pressure and it played great, my old cheap one took great lip pressure to play. My lip muscles were still in shape, especially with the bugle experience.

The band made a fair start, though we were short of a tuba player and had to start one man out on it as a beginner. At that, he was almost better than some players who'd claimed to be experienced. Many of these chaps could read and play the notes on the sheets in front of them but had no idea what the tone marks were for. When we had a good start, and after four or five practices, the tuba player and three other men, especially needed, departed when the 193rd squadron shipped out to Montgomery, Alabama. That killed the band.

Park Field seemed to be an unlucky place for me. By getting on as a bugler, I spoiled my chance to learn much about the aircraft, and I was in a poor place to be promoted. All the flying cadets were being taken from civilian life, and many were college boys, or the equivalent. Then too, I felt that I was not in shape to take any hard physical examination, until I had completely recovered from my pneumonia. It has been only recently that I felt like myself.

On March 7th, the wood pile caught fire. I happened to be near the guardhouse, but without my bugle, so I turned out and helped to run the hose cart down to the fire. Lordy, that cart was heavy. Its two iron rimmed wheels cut into the soft ground, and it took about ten of us to keep it moving. I would push away at it for about fifty or sixty yards, then swap with another soldier for a stint. The fire proved to be a fizzle. It was left over from a bonfire from the prior day, and not properly put out. It smoldered for a while, then broken out. We sprayed a tank of water-chemical on it and started back.

On the run out, we had followed the road in a semicircle, because there was a six-foot bank in our way if we'd cut straight across. On the return the bank was downhill, and shorter. Half a dozen men were pushing and pulling when we hit the drop off. I was on one wheel, another chap on the other wheel. We each held two spokes to keep it from rolling too fast, and causing a spill. The other chap stumbled, let go, causing the cart to rotate in front of me, rolling downward, men diving off to each side to avoid being run over! At the bottom the cart spun again on the lower embankment, teetering on its side. I'd continued to hold on, trying to slow it down. Others began to try to join in and help but the dang cart was so heavy, and moving. Up on the lower road, across and down into the other ditch, we finally stopped it but not before I felt some muscles in my legs and left arm seem to tear…and I was off to the hospital again!

Even the hospital had changed. Now there were three female nurses, Nurses Miller, Bush, and Vanderbaugh. They had taken charge of the patients by day, and it really looked like a hospital. My prior caretaker, Faber, was still there and had plenty to do but the woman's touch had definitely improved the hospital, like a woman straightening up a bachelor's quarters. Once done, the place is never the same.

I appreciated it, and those three lady nurses were so popular. There wasn't a thing those boys would not do for them, but as usual, the old army rule of "Officer's first" held good here, as I'd seen it everywhere. They treated the patients all the same, but in the evenings, if on a promenade, it was only officers present. Besides, it was against the rules for the nurses to walk with an enlisted man. Which became another very good reason why I disliked officers.

Saturday was visitor's day in the hospital. I can distinctly remember the Saturday, March 16th, that a Miss Conrad, came out from Memphis, with several other young ladies and sang songs for us. With my eyes closed, I laid there on my narrow bed, and listened to Miss Conrad sing a solo. I imagined being at a concert, for the ward was as quiet as any singer could wish. A distinct sigh could be heard as she finished. We sure appreciated all their songs. Another young lady sang, playing a ukulele, and we nearly died. She had a repertoire of over a dozen parodies on "Oh tell me how long, Do I have to Wait, etc.," and every one of them was a hot song, or hotter. Boy, what a hand we gave her upon finishing, and then for sure, I knew that the war was affecting our social life. Certainly, never before would such a charming young lady, from the best of city society, have sung such ritzy, risqué songs in public, let alone in a hospital.

Yes, when so many young men were getting ready to go over, and others already there facing death, the feminine population, following the male as much as possible, had adopted daring attitudes also. Not to say that they were immoral, the old "holier than thou" attitude was receding. The girl who would have ordinarily shaken hands with a sweetheart to send him off on a long trip, now felt naturally enough, that her lips were small favor, sending him off to face death. Across America, girls changed their code of behavior to correspond. Dresses were getting shorter, and the girl who had blushed at exposing her ankles, now showed her legs halfway to the knee, and smiled while doing so. Many hasty marriages were made at this time, and as a natural result, many hasty divorces occurred. At that, the girls were just following the same path, laid before them by their men. They became a bit more open, just as the men began acting all tough, and hard-boiled to impress themselves, and the ladies.

During the afternoon one old lady, a visitor, captured the Major on his rounds of inspection, and trotted along with him, asking all sorts of questions, as she tripped along following. They stopped at a cot beside me, just as she asked,

"Dear me, but this must be a tiresome life, with all these patients, isn't it Major? Don't you find it so, out here, so far from town, or do you have many serious cases to consume your time?"

"No, ma'am," smiled the old doctor Major, "Really it is an easy life, for we have but few patients, as compared to those in a hospital this size in a large city. We are well-equipped, to take care of all we have. We have had only one really serious case, and that was just when the hospital was opened. We were shy of a lot of equipment then, and nearly lost that case, but by calling in every available physician, we managed to pull him thru.

Really these soldiers are tough chaps, and with strong constitutions, at that, for that first case was won almost by the patient himself."

"What was that complex, first case?" asked the elderly lady, "Did some aviator have a bad wreck? I imagine many of them are badly hurt, with so many planes around."

"Oh no," smiled the Major. "We have not had any bad smash ups, as yet. The first case was an enlisted man with pneumonia. He was almost past hope at one point, but then recovered in record time."

Since Faber had said I had the honor of being the only pneumonia case, I now learned just how ill I had been.

The Major was just one day from being bad with his claim of no serious accidents. On Sunday, the 17th of March, a Capt. Mansfield and Lieutenant Jones collided while circling above the field. Their planes tangled, and dropped in a heap, deep in the mud. They were our first two casualties, and in a few short days the total grew to five, and with a few of them survivors, but seriously injured. There had been some laxity in allowing haphazard circling over the field but now that was restricted, better laid out, and no more accidents marred the Park Field record.

The next Saturday our visitors returned, and entertained us again with songs and ditties, as my leg and arm muscles, ligaments continued to heal. By then, I was a not as serious, and was moved to a tent outside, for the hospital began to fill with more serious cases.

The 193rd Squadron went to Montgomery, Alabama on March 17th, and the 65th left for some other place on the 10th of April. Someone told me they were going up to Michigan since it was now warm enough to open up a flying field there, snow melting and dry weather coming.

It was mid-April before I was released from the hospital, and Lord, had the field changed! A dozen buildings had sprung up and the field was now a little city. I saw movie, then went on fatigue detail for Lieutenant Borden, helping fix up a miniature battlefield, to be used as a spotting training range. It was to be used to train students as aerial observers on controlling battery fire, directed from a gallery above, to the miniature battlefield below them. Down among the hangars I could smell dope, oil, and gas all over. At the test shop, four or five motors were running their test time out all day. A motor that had been repaired had to be wired up on a test block and run for a certain length of time before being declared okay, ready for use again. I learned that engines were limited to a certain amount of time before needing to be overhauled, before reinstallation, and continued use.

A flagpole had been installed at the guardhouse, and we buglers had to assemble as a body, and blow "To the Colors", as the flag was raised or lowered. The guards were taught proper handling of the flag for such daily occasion.

Each day was an event in itself, as April showers turned into May spring breezes, and flowers showed that Spring was at hand. Spring even thawed out Minnesota, and I received several letters from Miss Marion. She seemed ready to forgive my faults, but didn't seem to consider that she might have any such herself. In fact, I began to think that maybe she was all right.

Another letter finally declared that a 6-3/4 lb. baby girl, she named Norma Jean, had been born on April 22nd. Say, but that made me feel funny! Perhaps, after all I had been wrong, and should have followed them to Minnesota, but no, that Doctor's statement had not been very definite. He had been unable to make any statement at the time as to the probability of motherhood. He'd also mentioned that there were insufficient medical reasons for him to order Marion to Minnesota for her health. He'd been vague, but certainly I was not completely wrong. Here I was, ready to go to France, if called, and unable to go see my new daughter. I had but little money, since my insurance and deductions came to so much that my net pay was but $9 a month. My insurance was a life insurance policy for a $10,000 benefit, was $6 per month. $15 went to an allotment which the government doubled, and then I was sending Marion $30 per month. If I had obtained a leave to see her, I would have had to borrow more just for the train fare alone, and repay it for months from my Army pay. Besides, the baby Norma Jean is all right, healthy, and there was no practical good that my trip would do. Feeling as Miss Marion and I did, perhaps it was best to remain in Tennessee.

I stayed at the field, perhaps, had I possessed more nerve, I may have gotten leave and bum my way home and back. A lot of folks did it, but it never occurred to me to try it.

With the changes that had come to the field, many activities sprung up overnight, movies being one popular one, boxing matches at the "Y", and another, one evening, we had the pleasure of hearing Madame Schumann-Heinke sing for us from the "Y" platform. Our band was broken up but I still had my Conn cornet, and one of the boys had a guitar. We found a guy with a violin, another with a juice-harp, and, with a player piano, we had an orchestra! We serenaded Madame Schumann-Heinke before she sang for us, and she complimented the field for its impromptu orchestra.

We did make a lot of noise at that, even if it was only the second-time we had tried it. I found it fairly easy to play by note from one sheet of music and yet follow the player piano in time, as it was running over the same selection. We weren't very particular whether we were in tune or note. Later on, we found a boy who could tickle the ivories and after that our little orchestra sounded better.

Saturday, the 27th of April, I went to Memphis again, with a minstrel show. A bunch of boys had organized a show, featuring some famous comedian from New York city, who happened to be in the photographic section at the field. They put on a fine performance at the Arthur House in Memphis that night, and since someone decided that a couple buglers might help, Monty and I managed to go along. We got a free trip just for the effort of blowing two short calls!

I borrowed two dollars from Sandbo, for pocket money, since autos from Memphis came out to get us and we needed no train fare. I was lucky, for a Mr. Young donated his car, and I happened to be one of the boys assigned to his car. He entertained us that evening at his home, at 1870 Vinton Ave., and after a delicious meal, prepared by their old black mammy cook, I promptly put down their address in my diary. The biscuits they served, piping hot, made me wish to stay right there! I could forget all about the war, and even my family troubles eating at their table!

We put on a fairly creditable performance, featuring the soldier comedian, then spent the night at Mr. Young's home. I lay awake half the night, being so unused to sheets, and the other half of the time I was dreaming of the delicious supper, and the breakfast to come. Sure nuff, that bacon, eggs, and more hot biscuits the next morning sure sold me on southern cooking! It can't be beat, not if it's all like that!

Mr. Young then took us around town, and later in the day drove us back to the field, that is, those of us who wished to go back. I had very little money to spend, so I returned with him. Monty, however, wanted to celebrate a bit, so he stayed overnight.

The next morning at roll call, when I answered, "Here!", the Top Sergeant told me to consider myself under arrest, in quarters. He ordered me to report to the HQ building promptly at 9a.m. That sure puzzled me, since I did not know what I had done to justify such action against me.

At about 8:30a.m., just as I was getting shined up to report at 9a.m., orders came that I was in good standing again, and that the initial order had been in error. Monty Gray had been the soldier they wanted, not me. I was quite relieved.

Come to find that the night before, Monty had gotten into "Dutch" in Memphis. We had each taken our bugles with us, but in the army, come to find out the bugle in considered a side arm, same as a pistol. They may not be worn, nor taken off post, without permission. We had permission to attend the minstrel show, of course, but not to do anything with our bugles. Monty had stayed in town, knowing that he could skip several days if he wanted to, since we buglers stood reveille and retreat at the guard house. He'd not be reported for days. He intended to return that same night but he got pretty pickled and then tried to find a room in a big hotel. What with all the officers and cadets in town over the weekend, rooms were scarce, and he failed to get one. The rejection made him angry and after several remarks to the clerk, the bell boys chased him out. He went out, but only as far as the door, where upon he turned around intending to cuss them out a bit. Realizing he had his bugle on his belt, he drew it and blew Billy Hell out of it. Starting with one call, he continued to every rally he knew. Of course, the bell boys and clerk got busy before he tried too long, and retreated under a shower of water pitchers! The bugling did get results. The hotel was full of officers and cadets that didn't know reveille from retreat, and after hearing all the blowing began to imagine that something was wrong at the field. Perhaps a fire, a crash or some recall to the field for immediate entraining to Europe. A thousand guesses could be had and when some of the boys tried to phone the field, they found the only line to the field busy. Monty found the bugling trick a huge success, and as soon as he started it, every window opened, questions and inquiries were shouted down. So, when he was chased on, he tried the same trick at another hotel and a few others. Soon every hotel was roused, and some of the excited guests even hired taxis to return to the field and find out what was wrong. The lone phone line was swamped and the hotels were in an uproar! The bugling stunt spoiled many a weekend guests' dreams.

Someone said bugler Gray was responsible, and if Monty had not been caught at the main gates coming in a taxi, so drunk that he couldn't pay the driver, I might have had a few bad hours that day! As it was, after my name was posted for appearance, Monty showed up and with him waving his bugle, they had plenty of evidence. He got thirty days exercise picking up cigarette butts and papers with a pointed stick, a shotgun armed guard 10 paces behind him. Poor Monty, but yet he was lucky it wasn't thirty years. Thirty days is a short time compared to some court martial sentences! Army life, dreary to exciting, even if he'd made it himself.

Aviator! My chance came at last, for on May 11th, with a number of others, I took my first examination, applying for a commission as an aviator in the Signal Corps, Aviation section. May 13th, the papers were approved. With a grade of "C" minus, meaning fair minus, my records started thru the mass of red tape necessary before obtaining my final examinations and assignment as a cadet. My first physical examination was before Lieutenant Wentworth, and Lieutenant John Jernigan, Squadron Commander. After review, they recommended my application to the board. There, Lt. Connor checked me over, passed me, and recommended me to the board president, Major Robins. He also approved me, and passed along recommendation to Major W.F. Jernigan, our C.O. He also approved my application and recommended it to the Chief Signal Officer in Washington, D.C. Whew, what a process!

Marion Gray, '16
160 Aero Squadron
Parkfield, Memphis, Tenn.

10

MOVING TOWARD OVERSEAS

I don't know how much more red tape has to be tied to an application, but what was how mine began. After thinking it over, I decided that about 1919 or 1920, it might get thru! Certainly, by the route it was taking, it would be months before I would be called for second and then final tests, and even then, I may be washed out. So, shortly after, when a call came for volunteers to go overseas, I was one of them. At first, it wasn't a call, but each Squadron commander picked out his undesirables, and listed them for transfer. Come to find out though, that many local Memphis sons had enlisted at the field, expecting to stay there for the duration of the war. They howled at having to endanger their sweet lives anywhere near those awful Germans.

The next morning, after that first list was published, I heard of several barracks where men had cried all night. Many were phoning their parents to help them out. Maybe it was this pressure brought to bear on the Squadron commanders and maybe it was because there were so many volunteers wanting to be on this list, that the first lists were torn down, and only volunteers were called for.

I was on that list in a hurry, and then blamed near lost out, for Red Smith wanted to go also and our C.O. Lt Jernigan, didn't want both buglers to go. I tipped Red off thou, and he didn't bother our office, and Lt. Jernigan. After the Lt. had approved the list, Red sneaked over to see Capt. Zimmerman, and got his OK for the transfer. The captain outranked our lieutenant, so he couldn't kick, and he had passed me, so we both got on the transfer.

One hundred men were on the final list to transfer to the 79th division, just preparing to go overseas. Later on, it turned out to be a mistake, being the 29th division, instead. The 29th, the famed Blue-Gray Division.

On June 10th, we were ordered to pack up to leave. With characteristic army speed, we stayed packed up all day, waiting. About 6p.m. orders came in for us to leave early on the 11th. Red and I played hooky that night, figuring on going to Memphis and coming back in the morning, or catching the train as it traveled thru Memphis. As for our barrack bags, well, if they didn't go with us, we should worry. We were feeling tough and didn't give a damn for anything. We hiked into Millington to catch a freight train into Memphis. We figured that even if we did go back to the field our bunk numbers had been checked in, so no one would miss us. Lordy, how those birds did hit it up, rolling down grade thru town that night. Not a freight train passed doing less than forty, downhill and no nearby stops. So, at 2a.m., we decided that Memphis was out, and we hiked back to camp. We still felt tough, and trotted right up to the main gate, checked in, and went to the barracks.

The usual procedure was that all names checked in at the gates as being out late were passed out from the HQ the next morning to each squadron commander. Thus, by regular routine it would be 8 or 9a.m. before our Top Sergeant could be after us for being AWOL. Now since we were supposed to go back to Memphis on the 6a.m. train, we figured we'd be safe.

We had not reckoned on the army red tape. That day, it was 6p.m. until we shipped out! For us, fortunately, Sergeant Wright conveniently "lost" our names until we were gone, or Red and I may not have been on that train. As it was, we stayed completely out of the barrack until noon, when Sergeant Wright tipped me off that he was holding our names away from Lieutenant Jernigan until we left.

Friends are hard things to keep, in the kind of army I found myself in. Shattuck had been great, and we were separated at Kelly field in Texas. Later I got a letter from him at Ellington field, near Houston, Texas. Betts had gone over a week ago, transferred to a mechanics training school, near St. Paul, Minnesota. That left me just two close friends, Red Smith and the other redhead, Red Jenkins, and we were all volunteers going to the 29th division heading overseas.

Monty Gray would probably have been among the volunteers going out but he was still in the guardhouse over his bugling stunt, and was not to be allowed to see us off. The 160th happened to be furnishing guard that day, so after arranging it with Sandbo, who was guarding Monty, he moved Monty behind 2 trucks near us, and we were able to meet. With Sandbo watching for officers, the two Reds and I were able to have a hurried handshake, and good luck pat from Monty. That was hard on Monty. He was unable to speak to a single soldier, except the other prisoners. Eating alone, doing disagreeable work, picking up refuse, chopping wood. He stayed game, wishing us good luck with no tears. He may have been noisy and lightheaded when mixed up with whiskey, but he was a game scout after all.

It was 6p.m. before we finally loaded out, and put in two Day coaches, headed for Alabama. We went to Memphis, with our coach connected to the work train, as it went back in the evening to Memphis. There we were attached to a train bound for Anniston, Alabama, the nearest town to Camp McClellan.

Summer was already present on that trip thru the south. With all the sunshine and smell of green grass and flowers, we were a quiet group of soldiers on our way to the Great Adventure. I dropped a short letter to Mother just before leaving Park field. I sent another letter and a small photo of myself to Minnesota for Miss Marion and my little Norma Jean, as a keepsake. It might be my last present to her.

It was lucky in a way that I sent those letters, telling of my transfer to a division that would soon be going overseas, for when we landed at Camp McClellan, about 8a.m. on June 12th 1918, everything was in a rush of preparation, and two trains a day were leaving for the coast and ships headed to France. We were rushed off the cars, lined up according to the way our names were listed as the read off roll call, and immediately assigned to other outfits. I lost track of Red Smith and Earl Jenkins right there. I was assigned to the medical detachment of the 104th Field Signal Battalion, with three other guys, Edwin Lane, Huber Reigle, and Thomas Price. It was called the Sanitary Detachment.

We four were picked out, and handed over to Sergeant Fitz, and he rushed us up thru the hills and valleys of the camp to the wooden floor tents of the 104th Medical detachment. There a short, spick and span Medical Captain McNenney, glanced at us.

He said, "Velcome to de hundret an fourt' Battalion". He told Fitz to see that we were outfitted. Fitz then hustled us off, and told us that Captain McNenney, our captain, was a Cuban, and though he had spent most of his life in New Jersey, he still spoke with a Cuban accent, twisting his words some.

Fitz was a big, heavy set, athletic chap, and he began fitting us out in a hurry. Our barrack bags had been in some baggage car, and had been left in Anniston, while our two cars had been pulled right into the camp. Fitz got ahold of a phone, and soon located them. He then got a truck and into Anniston we went, retrieved our bags and hurried back.

CHAPTER 10

Camp McClellan seemed to be dropped down among a bunch of hills, and the roads twisted and curved around them. I felt more at home in country like this than I did on the flats, but it did make me wonder how the infantry enjoyed it while drilling. I didn't get to see the camp though, for we were on the go most of the day, being issued medical collar tags to replace our Signal flags and getting the cavalry packs that were issued to the medical department. Fitz also issued us our medical belts, holding our small hand axes, scissors, tweezers, diagnosis tags, and a small bottle of spirits of ammonia, a tourniquet, and first aid bandages. He then explained the uses of each. The hand axe was for cutting splints, scissors for all bandage work, the tweezers for fine work dressing wounds. Swabbing out with cotton, or by using the lock on them, to clamp an artery shut. The diagnosis tags each had a wire on one end, and were to be put on each patient we attended. In the case of a minor wound, we filled out the lined tag, kept our paper copy, and tore the tag off minus the dark blue end. That made the patient a walking case, and when an ambulance was necessary, we left the blue part on. The blue was the riding ticket, and showed that the patient required conveyance. That was done in order that the ambulance drivers might pick out the seriously wounded men in a hurry. In some big battle, the men who were able to walk out would have to, until the rush was over. Then empty ambulances would return and pick up the walking wounded.

Fitz then showed us how to use the tourniquet, and explained that the spirits of ammonia helped quiet a wounded man's nerves. It was also good to settle the stomach after trying too much strong drink. I decided to remember that!

The bandage packages were the most interesting thing, for they were arranged so that when opened, the sterilized bandage was folded under sealed paper, and the ends of the tie strings dropped out first. By pulling these, the bandage could be opened, held, and applied without being touched by dirty hands. The bandage packs were folded twice, and by using the paper cover as a glove over dirty hands, the stitch holding them over could be torn out, and a bandage covering twice the regular area use.

We were also issued Brassards, or red cross arm bands. It was then that I realized I was going overseas as a member of the hated organization, the "Pill Rollers"! It was too late now.

At that I wasn't worry, for no matter what branch of the service I was in, I was not going to be a slacker. I was going over, and if a chance offered me a better outfit overseas, maybe I could transfer. Why worry till that time came? It had taken a year for that reckless "don't give a damn" attitude to strike me, and now I didn't care much what happened. When the future got to me, I'd take care of it as best I could. My family worries were a thing of the past, all but Mother, and Eve, just a shadow behind. A chap can dream of a pretty girl on a fine moonlit night, or when loafing along doing nothing. A busy man, preparing for this great journey ahead of us, had little time to think about "skirts".

At retreat the first evening, I had a chance to see what this Sanitary Detachment of the 104th Battalion looked like. We had Capt. McNenney, and the enlisted personnel consisted of a Sergeant First class, one Sergeant, three first class privates, and seven plain privates.

Sergeant Wester was the top Sergeant, Sergeant Fitz handled all the drill routines, and everything but the medical work. Wester was of medium height, round shouldered, and squint eyed. He did not look like a soldier. At home in New Jersey, he'd been a druggist, and in a medical battalion, he was made Sergeant on that account. He was the only man, outside of Lane, who was over thirty years old. My guess is he was about 35, and the rest of boys were about twenty.

Sergeant Fitz was the goat for all drill work, and the duty Sergeant also. He had been athletic director at some Jersey City high school, and enjoyed the drill work. He was a handsome young dude, and knew it too.

The three Private 1st class soldiers were Kelly, a slim faced, thin, black-haired chap, with a sharp tongue. Woods was a quiet, small fellow, medium height with brown hair and eyes.

Last of the PFC's was Radano, a dour-faced, grumbling chap of foreign extraction, and also a former druggist clerk. They had acted much as corporals in a regular army outfit.

Our regular Privates were, Long, a short barrel-chested guy. Noisy, hiding behind blue eyes, he liked to make himself heard. Carl Frederick Otto Stoehr, late a corporal of the 113th Infantry, who had transferred over to be with his buddies, Knorr and Louie. Carl was tall, slim, blond and fond of a uniform.

Knorr is short, heavy set with long arms and bumpy acrobatic joints in his frame. His hair hangs over one eye, and he was pretty easy going until crossed. A bull for strength to boot!

Kirwan is slim, sharp, strong featured of his face and outspoken. He kept to himself, an ex-bank clerk and he trusted no one.

Louie Schneider is very short, like Knorr, long armed and had well defined muscles. He is good natured, and needed to be with his quirky smile always on display. He was the captain's orderly, and that made him the joke of our outfit.

That was the group we joined. The four of us transferred from Park field were,

Huber Reigle, a friendly, small, dainty guy with dark hair and dark eyes to match. He was of Jewish heritage, and proud of it.

Thomas Price is from Mississippi. He's short also, with blue, sleepy eyes and slow going from all aspects. He had no business being in the army, as he was an inch below the minimum height. He lacked coordination, marching out of step and stayed that way.

Edwin S. Lane has a beaked nose, and at 36 years old, he claimed to be the oldest man in the outfit. He was still interesting, a jack-of-all-trades. He'd been an actor, tramp, sailor, and an expert in bowery and theater directory. He could recite the names of prominent actors and in what plays they had performed. He was bright, and likely knew more about Shakespeare than a college professor. He used his experience and nature to further his "gimme" game.

Last, and not least, myself, Marion. The guy with a girl's name, as I kept hearing.

Thirteen of us. In spite of the number, we ought to be lucky.

Actually, the dental assistant, Private Bryson, traveled with us, making our little troop count fourteen. Bryson was a small, slim, well-educated chap with glasses and usually a book at hand. The Dentist had but one assistant, and Bryson served him well.

For security of troop movements, a ban had already been placed on letter writing. The Division was shipping out, each day seeing two or more train loads depart for the coast. When our train pulled out about 3p.m. on June 14th, I had no opportunity to let Mother know that I was going over. I was glad I'd written prior. About that time, as I figured it, she would know from my last letter that I was in the 29th and she would probably worry till she finally got her official notification that I had landed safely in France, though that'll be weeks later. Mother and Miss Marion thought that I was somewhere in Alabama, and worrying as time passed without receiving any letters. Sometime a government postal would be sent, advising her that I was in France. After that, my letters would creep slowly through the censorship barrier, trickle home and calm them both. The censorship barrier was to keep aliens from knowledge of our troop strength, movement, etc. It's sad but it was necessary, after all.

11

ABOARD SHIP TO FRANCE

Monday, June 17th, was a sad day for me. The 29th Division was comprised of several National Guard units from New Jersey, Maryland, and West Virginia. Here we were in the coastal town of Jersey City, home town of the 104th Field Signal Battalion. Many of these boys had a chance to say goodbye to their loved ones, since they'd been tipped off that we were boarding ships for France. Other boys even got a chance to telephone their homes. Me, from the Midwest, could not see a single friend in the crowds around the Jersey City station, nor at the docks where we loaded on a ferry boat to head for the larger ships. I couldn't feel too bad, as I suppose a lot of the boys were not from this area. Those local boys were sent off by cheering friends and family, and that helped us all. Sadly, some of the local boys could not notify family and friends, so they were lonely like so many of the rest of us. That departure was difficult emotionally for many of us. The ferry took us to Government pier #4 and we were loaded aboard a ship, the Great Northern. I felt the peace and quiet of the ship a great relief, and a new adventure never being on such a vessel, and headed overseas.

That afternoon we had another examination. It was quite perfunctory, and we were each given one postal card to address home so that when we arrived safely overseas, these cards with their formal notification would be dispatched to our families back home. Censorship would not allow us to state we were aboard ship. I sent my card to Mother, and noted for her to "please write Miss Marion". I didn't feel any detachment about my wife, but I did my unmet daughter, yet in some way I wanted her to know that I had gone.

Tuesday a bunch of darkies boarded from Camp Meade. They belonged to some Artillery outfit, and their chatter and fun made life enjoyable, for a while. Trust those coons, they always seemed to enjoy themselves, kidding around, and having a good time.

Wednesday, June 19th, only eight short days since I had left Park Field, we were towed into the ship channel, and started on our outbound journey for Europe. Orders kept us below decks, but through one porthole I did manage to catch a glimpse of the Statue of Liberty, and believe me, with the four o'clock sun glinting about her head, and light clouds floating above, I was treated to a glorious sight.

Later that afternoon, when we were far enough out that observers could not tell that we had a shipload of soldiers, we were allowed on deck. The steady throb, throb, throb of the ship's great engine and the slap of the waves against her steel sides made for plenty of queer music on my first ocean going trip. A blimp overhead or dirigible, whatever it was called, and two aircraft made for a serious scene. Tales were that there were German submarines lurking off coast, and apparently our guardians were taking no chances. Several sub-chasers, those speedy little launches could be seen zipping about, till we left them behind as land began to fade over the horizon and we headed east. Then I noticed another ship about the same size and shape as ours, gliding along on our left, or port side as the sailors called it. She was camouflaged, while we were not, and the crazy quilt pattern painted on her was quite interesting. Some sailor said she was the Northern Pacific, sister ship to our Great Northern.

Our convoy formed up, consisting of two sleek, smoky destroyers, slipping and rolling through the waves as they rushed along, now ahead, now behind, changing sides, always on vigil watch. With the waves seeming to roll over part of the decks with each plunge, I could not imagine them as nice places to dwell on. The Great Northern was a Pacific coast mail boat, as was her sister ship, and the sailors were proud of her. She had the Pacific Ocean crossing record, recently set in the days before the war. After the war started, she had traversed the Panama Canal and up to serve as an army transport. The sailors were outspoken in stating that the Great Northern was the fastest commercial ship afloat, and they hoped to get a chance at the Atlantic record before she was sunk, or returned to the Pacific.

Certainly, those were two fast ships, for the destroyers kept plowing along, and we were making right close to thirty knots per hour, as mentioned by the sailors. The next morning, the two destroyers turned back, leaving us alone in the great expanse of ocean. Our two sleek greyhounds were too fast for any convoy and could show heals to any battleship. The sailors explained that we'd be on our own across, but pick up escorts meeting us some distance off the European coast and bring us into France. For defense, there were four rapid firing six-inch guns. Two mounted on the bow and two on the stern, all manned by sailors from the battleship *USS Oregon*. Their section of the deck was roped off, and hour after hour, they sat there or walked about. One always wearing the helmet and headphones to communicate with the bridge, and observation posts higher up. They were ready at a moment's notice to snap into action to shell any enemy sub that may appear.

I learned the meaning of sea sickness, when the boat began to roll a bit, but we were ordered on deck several hours a day, so I had to turn out of my bunk and like it. Added to that, Sergeant Fitz drew an upper and wanted my lower one, so as he outranked me, he ordered the change. I'd seen several occasions where, RHIP, rank has its privilege!

Red Jenkins was aboard in Company C, and I palled around with him most of the time. Red Smith was not aboard, so we figured he was put into some other outfit. I was interested in the sights, so I stayed out of my bunk as much as I could. Freighters were plowing back to New York with their water line showing high, revealing they were empty, and some so high that half their propeller was showing, splashing away. Our ships kept at a safe distance, after the first day, from all these strangers, as though fearing them a bit.

The first day out, we were issued our "tin" hats, overseas caps, and also items like salt water soap, red cross bags with toilet items and some Bull Durham chew tobacco. Someone must've thought we all loved it, for we each received a dozen packs. About half of these were used in crap games until no one would shoot for it. I gave mine away but saved the cigarettes, I could use them.

We took a northern Atlantic crossing route, passed several schools of porpoise at each of which our sailors took pot shots with a small one pounder amidships. I didn't think too highly of that. About the third day enroute, the Northern Pacific strung out a line with a target attached that plowed behind like a sub conning tower only faster. Our gunners opened up with their six-inch guns. Boy those things cracked and made the target jump when hit! They targeted below it, like they would a sub to sink it. One sailor claimed every shot was a hit!

The fourth morning, alarm bells sang out, and as we took our emergency stations on deck, we could hear the roar of the two bow guns, then a pause. Our funnels were pouring out a cloud of smoke as the ship quivered, tearing through the water at top speed. Then we heard the stern guns also commence firing, and for a moment the ship veered to starboard. I caught sight of a round mast like thing projecting from the water close off that side. We must have crushed over it or passed close. The rear gun poured shots at it.

We came to find out later, it was a stray buoy released from some distant location, floating way out here in the middle of the Atlantic in the shipping lane. Our ship had passed it on two previous trips but they took no chances and opened up each time. It was good practice they said.

Tuesday, June 25th, someone said that we must be close to the coast of England, but I could see no land. About 7:30a.m., though I saw a cloud of black smoke rolling along the horizon and gradually it came rolling toward us. It traveled like an express train, and suddenly snapped off short, as a destroyer shot out of the head of the smoke train, wheeled about and slid into position off our bow. Then I noticed another bulge of smoke, and yet another. In a few minutes, following the lead of the first, three other destroyers came slipping out of the smoke screens that they had laid, and took up positions on each corner of the square, with our two ships in the center. I realized that we must be entering the sub danger zone, and with others, we leaned over the rails, looking at the destroyers and open ocean, all searching for signs of submarines. It felt good to know we had such great protection approaching these dangerous sub-infested coast lines.

Those destroyers had a business-like look too, with the cold waves breaking over them. They rolled and weaved through the water. The waves were running high, and were blamed cold, so I didn't envy the few sailors I saw creeping about the decks of those relatively light boats. They seemed to be dunked at every plunge, the destroyer riding like corks, as they hit the waves. They were sure traveling right along, and our ships were also. The cloud of smoke roiling out showed that we were making all we could. The men of my group were restless that night. Most of us slept with our life preservers on, and with good reason, for early the next morning the alarm rang, and our guns roared a moment afterward. We rushed up to our assigned stations, and shivered for a half hour until we were dismissed. It might have been a false alarm but the tense, tight faces of the sailors didn't break out with any smiles. Perhaps, like I was, the soldiers were thinking of what probably was happening to the men who might have been on the receiving end of all the shelling. After we had passed the spot, two of the sleek destroyers slipped across it and in a crisscross manner. Behind each destroyer rose high spouts of water from explosives dropped.

Depth bombs. Whether death lay in their trail, we never knew. Out on that cold bleak ocean, our guardians fired off the depth bombs, and wondered afterward. No, I didn't envy the men on those submarines at all. Enclosed, dark, likely smelly, and edging toward death in any attack.

Afternoon, and a lighthouse appeared in front of us. It slid by far to our port side, and then dropped into the horizon. A dark cloud in front of us, turned out to be high banks, or hills as we continued to approach them. They appeared to be coastline in front of us, but they also slid to port. Closing forward, more coastline appeared but this time the coast became walls, appearing on both sides. A channel formed closing in on both sides, hills appeared and we began to see farms, separated by forest and clear spots. Word went around, we were approaching the town of Brest in France. In the dusk, the city appeared, the ship slowed, then stopped. We heard the loud clanking as our anchor was dropped. We were across, safely at that!

Even the darkies had quieted down while we were coming through the submarine zone, but now they opened up, joshing one another about the subs, the trenches, and what they would do to the Kaiser, and much other revelry!

We expected to get off the ship immediately, but we were held till the next morning. The evening we lined the rails and speculated as to what Brest looked like ashore, and to where we were headed next.

A big freighter was being unloaded nearby, and we watched an immense pile of mail sacks being unloaded onto a flat, raft-like floating tug. From the way those mail sacks were thrown out, I hated to think what might happen to a cake, if any had been shipped to some of these boys here! The sacks were tossed twenty feet or more from the deck of the freighter, landing with a solid "plop!" on the deck of the tug below. One item unloaded we observed was the fuselage of a plane. That, however, was swung out on boom, not dropped.

Several more ships arrived during the night and when we looked out the next morning, they were clustered all around us. On the deck of one, a sailor was wig-wagging his signal flags to beat the band. I had never learned this semaphore code, but the boys besides me, from the signal battalion, had and seemed capable of describing the communication.

"What's he saying?" I asked a Company C boy beside me.

He had not noticed the flag waving, but now I pointed out the sailor to him, and he watched a moment.

"Hail Columbia," he laughed. "They got a new captain on that ship and he locked up the company safe, but forgot the combination. Now they're signaling ashore to get someone to come open it for him!"

That made me wonder how many others knew the signal code, and enjoyed the joke with us. As soon as my friend from Company C, could catch the signaler's eye, he fished out two handkerchiefs and wig-wagged a kidding message to him. I could see the sailor double up with laughter, but being on the signal deck, on official duty, he dared not answer!

12

MOVING TOWARD THE FRONT

About 8 a.m. we were loaded off onto a tug and packed like sardines on deck, till she finally docked and we had our first sample of dry land again. On French soil at last. Somehow though, I was not enthused much over knowing that I was here at last. The excitement of the ocean trip, in the past few days had killed off any excitement possible at landing. Being in France was merely inevitable once we'd left New York.

On our march through Brest and up to the heights above, I wondered where were all the French girls that we'd expected to be welcoming us? By now the Americans were so common here that we were just a part of a regular day's operations. No one even noticed us, except the boys running about, and they gave us an earful!

"Who the hells got a cigarette?" shouted one.

"Gimme a nickel!" from another.

"Gimme two bits, and don't be a damn cheapskate," yelled another.

"What's the matter with you G—D--- S----, ain't you gonna loosen up at all? Or ain't you C---- got no money?" howled still another.

"Well, I'll be damned," said Louie, "Guess there must be some Americans living here, after all, or maybe that steamer made a mistake and took us back to America!"

"You're crazy, Louie," explained Lane, "those kids learn any new language overnight, and the doughboys going through here have taught them all that."

Maybe they had, but anyway those kids could sure cuss as well as any of us, and far better than many!

Three miles out of Brest, we landed at the old French Pontanezen Barracks, a relic it appeared from Napoleon's time. They were interesting, if one like relics, but I would far rather make my bunk in a new building than in such an old one. The amount of dust and dirt that have to be cleaned out always seems less in a new building. The collections of dirt in older buildings seemed very unsanitary.

I learned to appreciate Captain McNenney a bit better here, for he took us out on a hike, and he promptly asked the first M.P. he saw where to get the best wine. The captain was a wise duck at that, and by buying an extra bottle for the M.P., he bought us each a drink of white or red wine. "Vin Blanc", and "Vin Rouge", as it was called. Strictly against orders, of course, but who expects an Officer to obey such orders? Better to expect a politician to be honest first. The next day though, the captain hiked out by himself, and Fitz was our guide. Fitz led us to some small nearby town, and we bought bread and cheese at a hotel. Me, being from Wisconsin, found the cheese to be funny stuff. It was done up in a coat of mold that had to be scraped off, and with the odd bread they served, it all made for dandy sandwiches.

July 3rd, we had breakfast at 2a.m., and reveille and roll call at 4:30, after which we hiked several miles to a railroad station. Knorr had a sick feeling in his tummy, and I shouldered his pack with my own, so that by the time we arrived at the station, I was about all done in. Knorr and I are both broad and round shouldered, but most of my real strength lay in my hips. By the time we arrived at the station, my shoulder and hip muscles were twitching in pain. Here we got our first introduction to a French railroad train. Unlike American trains that loaded from the end, these had a myriad of side doors. Stoehr, Schneider, Price, Radano, and I were loaded into one side opening compartment of a third-class coach, and we started our journey eastward, with the destination unknown to us, as usual.

Our rations were loaded aboard just before leaving, and consisted of loaved of bread, canned corn willy, or corned beef, canned beans and tomatoes. Nick, being the only first class private in our car, appointed himself as chief of our commissary, and at each meal, he held an election to see what to put on the menu. Our service consisted of knocking a hole in a can with one of our axes, and passing it around. Each man helped himself. I never did like tomatoes, but if that trip had lasted any longer, I would have eaten anything, including tomatoes!

One or two times a day our train stopped at small stations, and we had a chance to refill our canteens. Finally, about noon, on the 4th of July, we stopped in some railway yards near a buvette, a small shop. Whatever they called it, they sold wine. At once several men made a dash for wine, but only a few got back safely. Major Hazeltine, Adjutant Simpson, and a dozen other officers were trotting about confiscating all the liquor that they caught sight of. Louie was the only one in our compartment with any money. He had raced over, bought one bottle, only to see it taken from him. There had been no orders given for us to leave the train. Major Hazeltine at once called out all sergeants and made them M.P.'s, telling them to allow no man off the cars, and then all the confiscated wine bottles were broken on some stones alongside the tracks. We wouldn't have minded it so much, but someone saw the little Italian cook who had charge of the Officer's mess sneaking onto the officer's car with an armload of bottles. Promptly, a lot of hoots and howls arose. If some of those officers could have caught and named the hooters there would have been some tough court martials later. Some of the other officers were so shamefaced that they quietly slid back into their car.

While all the other boys were grouped at the window on that side, I peered out the window on the other side. A string of freight cars had been moving along on an adjacent track, very close to our train, and halted beside us. Directly opposite my window, was a window in a freight car, and through it I could see one corner of a thin wooden box. I reached over, ripped off the cover, and part of the end. I was thinking for sure that I had a crate full of oranges. Mmmm, boy, I could taste a juicy orange, and then I saw that these oranges must be in square boxes. Odd, so I grabbed at one and found that the end only was square, for the box that came out was a 18 inches long. I jerked it out, then stopped to peer in wonder. I tore the paste board cover off, and shook out a rolled-up object, wrapped in tissue paper.

I looked, and gaped. "S...s...say guys!" I finally stammered, "Look what I found!"

The bunch turned and let out a yell!

"Wow! Where's the gal? Where'd you get em?" called Stoehr.

"My Gawd!" was all Louie could think of.

"Well, I'll be damned. Corsets!" snorted Nick.

Corsets they were, nice plain pink ones, with only a little lace at the top. Heavy, substantial corsets, nothing else. Each one of us tried them on, and I was about to replace them when Stoehr yelled, "Hell no, don't do that. Think what a fine souvenir they'll make. I want a pair myself."

But the freight moved forward, and out of reach, so I got the only pair out of it. Everyone in the compartment but Nick wanted a corset, and because they wanted them, I kept the one pair. If everyone thought they must make a souvenir, I'd just keep it.

"Yeah," snapped Nick, "They make a hell of a fine souvenir, all right, but when yuh show'em back home, who the hell's gonna believe that they came out of a freight train? Why even now they don't look like new, and by the time they get carted around in a barrack bag for the time we'll be here, no one'll know whether you stole'em off some girl or not. An who'll ever believe that a soldier in France was good? Some girl back home hopes you're staying nice and clean, but I'll be damned if she ever really believes you did by the time we get back from France."

Nick was right. The wild, fantastic tales told in army camps about the French girls had long since been passed on to the girls back home, and everyone openly doubted that we anxious soldiers wanted to go to France only to fight. So far though, I had seen only one French girl, and she was playing with a pet rabbit. She had been lying in the grass and we passed her on the march the captain took us on from our camp near Brest. She had turned her back to us, when noting that it was a party including an officer, but her position out there was open to question. She was too good looking to be hiding in waist high weeds and grass, at such a place, especially along a path traveled by soldiers.

Coffee was served us at several stops, by some USA women's organization and say but those American girls, in trim neat uniforms did sure look good to me! With the exception of the trips to Memphis, and the time I spent in hospital, I had hardly seen a woman in over six months!

At midnight on the 5th, worn out from trying to rest in those small, tight train compartments, we finally arrived at a place called Vaux, and marched out along the road, a little way from the station. There we pulled out our blankets and slept the rest of the night alongside the road. There was no traffic, and brother, how I hated to get up when the sun rose, and fellow soldiers all rolled out. We had been sleeping in our clothes, and it was a tired bunch that marched back to the station, and out another road to a village called, Montsaugoen.

Montsaugoen was a small town, set on a hill, with a flat, level plain surrounding it. The plain was cut up into small farms, and the owners lived on the hill. Each day they would walk to their farm to work. That morning, as early as we were, we met several old people, each with a long basket on his or her back, going out to work. They must have carried lunch, or done without for they stated at work until dusk. One aged chap seemed to have the job of breaking up little rocks to repair bad spots in the road. Several times, later on hikes, we passed that same old fellow, chipping away at his pile of rocks.

This town had no electric lights, and few other conveniences. It would have been an all-night effort to try and find our billets in the dark. That was the reason we had lain down beside the road, because in daylight we could be billeted in a hurry. Our Sanitary Detachment landed in a big, old house, which must have been centuries old. Stoehr, Kirwan, and I drew the attic, where, under gigantic old beams, we made our bunks on the floor. A day or two later, Louie, and Knorr were assigned into our attic group also.

France is so much different from the United States, or so it seemed to us. In the states we had always had steel or canvas cots, inside barracks or tents. Here, farm land was too valuable for tenting space, and besides, each home had space for one or more men, so we were boarded out. Beside each door in every town that was organized for billets was a white painted sign, such as "Hommes, 8, Chevaux, 3." Meaning that the place within, had room for "8 men, and 3 horses".

Each company or detachment was split up, and the old barrack rules went by the wayside, for who was to inspect these quarters daily, and make each man keep his bunk just so? True enough, we did keep out quarters clean, for that was a habit for us, and Sergeants Fitz and Wester inspected our billet anyway.

It was after noon when the cooks had the mess outfit set up and working. We got our first cooked meal in four days, then we went to bed. Our bunks, here as in most places in France, were wooden frames on legs with a wire netting across the bottom. When filled with straw, they made quite a comfortable bunk. The old army ticks were stuffed and used only a short time, but soon we learned to bunk right on the straw. Why not, when quite often the billet was in a haymow? Why waste time filling the army tick?

The next day I bought a map of France at a little village shop, and was surprised to find that our train trip had carried us nearly across France. Our division HQ, Prauthroy, was on the map, as also was the station at Vaux, but no mention was shown for Montsaugoen. We were in the lower edge of the Haute Marne district, and believe me, when I glanced back across that big map of France, then over to our location, near Switzerland, I began to believe that I was a long, long way from home.

I had made one short trip to Wisconsin one summer, and that was the only time that I had ever been away from Mother. I had been gone two whole weeks and later of course, when Mother had moved to Forreston, I had remained in Freeport, then later in Dixon, but always only a relatively few miles from her. Now though, with three thousand miles of water, plus more land in between I began to feel like a world traveler. No, I wasn't homesick, for those days had come and gone in Kelly Field, and later in hospital at Park Field near Memphis.

13

MY ARMY LIFE IN FRANCE

It was the next day that Stoehr, Knorr, Louie, and I began to get acquainted with our town. Cherries were ripe, and on a tour about the town, we managed to find several trees where we could fill our pockets without being detected. The army again forced us to be opportunistic. We ate all we could, and I even tried to make wine, crushing them in my handkerchief, draining it into my canteen. I figured that the juice would ferment if it was in my canteen long enough. Unfortunately, it didn't get to stay there very long.

The second night we weren't quite so tired when we went up to our attic to sleep and we were surprised to hear rats moving about in the dark, pulling and gnawing at our packs. They were after our emergency rations, and our biscuits, I knew, so we all got up and hung our bags up on nails and projections on the beams above. All was fine for a few minutes, till suddenly I could hear the rats again. Stoehr was cussing them for keeping him awake.

"Yeow!" Stoehr suddenly yelled, and then we all got up and lit candles. Stoehr was sitting up in his bunk, scared white, and a growing bump on his forehead.

"S'matter Doughy?" I asked, "Did you bite your toes off in your sleep, or what the hell happened?"

"My God," he gasped, getting back his wits, with the candles lighting things up so he could see, "Those damn rats must be able to see in the dark. I thought I could hear something up above me, where my pack was hanging, and damned if some big rat didn't slip and land right on my face. I damn near swallowed him. Gosh, he must have been as big as a dog!"

Perhaps the rat had landed on his face, but the thing that had made the bump on his forehead was his pack. The rats had gnawed the leather thong holding it. The dubbin, or grease on the thong must have attracted the rat's attention, and he had probably stood on the pack, and gnawed it free. Thus, Doughy had felt both the pack and rat land. To have a pack like that land on your hand, and head, even with no rate on it, is enough to make any guy yelp and turn white!

That was enough for Doughy. He put his pack way over in a corner, on a peg, and the next day worked a half day fixing brick pens and traps for those rats. I helped him and we spent most of the night listening till we thought the rats were in our traps. We pulled the string, letting our cover brick drop into the trap, but found our trap empty. Those rats must have been as old as that house, and as wise to go with it!

What with swiping cherries and gooseberries, and daily hikes out to other towns, life was easy in Montsaugoen. The adjutant decided we needed a bugler there, and since the regular bugler in Company C was ill, I won that job for 2 days. Blow as hard as I might, I could not get a decent sounding call out of one of those rotten bugles. Hard blowing, with thick, short bells, it was impossible to make them vibrate enough to sound a loud, far-carrying call. It was possible to make a fair sounding short, snappy call, like mess call, "Soupy, soupy, soupy, without a single bean." But when it came to drawing out a long quivering call, like taps, it was impossible to control the tone down to the dying out point. My taps calls sounded like some kid snorting them out. I imagine the towns folks hated our bugling, and with my meager efforts, especially so! Like many other objects, those horns were cheaply and quickly made.

My fine old style army overcoat was another item that I had to lose also. It looked queer among the short, new style garments. I had to turn it in and was issued one of the coarse, frumpy coats that came above the knees. Coarse, and rough looking, they kept one's body warm only above the hips, while my old coat, was sleek, smooth, and appeared neat. It was long enough to keep the breezes out to my knees. Maybe it was for the best, because many nights later, while marching mile after mile, with a heavy pack, my whole body would be soaked through with sweat, and suddenly those short overcoats flaps would lift, letting in a cold chilly breeze against my legs. The seat of my pants making me feel like someone was pouring ice water on me!

The French peasants in the village passed us by much as if we were animals. To them, used by now to the "Soldats American", we were a necessary evil, and few French soldiers were to be seen back here. The war was far away, and the only evidence of it was in the total absence of young men. Also, as far as I could see, there were few young women here, either. Certainly, I only saw one or two good looking ones, and they were minding their own business. They paid no attention to the American eyes continually turned their way. If they had any sweeties among the American Doughboys, they were quiet about it, and certainly were not advertising for more. The wild French girls I had heard such stories of, were not around here!

On Sunday, there was a special church service and since one of the boys was of the Catholic faith, he attended, and several of us went with him. I could make nothing of the droning voices during the services, especially since it was in French. I did enjoy looking at the old-fashioned clothing worn as the Sunday best by these people. Wooden shoes were worn on week days, but today they resembled a country congregation in America, being well-dressed, with far more lacy clothing in evidence among the older women. Perhaps these women did more hand work than our American women, for their clothes made me think of many of the lace-trimmed waists and dresses that Mother used to make.

A few were weeping when the services concluded, and as we wandered out, Sergeant Fitz asked a soldier who spoke French what it was all about. He explained, "Well, it seems they just got a letter here from some fellow that has been missing about seventeen months, and learned he is in a prison camp in Germany. They thought he was dead until now. He had been badly wounded, and been in hospital for a long time. So, he'll be coming back, sometime, but crippled for life. He told in his letter about two other missing men, who hadn't been heard from either for nearly two years, but they were killed in action. The letter was read in church, and the special services were for the men that were killed."

Church services for men dead nearly two whole years. It made me realize how long this war had already lasted for the French. Think what that meant to their families, living in dread for that long a time, not knowing where their loved ones might be. Here one family received good news, that their father, son, or brother, whatever he may be, was still living. Even though a hopeless cripple, he was still alive after two years. Could one call that good news? Certainly, a quick, painless death might have been preferred to over two years of agony, and in a prison camp hospital. Then perhaps a life of misery as a cripple after that. Then too, the families of the other two, hoping against hope for two long years, only to finally hear that hope was lost. Now, not knowing where the bodies of their loved ones might lie, and likely will never find it out.

This might be an old story over here, and a sad story, but it was due to be repeated more or less back in America in the months to come. There might be glory and adventure in war, and profit, too, for many at home, but the dread finger of doubt and death was already touching many of our homes back across the Atlantic.

We were a quiet bunch that day, wondering how our families would take it, if such a thing happened to one of us.

During our stay in Montsaugoen, I was on infirmary duty twice. That meant just taking charge of the medical office, keeping it clean, and helping the captain, and Sergeants Fitz and Wester during sick call every morning. At sick call time, every sick man was marched to our infirmary, located in a dreary, bare little room that once may have been a store room, each man was treated in turn, by the captain. If any of the men were too ill to come to us, then Captain McNenney and one of us, normally one of the sergeants, visited their billet and doctored them there. It was a pretty good system for care.

"Pill Rollers" was a good name for the Medical Corps, for most of our remedies were in pill form. The iodine came in a glass-tubes, done up in cloth. When one end was broken, the cloth acted as a swab to apply it to the wound. It wasn't really a glass tube but some compound that wouldn't splinter when broken. CC pills for one thing, formed part of most every man's prescription, for stomach trouble was the main basis of illness. The men seemed to think though, that the captain doled out CC's because he liked to, or he wanted them to suffer. 90% of our cases were for colds and indigestion, mixed in with a few cuts, and scratches. In Montsaugoen, I had my first two chances to help with bad cases.

One man, located in a bare, little old room, had pneumonia, and all morning I stayed by his bunk, trying to help him with what little I might. We waited for an ambulance to come from some distant hospital. We were supposed to have two motorcycles and an ambulance. My rating in the detachment was a motorcycle driver, but like many other items, the items were needed at the front, so little detachments never did get one. I knew that my patient should have dry, clean, fresh air, and in his little room, with but one door and no windows, a fresh air draft was impossible. There was a fireplace, and I carefully slid his bunk over in front of it, and covered him up to his chin with blankets, so that the draft, if any, would only come across his face and get fresh air if possible. That was as close as I could come to duplicate the treatment that I was given at Park field outside Memphis. They had every window in my room open in my room and covered me a foot deep in blankets allowing only my nose to stick out, and attempt to break the fever.

Finally, the ambulance rolled up, and my patient was started on his journey to better quarters and better care. We were first-aid men, not equipped for much more.

The second time I was on duty, some man in a hay loft was ill, and when the ambulance came for him, one of the other boys who had been assigned as his nurse, tried to bring him down the steep ladder to the floor. The poor chap groaned when the nurse tried to pick him up. I jumped in, and carefully rolled him from a sitting position, onto my shoulder and back, then with a single arm and leg hold, I easily carried him down the ladder. I carried him on out to the ambulance and placed him on a litter next to it. The ambulance men had arranged blankets on the litter, and as I slid him carefully onto it, he was covered in blankets. He reached out one hand to shake hands. "Thanks buddy," he whispered, "You didn't hurt me a damn bit bringing me down the ladder. So long."

He had only a touch of pneumonia, and like the other soldier, I never did hear of, nor from him afterward.

With no newspapers, and unable to understand French, nor read their papers, if there were any, information was sparse. Even the news callers, who with a drum or horn, called out all important news on street corners, but being in French gave us nothing. We got a little information from our battalion, along with the few letters from home that trickled in. Those letters seemed queer too, addressed at first to Park Field, and then forwarded. They asked about flying, and in a place four or five thousand miles from where I was. Being two, three or more weeks, they were like letters from the past.

July 17th I can always remember, for that day Knorr and I got in dutch, or at least I did, saving Knorr. The two of us had been out on a cherry swiping expedition, which was, one of the things we were strictly forbidden to do, according to orders from the Battalion Adjutant, Lieutenant Sloan. Such orders didn't bother us, so long as we didn't get caught. We had hit off to a fine place, where the trees were thick, over along the west side of the hill, just off the road. We each picked out a tree, and began filling up in fine shape, though we had to climb up quite high to reach cherries that had been left. Other fellows had long since cleaned out the lower branches. I had finished my tree, and climbed down to pick out another, when suddenly up the road I hear the tramp, tramp, tramp of marching feet. And peeking through the bushes, saw the O.O.D. marching around with the guard detail, changing the guard. There was no time to get Knorr down, so I picked up a small stone and threw it at him to get his attention. He looked around and I held up a finger to my lips, then pointed up the road. He had been making so much noise that he had not heard the marching guard approaching. Now he caught on and kept still.

The dickens it was, though, that he had not time to come down, and I, being on the ground, under the trees, would draw attention to him. My coat was off, but I grabbed it up, slipped it on, and while buttoning up strolled out in the road across to the other side, acting as if I had not seen the approaching guard. I was making a great effort to button up my coat, trying to get the attention of the O.O.D., so he would not look at the other side and see Knorr. The devil of it all, though, that blamed O.O.D was Lieutenant Sloan, and he never had liked our Sanitary Detachment bunch, so he hustled up. When they were right behind me, where I could not avoid hearing them. I had to turn around, salute him, with two buttons still unbuttoned.

I stepped to the side of the road, as if nothing were the matter, turned around facing the detachment, and saluted.

"Detail....HALT!" the Lieutenant snapped, as he answered my salute.

"What organization do you belong to, and what do you mean saluting an officer and appearing on the roads with your coat off, or unbuttoned?" he snapped at me.

"Private Gray, Sanitary Detachment, 104th Field Signal Battalion, sir", I answered, forgetting to answer his questions.

"What do you mean, appearing with your coat unbuttoned, and daring to salute an officer that way?" he barked at me, showing that he meant to get an answer.

"Why, I was just loafing along and didn't see you birds coming along, Loot." I responded, "I was just having a walk around and didn't figure running into any ossifers on this road." I used those words, "Loot, birds, and ossifers", figuring on getting him hot, or keeping him so, in order to keep his attention on me, so he wouldn't look to where I had been, and maybe find Knorr.

But he had his own idea as to why I had been among those bushes, and wasn't eager to go searching there, and the only thing worrying him was because my coat was unbuttoned. The guard detail behind him began snickering, and he snapped around at them: "ATTENTION!" he roared at the detail, "and remember, I said ATTENTION, not AT REST." then he turned back to me.

"Private Gray," he snapped, "Report to your quarters, at once, and consider yourself under arrest. I am going to prefer charges against you for being disrespectful to an Officer, and for insubordination. You are not to leave your barracks without authority from your commanding officer."

"Guard detail, FORWARD MARCH!" and on they went.

That was enough for Knorr and I to think about, so when they had disappeared, he came down, and we trotted up to see Sergeant Wester, and relate our story.

"Oh hell, forget it!" he laughed. "I'll tip off the captain, and he'll land on the Looie with both feet. He outranks Sloan, and Sloan never did like him, so you don't need to worry a bit. He'll take care of the Loot, and in a hurry."

That made me feel better, but I was worried for a while, until moving orders came out the next day, and we packed up and left about 3p.m. without a word being mentioned about my court martial. I think the captain meant to say something, for he grinned at me several times. At Reveille, the next morning he grinned again like he meant to tell me a good joke, but when he did get a chance, he must have forgotten all about it.

Back to Vaux we marched, and this time we figured we were going to the front, for our equipment had been cut to our packs only. We found our barracks bags had been packed up, and shipped away to storage. On our backs we packed all necessary equipment with the understanding that sometime later on, whenever we were back in some rest area, we might get our barracks bags back again. I left an extra blanket, heavy underwear, my corset, souvenirs, book, and other things in the bag. I did remember to throw away the bottle of ink that I had, for fear of it spilling over my other items. I had a pair of spiked track shoes, and a dandy black leather baseball mitt in my bag, among other things. My little gray memo book was the only unnecessary possession that I kept with me.

This time we won the use of French box cars, the famous "Hommes 40, Chevaux 8", affairs, and I'll be damned if I believed forty men could live in one for a whole day. We loaded about thirty men in each, and it was a hell of a life on the trip. There was just about room for each man to sit down, and even with straw in the car to use, a few hours of sitting down was plenty. There was no room to move around, and if one stood up, he was liable to fall over onto others as the car bumped and swayed along.

Rations, as usual, were passed out to each car, consisting of the inevitable canned willy beans, bread and tomatoes. This time we drew also a few cans of Australian jam. A mess sergeant was appointed to take care of the cans, and he counted them, then divided them into four groups, covering four meals. We were supposed to be on the cars not longer than overnight and the next day. That evening one pile of cans was opened and the other three were stacked aside, about six feet from where I was sitting. There were whispers in the car, mentioning that most of the boys near that pile of cans figured on having jam in their packs if the "All out" call came during the night. Lord, what a weary night that was, packed in with that tight bunch of soldiers, trying to sleep sitting upright, or on some other chap's legs till he got tired. At that point, positions were reversed and then it was hell keeping the blood circulating, and keeping my legs from "going-to-sleep", as we called it.

About 5a.m., the train stopped and after five or ten minutes, someone down the line could be heard shouting, "ALL OUT! EVERYBODY PILE OW—UUU—UT!"." Immediately I made a six-foot leap for the pile of cans. I was a bit slow for others arrived first. More like 15-20 soldiers grabbing for the cans. I grabbed two, with no idea of what I got, being in the pitch-dark car. I put them under my coat as we piled out. Then I hustled to one side, Stoehr with me, to light a match, and see what I had. Stoehr lit the match, and I peeked under the overcoat over my arm to see two nice big, beautiful cans of tomatoes! I hate tomatoes. Yep, nothing else. From the whole pile of cans, I had to succeed getting the only thing I couldn't stand to eat! Boy, how I cussed!

I was going to see how I could throw them, but Stoehr wanted one can and then I quieted down and trotted back to our bunch to toss the other on the growing pile of cans. There among the cans was the noticeable absence of those Australian jam cans.

In the early morning light, we were lined up in the town of Belfort, right near Alsace. and marched out of town. On the march through town, we saw several places where air raid bombs had torn out whole sides of buildings. One building too stood there, with the whole front wall gone. On each of its four floors, there was furniture and property showing in each room. It was like taking a knife and cutting off the front wall, leaving the interior intact and visible. We marched along a beautiful, winding road, lined on each side with tall trees. We marched about six miles, or ten kilometres, as they used in France, to a place called Chatenois. For this hike, the Sanitary Detachment was placed in the rear, to take care of any sick men who might drop out. Into the future, the Sanitary Detachment was always placed at the rear of the column. That hike was our first long one in France. Cliff Price, was a wee, little chap who was under-sized compared to the average army soldier. He was unable to keep pace and later that day got a lift in some officer's car, that traveled to Hericourt, so he didn't get to Chatenois until late on July 20th. That trick of dropping out and showing up one or two days later got to be the habit of several soldiers. After each hike, there would be men rolling in for several days afterward. Cliff Price was always among them.

At Chatenois, some chap from one of the companies asked if, "OLD AVEZ VOUS" was in our detachment.

"Who the hell is 'OLD AVEZ VOUS'?" I asked.

"Oh, he's an old duck with an eagle beak, that had learned French, and the first thing he learned to say was, "Avez vous une petite dis tabac pour la peep?" because he found that he could borrow that damned French tabac from the Froggies, he's a regular 'gimme' guy" this guy explained. That French phrase meant "Have you a little tobacco for the pipe?"

"Well, I'll be damned, I bet you mean old man Lane," I laughed. "Sure, he's one of our detachment, and he'll borrow anything he can. He sure must like strong tobacco, if he can smoke that stuff."

"He'd smoke anything, if he could borrow or beg it," said the other chap. As strong as that French "tabac" [tobacco] was, Lane earned all he smoked. That was the first of several such nicknames for him.

It was near noon on the 19th when we lit into Chatenois, and in the early evening Doughy and I trotted around, looking over the town. Only one other bunch of American troops had been there, and the girls were not out of sight, and quite evidently interested in us. Doughy and I soon became acquainted with several, so we tried out the little French that we had picked up. The girls managed to understand part of what we said. Suddenly one girl came up and popped out with, "Plissed to meech youse, and I'd be glad to spit in yore mess skit!"

Another with her spoke out with, "Glad to see your ugly mug, youse can sleep in our pig pens ennytimes."

Still another, "Pleesed to see your underwear, bee glad to show youse mine."

Doughy and I looked puzzled, till Captain McNenney popped up behind them, and said, "Say boys, there's been an outfit here before us, teaching these girls phrases like, 'pleased to meet you', 'I like your looks', and things like that. They learn English quickly, don't you think? Especially that first one, who said she was glad to see us over here."

Doughy and I managed to keep a sober face as these girls sprung other sentences that some doughboys had taught them, many of which, were unprintable. We complimented them on how quickly they picked up our language. Meanwhile, we were wondering what those girls would think when they sometime learned just what they were really saying! Such phrases as they spoke coming from nice, respectable girls, proved too much for us though, and we excused ourselves and beat it to where we could have our laugh. Captain McNenney though, was right at home, and could face the worst remarks without the quiver of an eyelash, and then respond, "Tres bien," very good.

Later on, Doughy and I met two nice little girls, and walked around quite a bit, learning a little French as we went. We even made a date for the next night, planning to bring our French-English dictionaries with us, so that the girls could look up the words they pulled on us, and the dictionaries would give us their meaning. We spent half of the next day picking out sentences that we intended to use, only to be ordered to pack up by 3p.m., and be moved onto another town, Vourvenon, a few kilometres away. No date for us!

Vourvenon was distinguished only in that our mess sergeant must have been on a spree there, for the stuff the kitchen served there was rotten! It must be difficult to move, set up and obtain local vegetables in short order, but still, they must know the troops depend on a decent meal once-in-a-while. Canned stuff in between.

Gas masks were issued also, and a gas mask drill became a part of our daily routines. At first, it was torture to put on one of the blamed things, but I got so tough that later on, I could wear one for an hour or two without much effort. With a clamp on one's nose, and a rubber mask tight over the face, it's a trick to learn to breathe thru the mouthpiece.

Doughy and I did get to hike back to Chatenois one afternoon, but did not see our girls, and all we managed was a few glasses of 7 cent beer. I couldn't say that I really liked it.

July 25th, however, we hiked to a little place called Brebotte, and there, our billet was in a barn haymow, above a stable. The hay was nice, but we were right above a horse manger, and the smell was awful. Like anything else, though, after a few days we did not mind it.

Brebotte interested me because the people living in the house next to our stable all spoke German. I had learned German in high school, and could make myself understood quite easily by Madam Pauline a' Gasser, the daughter. Her mother-in-law was an older woman, and she spoke low German, which was difficult to understand. Pauline was a native of Alsace, and had married Monsieur Gasser just before the war. He was now a prisoner in Germany, and she lived there in the Gasser home with his mother, and a half-baked brother. He was a bit odd, and us soldiers, called him Charlie Chaplin. Pauline was a neat, young woman, but her mother-in-law, and her young baby, kept her busy, leaving little opportunity for us to talk. Anyway, not as much as I desired.

A Y.M.C.A. man was attached to our battalion at last, and in his little room he carried a supply of tobacco and chocolate, so at last we had a

CHAPTER 13

chance to buy candy and American cigarettes. They were to be purchased and not given away. It had been bought by the Y.M.C.A. from money that was donated back home. It seemed that the sweets from them should have been issued out free, but they never were.

About every two weeks the Battalion Adjutant, or someone else would howl because the Sanitary Detachment didn't have a regular drill and hike schedule, as the regular companies did. Captain McNenney would call Sergeant Wester on the carpet and we would hike out of sight on some pretend drill, only to find some quiet spot where we could loaf for the two hours that had been assigned for the drill. If we happened to be loafing along some roadside, and one of the regular companies came by, we would pretend to be at rest, perhaps move on a bit after they marched on by. On several occasion we went fishing, but the canal near Brebotte didn't seem to have any fish, or maybe we didn't try very hard. Certainly, our bent pins and twine string wouldn't have worked too well landing a big fish. We even tried swimming on several afternoons, but that canal water was far from warm, and since I couldn't swim, I kept in the shallow water. Those canals were interesting to us. On several occasions, we saw boats on them, especially going thru the locks, and we always stopped to watch.

One afternoon we stayed out till after 4:30p.m., and on our way in stopped at a small buffet, or drinking place, for wine. Those places were all closed to the soldiers until after 4:30, so that everyone was kept out during duty hours. They had plenty of business in the evenings! This evening Wester and Bryson stopped at one table and ordered champagne. Stoehr, Knorr and I landed at another table, ordered wine which was cheaper, for we had little money with us. We had several bottles, mostly of that cheap, red wine which I never did like too well. It was too sour for my taste. I still drank plenty of it that afternoon, enough anyway to make me sick, as we left the place. In a few minutes I was alright again, only feeling pretty good. Any drink always affected me that way. I never could seem to get dead drunk, or unconscious, from drinking. Doughy and Knorr kidded me a lot on the way back to our billet because I had been sick. The rest of the bunch had left us when we dropped in at the Buffet. Wester and Bryson were still celebrating on champagne when we departed and we expected them later.

Six, seven, eight o'clock, and no Wester nor Bryson. Finally, at nearly nine o'clock, a motorcycle with a side car stopped in front of our billet, and the driver called us out to help carry in Bryson! He was nearly dead on his feet, stumbling along, and when we piled him in his bunk, he lay without moving.

"Where's the other guy, Wester?" I asked the motorcycle driver.

"You mean that Medical Sergeant?" responded the motorcycle driver, who was from battalion headquarters.

"Sure, Sergeant Wester, our Top Sergeant." I answered. "He and Bryson were together."

"Yeah, I seen him there. While I got that other guy in the sidecar, I returned, but damned if I could handle him alone. Some of you guys help me, and we'll go get him."

That motorcycle chap was sure obliging, for if we could get Wester and Bryson in alright, the captain might not say much about it. True, they had been absent at Retreat and roll call, but Captain McNenney was easy on us and would probably pass it up.

Sergeant Fitz volunteered to go with the motorcycle driver. In about an hour they returned, dragging a fighting Wester out of the side car. Brother, did Wester stink! He was kicking and yelling about being dragged away from his 'friends' and when we asked Fitz who the friends were, he said that they had found him in a pig pen, on his hands and knees, talking to the pigs. He was stating that now that he knew who his friends were, he'd wanted to stay with them!

That story sounded queer to me, but anyway, Wester was so dead drunk that both he and Bryson could not be awakened till a day later. Upon awakening, they were in real pain, and could not believe that they had slept a solid thirty-six hours. Champagne is like that. The captain refused to take it as a joke, though, and confined them to quarters for a week. In reality, that was slap on-the-wrist, and could've been worse!

Stoehr, Louie, Knorr, and I started out on a hike the second day at Brebotte. About a mile out of town we hit a long, open stretch of road, leading from a group of trees. We continued out over a hill about a mile out of town. We had nowhere to go, nothing to do but walk around and see what the country was like and wait until the division was moved to some active front. Alsace was a quiet place, and though part of our division was already on the front lines, we of the Sanitary Detachment didn't know anything about war, yet. We might be only twenty or thirty miles from the front, like some of the boys had said, but not a single gun had been heard. Other than the signs and language, we might as well have been in the United States. We'd seen little evidence of war. Ahead more open space. In that next mile of road ahead, there was single old tree was visible, set apart from the forest. It was a big, spreading giant about a half mile from the forest. We were about a hundred yards from that big tree, walking along, and joshing one another, when suddenly "WHE—EE—EEEE—EEE!", something came whistling thru the air. If you've ever heard a spent of deflected bullet whistle, you know what I mean.

Everyone chimed in,

"What the hell was that?"

"Who's shootin' at us?"

"Where'd at come from?"

"What'll we do?"

We were all talking at once, and didn't know what to do. It was nearly a half mile to the group of trees behind us, and whoever had let that bullet go might be hiding in them. It took a moment's figuring to see that he couldn't be in the big tree ahead, for that bullet had sounded spent, and we had heard no gun report from ahead.

Stoehr, being an ex-infantryman, realized that first.

"Let's run for the tree ahead," he yelled, starting off. "He may be in those trees that we came out of, and we can't stand here in the open."

We didn't, but we had barely started when another "WH EE EE E" sounded, this time closer than before.

On the way to the big tree, a third round passed, and then I noticed a faint "whump" from far away, like the sound of a bursting shell from a six-inch gun, like those we had noticed on the Great Northern. I stopped, and looked up in the air, in the direction from which I had heard the "whump". Sure enough, way up in the blue sky above, a black puff of smoke was breaking out, with two smaller ones following. Even as I watched a fourth and fifth erupted, being more pencil dots at first, then gradually spreading out to fair sized black clouds. Following their line of fire, I saw the wings of a plane glisten, as it banked in the air, far ahead of the last shell and off to one side.

I called to the boys, and we watched. In a moment, other whistling pieces of shell came hurtling down, but far away from us. The second one had been the closest, and we had been at nearly the right angle to be under the failing pieces. Looking up, we could see the dot, dot, dot as shells followed that Boche across the sky, but he remained far ahead of the dots. It was nearly a half minute after each dot appeared that we heard the faint "whump" of the exploding shell. The gun firing at the plane must have been quite a distance from us, and behind some obstacle, for we could only faintly hear the "whump" as they launched each shell.

That ended our hike. We looked around for pieces of shells, but could find none. Then we hastened back Brebotte, to relate our story to our gang of being the first to see a Boche airplane. We found that they had also had their eyes open, seeing the shells, but not close enough to hear the gunfire.

After that, fights in the air and antiaircraft gunfire became a daily occurrence. Always high up and never down low. This seemed to be a training sector for planes also, and we never saw one fall. Maybe they were just playing at fighting.

Payday came at last on August 5th, and I proceeded to take a neat hundred francs from the bunch with Knorr's dice. Only then, to have Bryson stroll in after it was over, and take a hundred and ten from me!

Such is life. A wise crap shooter would have played heavy against Bryson, since he started with only thirty or forty francs. He threw five or ten francs down for each roll, while my cue would have been to shoot twenty or more per roll. I ambled along at five or ten also, till he was even with me, then he boosted the betting, and cleaned me out in a couple of passes. I kept remembering the little coon in Park Field, and almost daily practices with the dice. Everyone else tried to spin them, but I remembered how he had rolled them straight out on that cement floor and finally I thought I had learned his trick. It was simple but good only on a hard surface, while we shot usually on a cleared space on the ground, or on a blanket over hay. No chance to try it there.

Our opportunistic talents came to light again. Plums were now in season, and also apples, and behold, we found a plum tree right at the side of our barn. The blamed thing happened to be in the back yard of an old house on the next lane, or street if you could call it that. The captain happened to be billeted there, but he was notoriously slow at speaking or understanding French, so we figured that the old woman would have a hard time telling him about us swiping plums and apples. We sure did swipe them, those on the lower branches were too high to reach, and it was poor tree to climb. We would toss up a stick and gather whatever fell, then we'd beat out of there, as the old woman could hear us tossing the stick, and she'd some out and holler at us.

That stunt got tiresome, for though we always ran away from our billet, to make her believe that we're not some of the soldiers billeted right next store. Sooner or later, she was sure to catch one of us, and be able to prove that we were the guilty party. I began to look around, and soon noticed that the plum tree stood right beside our barn, and from the roof one could reach right out into the best part of the tree. Also, the best of the apples could be reached from the roof also. In back of the barn which sat on an incline, was a ditch, and the outside wall of the ditch, came part way up to the eaves of the roof in back. It wasn't really a ditch, but a space dug around the back wall of the barn for a walk since the ground rose so sharply there that otherwise the back door would have come out from the loft. From one part of the high bank, beside the ditch, I figured I could leap to the roof. I removed my shoes, and tried it, and sure enough, in a minute I was up high on the steep part of the roof, filling up with plums.

That first trip was successful, and I filled my pockets before I came down, so that I had proof of the success of the raid.

"Where'd you get them plums?" yelled Knorr, when he saw my filled pockets. The rest of the gang wanted to know also, so I told them.

"Why, out of the tree back there. Just throw up a few sticks, and pick 'em when they fall, I lied. Easy. The old lady is getting' deaf, or don't give a damn. Go get yourselves some."

They did. At least, they tried to. For in about ten minutes back came Doughy, Knorr, Louie, Kirwan, and Long.

"Hello boys, where's the plums?" I asked.

"Plums, hell!" snorted Knorr.

"Yeah," growled Louie, "That old lady is deaf as the devil. She knows me, 'cause I got to go over there for the Captain's things every day, and she damn near saw me. I almost broke my neck getting' away when she pulled the door open. If Knorr hadn't been so slow, she surely would have seen me, but she was watching him!" I laughed, and kidded them quite a bit.

The next day, parked on the roof again, I saw Kirwan down below, looking up hungrily at those plums, and I hastily rolled back out of view. The high bushes in back of the barn hid me from them seeing me. Unless he looked right up at me, through the dense growth, I was invisible. I had kept my stunt to myself, as yet, planning on having some fun, and I sure did. I had several stones in my pocket and as Kirwan raised a pole, to try and quietly shake a lower limb, I dropped a stone on the old lady's back porch. Kirwan thought it was a plum that he'd shaken loose, and stood still a moment, trying to figure out whether to leave or not. He had just decided that the old lady had not heard it fall, and stooped over to pick up a few plums that had dropped, when she jerked the door open, and came out with a broom winging. Lordy, how he did leave there. He damn near tore himself in two, reaching out for the next step ahead! I rolled back out of sight, around the other side of her house, and up thru the brush. After she had gone back in, I filled my pockets, skipped down, put my shoes back on, and went thru the barn, so as to be out in front when Kirwan showed up. In a few minutes he came in, still panting.

"Hey Kirwan, what yuh been doing?" I asked. "You look like you have had some heavy work, for once. Here, have some plums." And I offered him a handful.

"Damn the plums," he snapped, and trotted inside, while I doubled up laughing.

I pulled the same trick on Knorr, and Long, and then twice on Stoehr before I finally let them in on it. There were plenty of plums, and I kept the gang supplied for a while. The apples weren't so good. There was hive of bees in another backyard nearby, and we did plan on raiding that for honey, but I couldn't get anyone to help me, so that idea blew up.

I might be only a fair soldier, but when it came to extra foraging, I handed it to no one, except perhaps Doughy. If there was a chance to get anything to eat for free, we got it. What little pay I drew usually went into some crap game, so my extras I had to provide. Funny, isn't it what an otherwise honest guy will do in the army? I think scroungers have always had a place in any army, likely back to Roman times. At home I was always extra careful that I never took an unearned penny. Here, I helped myself. If I could find anything edible that could be had for free, I was never last in line.

At Brebotte, we had our first casualty. Some chap in the Charlie Company, got a piece of shrapnel in one hand. It was numbing the cords in his hand, so that he could hardly use his fingers. He had been with some infantry company in when lines when it happened, and had been treated there first. The captain got him to exercise his hand, and he began to be able to use it, so he was kept in the battalion.

Major Hazeltine, our Battalion C.O., was made chief signal officer, and Captain Heidt soon took his place, later being promoted to Major Heidt.

At Montsaugoen I had checked in all extra supplies, and since I had then three pairs of shoes; one barrack pair, and two pair of trench shoes. I had foolishly kept the barrack pair, because they were easy on my feet, and one pair of trench shoes. Now my pair of barrack shoes began to get thin, and when a crate of shoes came in, I went down to the supply office to get me a pair of number nines, or sometimes a bit larger. I usually wore a nine and a half, and after searching thru the crate, we found one pair my size, the last pair in it that fitted me. I got them half way back to the billet before I remembered that I had tried only the left shoe, and glancing at the other, I saw that it was a left also. I trotted back only to find that I was out of luck. So, I kept on with my single pair of heavy trench shoes, and the thin barrack shoes. Those thin shoes were nice on sidewalks, but they're hell to use hiking over rough roads.

14

ADVENTURES PASSING TIME

We celebrated August 9th by hiking to Montreux Vieux, which was just across the old Alsatian border. After changing billets twice, we finally got settled in one attic, where I, at last, found a good "cushea", or bed. It was the first time so far, that I had a comfortable one to sleep in. We made ourselves at home in Montreux Vieux, for we stayed there for some time. It was quite a large town, and since everyone spoke German, except the French soldiers, I enjoyed myself quite a lot using the German that I had learned in high school. The second day we were there, Louie wanted a dozen eggs, figuring on having some old woman cook them up for him, or rather for us. I went with him to the shop where we thought we could get eggs.

"S'il vous plait, donnes moi a doze d'eff" I said in French, for Louie couldn't get his French by at all. The old chap behind the counter couldn't seem to understand me, and jabbered something at me.

I repeated, but he still could not understand, or didn't wish to, so I flapped my arms, then squatted down, then got up, flapped some more, and said, "cuck-a-cutaw—kwett!" As near to chicken sounds as I could make, and pointed at the spot where I'd squatted, then made motions counting out twelve on my fingers.

The old duck looked at the floor, but couldn't see a thing there, and seemed to think I was kidding him. Finally, he dragged out a string of boloneys, but they weren't what we wanted. Some other old fellow came in the from a back room, and they jabbered for a minute, while Louie tried to figure out what to do. Neither of us had a pencil, and how was I to ask for one if these blamed ducks couldn't understand such a simple word as egg, "eff" in French. Even with a pencil, maybe his picture of a hen that we could draw might resemble a rainy day to him, and he'd give us some milk!

I thought I'd heard a word of low German in their talk, and so I tried my high German.

"Sprechen sie, Deutsche?" I asked, and he nodded quickly.

"Ja, mien Herr, Sehr wohl," he answered.

"Damn, glad you speak something," I said, "Gimme a dozen eggs."

"Hell, he can't understand that," said Louie, and then I remembered, so I got into German. "Bitte, Mein Herr, zwelf euer, s'il vous plait."

He understood me then, for all the "S'il vous palit. That was the devil of it. I never could speak German without mixing in a little French, nor speak French without mixing in some of my high school German!

We got our eggs, after all, and since it quite a large town, and everyone except the French soldiers spoke German, I had quite a good time from then on.

I had never been to the border of the U.S. near Mexico, but I wondered if it were the same there. Here, only a stone's throw from French soil, these Alsatians, some with French ancestors, had been so completely under German dominance that they could not understand even a single word of French, even as simple as "eff", or "oeff," meaning egg in French. That gave me a new slant on this war game. Perhaps these Alsacians had been satisfied with German rule, after all; or else there must be some reason why they had forgotten all their French.

Our infirmary was located in a swell place in Montreux Vieux, being in an old barber shop, in back of the main hotel and bar-room. Our front window was an immense plate of glass, much the same as in any American shop, but this had a steel shutter, like the top of a roll top desk, only of steel. That roll could be pulled down on the outside at night. The glass did hold a memento of war, a bullet hole right thru the glass.

The sign on the hotel was funny. "Heinrich Schultze", it had at one time read, but the proprietor, being now in French territory, had merely painted out certain letters, leaving blank spaces.

"He nri S hult e" it read, making it a French name! It was perhaps a changed name, but believe me, the beer they served was the same old Alsatian or German beer. It was the only time I ever drank beer, and say I really liked it. I always did prefer a smooth, neat wine better than beer. We got to arguing about beer one night in our billet. Long said that it was impossible to get drunk on beer, and boasted how much he could drink.

"Hell, I can drink a barrel of beer," he boasted, "an' still find me way home in the dark."

"Like hell you can!" snorted Stoehr.

"I don't believe that either." I put in.

"Tell yuh what I'll do," volunteered Long, always willing to bet. "I'll bet youse guys I can drink more beer than either of youse, or both put together, and not get drunk at that."

We took him up, at that, but no bet was made, for instead of betting we pooled our money, and set out to see who could drink the most.

The next afternoon, right after Retreat, we hiked off to a small beer parlor, and grabbed a table.

"Gimme three beers," said Long to the cute little girl taking orders, and off she went, returning with three big glass mugs, foaming high with real Alsatian beer, that really tasted nice. We sipped ours to taste.

"Three more," said Long to her, as he paid her for the first round, and then tipped his stein up, drinking it all without a pause. "Here's to yuh, go to it, youse guys." He challenged.

We all chugged away, and the little girl returned with the second order of three beers, setting them down, collecting the first set of empty glasses.

"Gimme three more," requested Long, puffing out his chest, and sticking our coins in front of him, paying for each round. "Nope, better make it six." He corrected.

The girl understood English, at least enough to answer her customers, and she shook her head, "No," she said, pointing to the three full steins before us. Three glasses on a table for three customers was enough at one time, so she thought. Long persisted, "Gimme three more," he said, "and don't shake them cute curls at me now. I'm on business tonight, trying to teach these guys what beer is for. Gimmer three more."

She shook her head again, but when Long showed a few francs in front of her, she decided that it ought to be all right, since we were paying for our orders. So, she kept on bringing beer after beer, till finally we had six glasses lined up in front of each of us. We had slowed down in our drinking, right after the second one, and began to take our time. It was a joke to our server girl, but other soldiers and the few Frenchmen in the place paid us little attention.

With the count at seventeen each, we went out for a walk, and to get a breath of air. Then back again, to run it up to twenty-three each, when we had to ramble out again. Drinking went slower, there, and we made a longer time still between beers. It was a full hour from beers twenty-three to twenty-seven, and when we hit that, Long was ahead having thirty, to my twenty-nine, and Stoehr's twenty-seven, but we didn't stop there.

We exited for another walk, and sang a few songs. There might not be much kick in a glass of beer, but we were beginning to feel funny, at that! At thirty-four for Long, I was at thirty-one and Stoehr went out dead drunk, after twenty-eight. Lord, but that was a long drink for him. He tried to down it for a half hour, but finally had to give it up. Then we were in a pickle. There were two roads back to our billet, one thru the main part of town, where we would surely meet Officers, and the other, a short cut, but past General Morton's headquarters. We were up against it, and since it was barely dusk, now at nine o'clock, we had to try one or the other, for after nine-thirty the M.P.'s would be out, patrolling streets and we would be caught out of our billet.

The only thing to do was to try the route past General Morton's H.Q., which we did, without getting caught, but Lordy, what a load Stoehr was! His legs were limp, and his whole body likewise. He was absolutely dead on his feet, and since he was even taller than I was, it made it hard to harry him between us, and yet make him appear as being only ill. Long especially, was so short that his head came just to Stoehr's shoulder, tipping us all around. Somehow, we managed it, and everything was fine. Stoehr was "sick" at Reveille, but Sergeant Wester tipped Captain McNenney off, so nothing was said, and the captain didn't come to our billet to treat him.

Lane, our oldest trooper, was a funny duck. He hated like the devil to carry his pack, and on all hikes, when we were moving from town to town, he often tried some excuse to get out of it. Throwing objects away, rather than carry them. One day he saw two safety razors in Reigle's kit. Before the next hike, he threw his away, and then borrowed Reigle's. He even went with one blanket, rather than carry two. He was chilled many a night, punishing his comfort at night to save weight occasionally.

When First call came each morning, we all hated to roll out on those frosty August mornings, Lane was out like a shot, and hurried down to the hydrant in the little park in town, where we washed up every morning. There, no matter how cold it was, he promptly stuck his head under the cold stream of water from the hydrant. He had his head shaved almost tight, till he looked like a bald-headed eagle, but while we shivered at the contact with the cold water, Lane waded in head foremost.

One afternoon the bunch headed for a bridge over the canal, about a half mile from town, and we all went swimming. It was a deep canal, and Lane and Fitz tried to teach me how to swim. I finally managed a breast stroke, or dog-paddle most would call it. That carried me along a bit, and at last I tried going across the canal. Lane and Fitz were right behind me, and I got almost to the edge, and figured I could let down my feet. Out of breath as I was, I could not even close my mouth. The bank was stepped, and I had misjudged my distance and thought I was in shallow water. As I let down to the bottom, that I thought was there, I dropped under, over my head. Lane was right behind, and as I bobbed up, he hit the back of my head. I had popped up backward, and that smack tipped me forward, and one pull of my arms brought my hands within reach of rocks. There I hung, spluttering and blowing water like a whale. I had a gone feeling for a little while.

I had forgotten a primary lesson on having nerve, don't wait. I fiddled around for long time before trying it again. I knew that I could get across easily now but that scare made me hesitate, and it can be fatal to hesitate. I blamed near gave out from pure fright, on the fifteen-foot trip back. Deep but narrow that canal was. At least I had learned to swim, a bit, all fifteen feet!

Woods and Price won the first detail at the front. Our detachment was ordered to send two members up to some small station, Woods and Price had all the glory for a time.

The town of Mulhouse, held by the Germans, across from us, lies in a valley, with impregnable heights beyond it, and swampy land in front. An adjacent village, Belfort, was ringed with forts and natural defenses, especially that same swampy land in front of Mulhouse. So it was that the Alsatian front was merely a training front, for neither the Allies, nor Germans were foolish enough to try anything there. Being that far from any important or strategic points, like Paris, or Berlin, even a considerable gain there would have amounted to little gain.

At this point, I did not realize just how close we were to the German lines. We seldom heard any big guns firing, until one day I saw a camouflaged train go thru the station at Montreux Vieux, with sailors on the cars. As part of the train, it pulled two cars containing a big naval gun.

That night Mulhouse got a taste of war, for those guns were large, 14-inch rifles, and they lofted a few shells over at the breweries there. At least it must have been the breweries, for we couldn't figure out what else there would worth firing upon. By morning the big guns had returned, moved far to the rear, and brought Boche aircraft buzzing around in the air searching to locate them. If sighted, I imagine they'd have sent return music.

Back at our hotel billet, the hotel man's twelve-year old son, Henri Shulte, was popular in our infirmary. He was a neat lad, and learned English in a hurry. We likewise spoke German to him, brushing up on it ourselves. Henri often acted as a waiter for us, bringing in glasses of beer when the bar was closed to us, and we tipped him with small presents, as we could.

One evening, while I was on duty, Long had dropped in with me, a Frog soldier trotted in. Fresh from the trenches up front, he carried a pair of decorated shells that he wanted to sell. Little Henri acted as interpreter, and said that the old duck wanted forty francs for the two shells. That was twenty francs each, and they were sure worth it. Each had a wreath of oak leaves, raised out on the shell, with a raised boss inside the wreath. On one was an American soldier's head, in the old-style campaign hat, while on the other shell was a French Poilu, with his tin hat on. They were decorated around the rest of the shell, outside the wreath, with little triangular dots. All hand engraved work. Problem was, we didn't have forty francs!

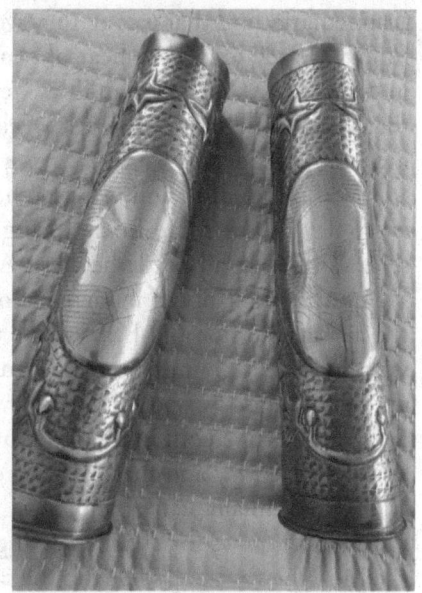

Two souvenir 75mm shell casing art

"I get monee." said Henri, and off he trotted, upstairs to his mother, and blamed if she didn't come down with his bank in her hand. She was willing to let him loan us the money to pay for those shells. We couldn't do that, because we may have to move before payday.

I did have a happy thought. Those shell casings were worth double what the Frog wanted, so we let Henri buy them, with the understanding that if we moved before payday, he was to keep them, and by displaying them in his dad's bar, he could easily double his money. If we did stay till after payday, each of us would buy one shell, at forty francs each, again doubling his money!

His mother didn't want the profit, but we had our way, and Henri carted the shell casings off to bed with him, while the Poilu went whistling on his way. He must had been on the front a long time for he looked like it might cost him the whole forty francs for a shave, if he ever got one!

Woods had lost his coat at some cognac party a while before and Captain McNenney busted him, so on September first, he made me a First Class Private to replace him. Stoehr had made 1st class in August at Brebotte, so now I began to feel like somebody.

Doughy and Kirwan earned the next trip up at the front, and our beer party was the reason Stoehr was chosen; that was his punishment for losing the bet. Each team consisted of one PFC, Private First Class, and one ordinary Private. Woods and Price had taken the first trick, up near the town of

Dannemarie, and that was all they would talk about for a while. It seemed funny, as they told it, to hear of peasants plowing and tilling their fields in plain view of the German lines. Yet in that sector, things had carried on that way, up till lately. The last week or so small guns had boomed with increasing frequency.

My special diversion was watching the planes in the air, and almost every day I'd see some Boche being chased by anti-aircraft gunfire, and several times an air battle between Allied and Boche fighters. I never did see one brought down in that sector, though quite often the battles in the air seemed hot and heavy. One plane would break away and sail off with the other giving chase. The most interesting sights were when an anti-aircraft gun was popping way at a Boche plane. We could see the little dots of shells open out in the sky above, as the plane that they were aiming at swung this way and that, keeping easily out of the shell streams.

Payday finally came before we moved. Long and I each gave little Henri forty francs for the shell casing art. Up in our billet, I looked at my shell and then at Long's. He did the same, looking at his, and then at mine.

"Hell," he said, "they look better together."

"I was thinking that myself," I admitted.

He rattled his dice. "O.K., high dice gets'em." I suggested.

"Let's go!" said Long.

"Best two out of three rolls," I stipulated, "and the winner pays the loser for the other shell. That way it's not the money we're rolling for, 'cause forty francs is one pile, right now. The loser can pay at the next payday."

"Fair enough," said Long, and rolled a dice.

"I remembered the little coon at Park Field, and his rolling style. For months I had been figuring and wondering as to how he managed the dice. Now at last, I believed I knew, and here, on a hard billet floor, fairly smooth, I tried his trick. I could set the dice in my hands, easily, and as I rolled, the two cubes straight out from me, four or five feet away. Long grinned, till he saw the six and five that I turned up. The next roll, I laid out two sixes, to his pair of fives, and so it was, that I got the shell casing set!

Gambling was an everyday occurrence in the army. We gambled for anything, and everything, from matches when we were broke, to a hundred dollars a shot, when we had that much. What did any possession amount to anyway? We were due any day to move to the fight up on the big front.

Montreux Vieux was a cinch, but all good things must end, and at last, on the 13th of September, we packed up and rode back a few kilometers to Montreux Chateau, just across the old frontier. There seemed to be three Montreux towns here. The one on the German side being Montreux Vieux, and the twins, really two connected towns on the French side. Montreux Chateaux and Montreux proper.

This was apparently our first hike back from the Alsace front, where some other Division was relieving us, and soon we would be handed up to the big front, as an experienced Division. This had been merely a training sector. Certainly, the Signal Corps had got some training, for the Telephone and Telegraph companies, even the wireless company practiced daily. The switchboard men had taken over many of the P.C. switchboards (Post of Command), throughout the area, and as a whole, the battalion was in fine shape, but certainly, our Sanitary Detachment, had really gotten no practice. Not that we wanted practice on dire situations of wounds nor the death of many, but it would be better in the long run. We were content to be the time killing, crap shooting experts of the battalion. Under Captain McNenney and Sergeant Wester, "Lights out" was an obsolete order to us. Taps might sound, but we went to bed whenever we pleased. Sometimes when our billet windows were too prominent, we did have to put out our candles at taps, for then the night guard would raise cane. Usually, we were billeted off to one side, out of notice, and did as we pleased.

The billeting in Montreux Chateau was as usual, and as far from perfect as possible. The captain's room was on the east side, and we stopped the truck while he pointed them out to Louie. On down the street and over the railroad bridge rolled the truck. We dropped off in the main section of town, and unloaded our medical supplies into a shed near a restaurant. We were due to move out the next morning, and it was 5p.m. then, so for some reason no infirmary detail was named. Usually, it was custom to establish the infirmary, then place one man on for a twenty-hour detail, he having to sleep on one of the litters, and only relieved for meals.

After disposing of our infirmary equipment, we hiked way out to the west end of town, a good half mile. We were billeted in barracks once again, and as usual the beds were the "cusheas" with wire bottoms. Half of them were broken, and Knorr drew a bad one. He got busy at once patching it up, and when he was finished, he bragged so much about his fine handiwork that Doughy and I put one over on him. We pulled the main support of the bunk off, and braced it back up but tied a wire to it so that we could jerk it down at will. Doughy's bunk was just about in the right position, so we ran the control wire to the end of his bunk. Doughy could do the pulling.

About half of the battalion was billeted there in two barracks, and we had to go to bed when they did. Wester, Kelly, and Long however, went out on a little spree and came in just before taps feeling good. Taps was sounded by the whistle of some sergeant, and a shout, "Lights out!". Since we were excited at moving to some big front, that didn't mean being quiet to us. Not by any means. Certainly, those boys there, real vets now, were far easier going than us rookies had been back in Jefferson Barracks, where the night guard had a fit if any one whispered. Here we even sang, till some sleepy heads yelled for quiet. They'd throw sticks and perhaps send buddies' shoes sailing in our direction. Then we'd finally dropped our noise to a more conversational tone.

Doughy yelled over to Knorr, "Say, you bum carpenter, is that tub of yours still holding up yet? You must be a real carpenter at that, if that thing of yours can hold all your beef! You must weigh most of three hundred or more now, don't you, Knorr?"

"Aw-w, shut up!" snapped Knorr, who was getting sleepy.

Everyone in the detachment but Knorr knew what was coming. We took turns kidding Knorr, till finally I thought the time was ripe, and signaled Doughy. My bunk was right beside Knorr's and I was sitting up, my back against the wall, my hands behind my head. Knorr could see that I was not doing anything. While he was watching me, Doughy, two bunks away, was set up to pull the wire when I gave him the signal without Knorr catching on.

When Knorr was finally comfortably settled, lying there with one eye on me, I raised my hands high, stretched, yawned and yelled at him, "Well, good night William, my dear. You're a swell carpenter at that, Sweet William." That was the signal, and Doughy was ready, pulled the wire, all the while Knorr watching my hands still above my head. He had caught on from our kidding that something was up. He was watching me, suspecting that I was at the bottom of something.

Crash! Down came the bunk, for with one leg off, the others weakened as we had left them, they spraddled out and Knorr made a beautiful ten-inch drop, right to the floor! None of our "cusheas" had straw in them, and he had but one blanket between the wooden floor and his body.

The whole group roared, and howled in laughter!

"OH YOU G— D— X— X— X—!" howled Bill, and he kept at it, even repeating himself a bit. He sure could swear when he got mad! It took him ten minutes to say all he cared to, while we howled our heads off in laughter! He finally propped his "cushea" up on some handy bricks, and also a few odd pieces of wood till it was two or three inches off the floor, allowing a little bend in the wire support at the bottom.

Doughy had removed the wire from the key leg and thrown it out in the aisle so that Knorr could not figure for sure just who had pulled him down. He suspected that I was partly responsible, and figured Doughy as my helper, so he was about right but not positive.

15

FIRST TASTE OF SHELLING

With all the excitement it was 11:30 before we quieted down, and soon after that time we suddenly heard a far away, dull, heavy roar. "Whaap", and immediately after it the heavy, shrill reverberating scream of a big shell. "Whoooeeeeeee—EEE Yup-Whupp!" As it tore thru the sky somewhere above or near us, then landing, and after a short half-second, exploded. The cracking, booming thunder as the sound rolled across the town. Like iron clouds crashing into one another. The nearest thing to the shrill "WHEEEE" of a heavy shell coming thru the air, that I can think of, is the sound made by an express train, suddenly applying the brakes. To appreciate the resemblance, one would have to lie down next the tracks as the train screeched while stopping.

The rolling thunder across the sky is the same that one would hear near a rock quarry, after a heavy blast was set off. The sound from a heavy shell can be heard twenty miles or more, and some up to fifty miles, we were told. It's a damned unpleasant sound to hear, even if one knew that they were safe. We knew at once that a heavy shell had come over, but whether it landed a mile away or ten, we could not tell.

Some of the boys were sitting up in bed, others lying with their heads completely covered, and probably put their fingers in their ears.

"Whew," said someone, in the dark, "That was a damn big express package for somebody!"

"Special delivery letter from Big Bertha," said another.

"Damn glad it wasn't addressed to me," from another. Others floated many more similar comments in the darkness of the billet. These boys, as usual, displayed or tried to display their nerve by kidding about everything, even death itself.

CHAPTER 15

It seemed that the shell had impacted near us, but the others didn't seem to think so, and since they had been nearer the front than I had, I conceded to their judgment. In about ten minutes another passed over, and later another. Some of the boys spoke about getting up, but some Sergeant vetoed that idea in a hurry.

"Yeah, get up and have some damn officer on our necks for chasing around after taps. Like hell! G'wan back to sleep, till someone calls yuh!"

Wester seemed to have the same idea, but just the same, I quietly slipped on my shirt and trousers and laid there listening. From the chatter in the barracks the boys figured that perhaps Grandvillars might be on the receiving end of the shelling, or maybe Fontaine. I did know exactly where either place was, and they weren't shown on my map, so I could only lie and listen.

Suddenly someone came up to the barrack door, and jerked it open.

"Anybody in here?" snapped an Officer's voice, which I recognized as being Captain Heidt's, our C.O.

"Yeah." Someone responded.

"Well, dammit, get out. Don't you damned fools know the town is being shelled? GET OUT AND DAMN QUICK! SCATTER! Anywhere but get out of town. Go out in the fields but don't bunch up! DON'T COME BACK TIL IT'S OVER! Sanitary Detachment You there? Sergeant Wester, get your men up at once and report downtown to Captain McNenney! First man dressed, goes for the captain, the rest of you report to the infirmary! HURRY!"

That meant business, and was all we needed to hear! There was no more talking in the billet. Believe me those boys pulled on clothes in a hurry. I had only to slip on my shoes, flip my putters around my legs. I always kept them rolled, handy, put on my coat, tin hat, medical belt, gas mask and out I went. Being the first dressed, I went to go get Captain McNenney.

The moon had been shining an hour before, but now it was hidden behind clouds, and as I raced down the street, my white brassard gleamed on my arm in the darkness, against the olive drab of my uniform. Those red cross arm bands sure do show up at night. It was the only bright thing on my uniform.

I went at a trot, for I could not see well enough to run any faster in the dark and deemed falling and getting injured not a helpful thing. On the way down town I passed bunch after bunch of outward-bound doughboys, some half-dressed, and a few with only a blanket or overcoat on them.

Usually we slept in our underwear, and I could see from the looks of these boys that the shells must have lit close to them, for they hadn't stopped to put on anything at all. Some were even barefoot!

One stopped as I went by, and yelled, "Luck to you, yuh damn Pill Roller, and I'm glad I'm not in your boots tonight. Yuh don't catch ME headin' back into town this night!" He wasn't cussin' at me, so much as for me.

"Plenty of work for you tonight, Sanitary," yelled another fellow. "They blew hell out of the barracks at the station."

One or two others said things to me as I sailed by, but for the most part they were silent, panting and puffing, in their scurry to get to the fields.

The "Big Bertha" guns that were entertaining us, were not finished, by far, for about every ten minutes a shell came rocking over, and as I heard each start, I dropped to the ground, if possible, near a tree. Sound traveling in a straight line, always beat the heavy missile that arched high overhead by seconds, so that I could always hear one coming five or six seconds before it hit. I was just starting when one came over, and others hit when I was half way downtown. In the main part of town, where the doughboys had already left, everything seemed quiet. Only some rudely awakened rooster was crowing up a storm in the blackness of the night.

Men might have been hit, and might be lying wounded or dead somewhere about, but I did not see any, nor hear any moaning. I knew that there were a few barracks in the yard at the railroad station, for I had noticed them as went by earlier in the day but I was not sure how many of them had been occupied that night.

Now that I was outside, I could tell by the awful flare from the main part of town that most of the shells were landing there. Each shell, as it exploded, lighted up the country for miles around, with a flare like a flash of lightning. It was visible easily for miles. The flashes of heavy shells exploding above ground can be seen for maybe twenty to thirty miles, showering shrapnel down all around. It was by all these flashes that I could see the half-dressed doughboys on their way out. The huge shells continued to rain down every five minutes or so. So big, it must take minutes to reload the gun.

Going over the railroad bridge I met two soldiers, buddies, apparently, for one seemed to be crying, and the other comforting him, as they trotted along. They had come off some side street, and were going my way.

"Better get out in the fields, you boys!" I yelled at them. "You aren't wounded, are you?"

"No, we're all right," answered one. "We just lost our way, and got into a blind street. We're getting' out as damn quick as we can."

I had thought that the little fellow must be hurt, but he might have only been sobbing from being out-of-breath. It sounded like a chap crying with pain. Later I wondered if he had lost a buddy back where the "ash cans" were dropping.

"WHAP!" another one started, just as were on the center of the bridge. From the sharp sound of the gun, I knew it was headed our way. Funny, but that night I learned that one thing. A gun, like a megaphone horn, throws sound best right in front of it, and that night one or two guns were firing right at us., while others were busy on Fontaine, or some other town. The sharp "WHAP!" always preceded a shell coming our way.

I dropped on the bridge, and the boys ahead of me did also, the shrieking crescendo of that big giant shell rose and rose. It seemed that the shell must be right on us, when "WHUP-WHAM" right below us! A high pitched "Wheeeeeee" telling of its inbound flight, then the blinding flare or the explosion. It came from a spot on the tracks, past the bridge, a bare hundred feet or more down the line from us. The ground heaved, and the bridge rocked and shivered, as the thunder of the shell rolled through the clouds and a glancing piece of shrapnel whizzed by. I leaped up and ran on. That bridge must surely have been one target that night. And I still wonder that they missed it. I was damned glad they missed that shot anyway!

Down one street I went, turned into another, and at the corner, near where I thought the captain's billet was, I ran into a motorcycle, slowly chugging up. Its driver sitting there looking around in a puzzled manner. The moon was out again, and I could see him quite clearly.

"Hey, Sanitary," he yelled, see my white armband and red cross. "Was you looking for Captain McNenney?"

"Sure." I answered, trotting up to him, "Have you seen him?"

"Nope, I came over after him, but his room is locked, and he must have gone. They're looking for him down town."

"Are you sure you looked in the right billet?" I asked.

"Sure. I asked a woman there, and she said he was gone. She knew his name and said he had a white arm band. Second door there, and his room is that one with the window sticking out, on the second floor."

"That's it," I responded, recognizing the window when he pointed, as being the one the captain had pointed out to his orderly, Louie, on the way over.

"Nothing for us to do here then, for I was looking for him also. Run me back to where the infirmary stuff is stored, will you?"

"Hop in." he said, and off we went, tearing thru the dark, back to where the shells were still crashing down, all of them seeming to land in the railroad station vicinity.

The station proper, a three and four story, stone building, was on the north side of the tracks. North of it was a space about a hundred feet wide, perhaps more, where the barracks were located. The main street, a mere road, came next, with a row of buildings on the side opposite the barracks. Right there, beside the restaurant, our infirmary stuff had been stored in a shed. That was our destination.

There were two or three big stone warehouses or buildings on the near side of the station, and as we passed the first of them, some soldier ran out to us, from the gate way leading into them.

"Oh, doctor," he yelled, seeing my armband, "I've got a man back here, badly wounded. Come in and see what you can do for the poor chap."

I noticed the gleam of a Lieutenant's bars on his shoulder, and slipped one leg over the edge of the side car, as the driver slowed up.

"Anybody look at him at all yet, Lieutenant?" I asked, knowing how little I could really do with my meager first aid bandages for a badly wounded man.

"Just some first aid man," he answered, still seeming to think I was a doctor, because I was in a side car.

"Well, that's all I am, so I can't help more than the other already did. There may be others needin' me down here. If not, I'll be back. Catch the first ambulance you can." Then I patted the driver on the back, and motioned ahead.

"But dammit, can't you do SOMETHING?" pleaded the Lieutenant, reaching out to stop us, as we started off. Then as we went by, he yelled, "COME BACK, DAMMIT. COME BACK AND DO SOMETHING, ANYWAY."

"Go to hell!" I yelled as we tore on.

I knew he was just crazy with grief, with some poor chap wounded, and unable to do a thing for him, but since another sanitary man had been there, it was no place for me. An ambulance was what he needed, to take the soldier to a hospital, where he could be handled properly.

Down by the shed we stopped, and the noise and bustle inside the restaurant drew me there. Blankets had been nailed over all the windows and doors. Inside, working by candle and lamp light, was Captain McNenney and part of the detachment. Tables and floor were littered with wounded. I didn't stop to ask questions, but took the first man handy. On a table, off to one side of the door, lay a man, apparently just brought in, with a blanket partly covering him. He was barely moaning, and seemed either unconscious or unable to answer my questions, as I stripped the blanket back, and asked him where he was hit.

He had both shirt and trousers on, and his trousers were soaked in blood, from a space about four inches below the waist band, on down his legs. I opened his belt, and drew his trousers nearly off, but I could find no sign of a wound. Carefully, I rolled him over but still found no wound. Then I drew up his shirt, and still found nothing. I rolled him on his back again, and searched his body clear to the next, and still no evidence of a wound; where all this blood was coming from. Finally, as I rolled him carefully on his face again, I found it, right in the middle of his back, between the shoulder blades. It was a red, raw spot of flesh, about six inches wide, and ten inches long. I knew it was probably hopeless as I ripped open a bandage to place over it. All I could do with my bandages was to prevent any further infection. If a piece of one of those giant shells had hit him in the back, and spine, it may have crushed his spine, and then little could be done for him anyway.

I heard one barely intelligible word pass his lips, as I worked to stop the flow, and that was, "Mother!" Perhaps he tried to say something else, but that was all I could make out. As I arranged my first bandage, I felt his body grow tense, and go limp, then his breathing stopped.

I turned him gently over, pushed the table back into the shadow, and pulled the blanket over his face. Others were waiting.

Across the room a boy on a litter was gripping the edge of it and he groaned as I drew his trousers down, and the cut them off. About half way between his thigh and knee, a shell piece had torn between his legs, leaving a bruised, raw section on each leg. Both legs were already swelling and in bad shape. Even the lower part of his abdomen was swollen, from the terrific blow he had received. A few inches to either side, a femoral artery strike and he would have lost a leg, and undoubtedly bled to death. He eased up while I opened a bandage.

"Smatter with the guy on the table," he asked. "He passed out?"

"Just unconscious." I answered, lying like hell. It wouldn't help his spirits to tell him the truth.

He looked around at the other fellows, some crying with the pain.

"I getcha. S'too damn bad." Then he groaned in pain himself, as I put the first pad on. Like myself, he realized that the chap on the table was no cheerful subject, with all these other men lying about.

In a few minutes, I had him bandaged, so that no further infection could bother the wounds, and as I packed blankets about him to keep him warm till the ambulance rolled in, he leaned his head back, to see another soldier at the head of his litter.

"Where'd they get you, buddy?" he asked "They got me in the legs, but somebody'll pay for it! Got a cigarette handy, buddy?"

Grit he certainly had, to start cheering up others, when he certainly was in awful pain himself. I passed him a cigarette, lit it for him. I then passed on to a chap in a chair, with a shoulder wound, in his left shoulder. He was due for a few weeks in the hospital, but outside of the pain, he really wasn't damaged much. The shell had missed the artery, and just cut into the muscle, which will heal fine, if infection was avoided.

The next case was a nasty one. Helping Captain McNenney clip a man's hair and bind up his head. Unconscious part of the time, it was a question as to how he would pull thru. The rip along the side of his head might not appear bad, yet it was extremely dangerous, for his skull was certainly fractured.

Then I noticed Lane passing out spirits of ammonia, to help these boys keep their nerve up. As for me, that stuff would spoil all the nerve I ever had.

Captain McNenney used to work in some large New Jersey hospital. He seemed overcome, trying to give adequate help to these boys out of one medical chest. West and Kelly were missing, and the captain had been carrying the cocaine and strong drugs in his belt, along with his hypodermic syringe. In all the excitement, these he had left in his billet. Long went for them, and the captain forgot to give him the key, so Long had one hell of a time breaking into the room. By the time Long got back, the ambulance had taken the man needing the shots.

Little Cliff Price was trotting around, doing all he could, showing up some of the others with the way he worked. A man may be a poor soldier, a rotten marcher, and may be awful in many ways, but when the big shells begin to drop, they excel. You'll damn soon know what guts he has. Cliff and Lane had their share, and more.

The town must have been nearly empty, by then, and no more bad cases rolled in. Ambulances were coming up, and our worst cases were sent back to the hospital, which I think was over beyond Montreux Vieux, about six miles away. In the first rush of artillery fire, two wounded men had been taken to the basement of the restaurant. Now I helped others, and we carried one up and rearranged his bandages, and then the other. They'd go back to the hospital eventually.

Back in the kitchen, I had noticed a French girl, and at times she'd been helping to bandage the wounded, bringing hot water, etc. for Captain McNenney, as he needed it. Now she and her sister were making coffee and back in the kitchen I discovered our Y.M.C.A man. With no orders holding him there, he had been doing his share, and was now promoting the coffee idea. It helped morale.

Not all soldiers are good, and few are real heroes. Y men were the same. Their plan of handling supplies heaped criticism on their heads. Among the good ones was men like our Y man. Later on, he issued us candy and smokes on I.O.U.'s, which he would be required to pay off, if we failed to. He was the kind of a man any organization could be proud of.

Volunteer squads were formed, and began searching the barracks and through the town in the darkness, looking for wounded men, or worse. They kept dropping by the restaurant. One chap borrowed a light from me, as I stood back in the shadows, and we talked a moment. As he turned away, I noticed his rank, the shoulder ornaments of a Lieutenant Colonel, and grinned because I hadn't saluted him. I wouldn't have, that night, had I noticed his rank, for that night, rank didn't count.

The smaller shells were still coming over, but slower, and one rocked our little hospital. "Screeee — Boom!" Going out in back, we saw a cloud of dust rising from behind. It had missed us by thirty feet.

One of the French girls had been at the backdoor, when it lit off. She was shrieking and yelling. Her sister ran to her, and then the rest of us gathered around but could do nothing. She was not injured but it was a case of pure fright. Shell shock from being so close to a bursting shell. I don't wonder it shocked her, that immense blast almost right in her face. It landed just across the back alley and tore a crater out of the ground, big enough to bury an auto truck in. Dirt and debris kept falling for minutes, as we dragged her back into the house, her sister took her into a side room. It was an hour before her shrieks and sobs quieted.

It was slowly beginning to turn light outside now, and the shelling stopped at last. Men kept coming in, showing tin hats bent, or with holes in them. Torn clothing, and odds and ends of souvenirs from the shells. One more patient came in, with a hole in one foot. He had gotten it while leaving town, and had not stopped in then.

The front room of our restaurant aid station was quiet now. The stretchers remaining there were covered. Those men needed no medical attention. There was a shed up near our barracks, and the captain had decided to use that as our morgue. In the very early morning light, it was mostly dark. Four of us took up the first litter, and went up the street. It was still so dark few objects could be seen, and only a few soldiers were returning from the fields.

On our second trip, when day was breaking, many of the inhabitants were out, and doughboys were out. The doughboys were coming back, dressed in all sorts of clothing. I had a chance to see how quickly they must have left their billets. Many were barefoot, having left without even taking shoes. Several had nothing on but a blanket, some only an overcoat, and under one blanket, two men were hidden.

On that trip we noticed one thing. Each Frenchman, as we came upon him, as soon as he noticed our silent party coming, stopped, removed his hat. They'd stand at attention, head bowed, as we passed. The Americans we passed, rolled noisily on, a few uncovering, many paying no attention. Some asking who it was, and one or two even making remarks as "Who the hell yuh got there, guys?" What is it? 'Nother stiff? Where ya goin'?"

We answered no questions, but kept on our way.

Louie Schneider was on one litter squad, and was surprised to find, after one trip in the dark, that all three of his litter companions were officers, one a captain. We began to think the blamed officers might be human, after all.

Most of our casualties had come from Company L. of the 115th Infantry, their billet was a sight. In one barrack a giant shell had lit in almost the dead center, and blown up a space about ten feet square. I would have expected a crater ten times that size, but the ground was hard, and the force of the explosion had been more sidewise that if the ground had been softer. The morning, outside one window, one searching squad picked up a man, blown clear out through the window, and into a ditch and nearly every bone in his body had been broken. He likely died instantly, and I certainly hope so for his sake. Fitz knew him, and said his first name was Bob, but he could not recall his last name.

Our detachment, with the help of one first aid man from the infantry companies located near the station, had handled nineteen wounded men, and we had six dead. Later I heard that the night's casualty total, had amounted to forty-two wounded, and thirteen dead. That meant that our unit had borne the worst of the shelling, though several villages had been shelled. We were not given any indication of civilian casualties, though, sadly, I'm sure they suffered also.

Back at our barrack, mess was almost ready when our litter squad came up, after leaving the last man at our morgue. The boys who were lined up waiting for the mess whistle, yelled question after question at us. We had bloody hands, and the nearest water was a block away. By the time we were cleaned up we might be late for mess. One of the cooks yelled to us to hurry, and said that he'd save some stuff for us.

"Hurry, hell," yelled somebody in the head end of one of the messline, "Looks to me like the Pill Rollers rate the head of the line today! How about it boys?!"

"Sure!"

"You bet!"

"Damn right they do! They earned it."

And a lot of other calls much the same. That was the highest tribute those boys could give us. We had stayed right where the shells were falling, to care for the wounded, while they had beat it to the fields. For once the despised pill rollers were kings, and with waiting to wash up, we ate that morning with dried blood still caked on our hands. As each Sanitary Detachment man came up, he was showed to the head of the line, with cheers from the boys behind. For once the "Pill Rollers" had proved themselves fit, and ready for the front.

There was one aftermath to that night's shelling, that never did sit right with me. That was that three Sanitary Detachment men had slipped out into the fields, and not going down town, as ordered. Practically, they were deserters, but nothing was done about it, since they claimed to have attended wounded men in the fields. Captain McNenney might have been lenient because he himself had forgotten his first aid kit with his hypo needle and the drugs, but that was an accident. He certainly had not shirked his duty. I, for one, knew just how much pure guts it took to trot on towards those falling shells, in a pitch-black night, with the rolling thunder of shell bursts making every nerve in me quiver and shake. With my single-track mind, I would have trotted on, into death itself. Thinking of it later, I could hardly blame the other chaps that had turned to the fields. Perhaps I would have myself, had I stopped to really think it over.

Most of all, I had to hand it to Lane and Price. Those two we would have soonest suspected of cowardice, yet they had been most prominent at the restaurant aid station. We had no real reason to suspect either of cowardice, but each had faults only too evident to us, and that they did not possess.

Later that day, we were moved over to Montreux proper, into billets, in place of barracks. That night, tired though I was, I awakened several times to watch a Boche night aircraft. Along in the early evening he flew over, and from the crack and roar of anti-aircraft, there must have been ten anti-aircraft nests scattered across town. The Boche was flying low, for as each gun let go, the burst of the shell followed right after, instead of a delay when they fired higher.

From the shelling we had gotten, and the plane flying over, it was apparent the Boche feared that we were up to some night work. This flyer was probably inspecting the ground below, trying in the bright moonlight to see if any large bodies of troops or long supply trains were moving about. If he had located any movement on the ground below, undoubtedly, more shells would have come screaming over.

On the 16th of September, we received a nice little official letter of commendation, from the Division Signal Officer, Major Hazeltine, to Captain McNenney and the men of the Sanitary Detachment. After keeping the original, the captain had copies made, adding an endorsement to we men of the battalion, expressing his thanks for our cooperation, and to each man he gave a copy of the original, bearing his message also.

```
                HEADQUARTERS, 29th DIVISION.
           American E.F.          Army PO 765
                    15 September '18.
From:  Division Signal Officer, 29th Division.
To:    Captain Claudio E. McNenney, M.C., 104th Field Signal
                                                   Battalion.
Subject:  Commendation.

        1.  I wish to express to you my appreciation of your
excellent work on the night of the 13th--14th September.

        2.  Your conduct during the bombardment and attention to
your duty was in keeping with the finest traditions of the Corps.

        3.  As the surgeon of the Signal Battalion, the work of you
and your men reflects credit on us all.

        4.  I wish you would convey to your detachment my apprecia-
tion of the excellent work done by them and yourself.

        5.  The devotion to duty displayed by both you and your
detachment is worthy of great praise.

                       (signed)    C.B.Hazeltine,
                                   Major, Signal Corps, U.S.A.
           Ind.
From Claudio E. McNenney, Capt., M.C., 104th Field Signal Battalion,
Sept. 16, '18--to the enlisted men of the Sanitary Detachment, 104th
Field Signal Battalion.

        1.  I want to thank you for the hearty cooperation you
rendered me under the most trying circumstances.

                       (Signed)    Claudio E. McNenney,
                                   Capt., M.C., U.S.A.
```

CHAPTER 15

On the night of the 18th, we left Montreux proper, going by truck to Cravanche, a little town outside Belfort. That night the Signal Corps was moved piecemeal, so our solitary truck was all by itself, and later I was glad that we were, for our Boche night flier appeared just as we were moving nicely along on a level road. It was bordered by a stately row of trees, and sighting a truck some ways ahead of us, the Boche peppered them with machine gun fire.

Our driver stopped our truck dead, and a few of us piled out, but it was over so quickly that only a few had managed to get to the ground. We were packed in like sardines, and I hate to think what damage a few steel-jacketed bullets could have done had they pierced the light sides of the truck. It was a moonlit night, and the Boche had suddenly roared out of the darkness, skimmed along one side of the road. He was level with the treetops and hopped over to the other side before reaching us, and a little beyond us, peppered some object that the aviator thought was moving. We, in the truck, could not see or hear anything ahead that resembled a truck, so he might have intended those bullets for us. I rather believe some cluster of trees, or shadows along the road, had drawn his attention. Perhaps he thought he saw a column of marching men. Anyway, I was glad he had passed us by.

Armed as were, with only hand axes, being fired on made me feel like someone had tied my hand, and then hit me. There may be honor and even some joy, in a fight where both parties are armed. If one is a plane with a machine gun, and the other on the ground, with a pistol or rifle, I'd at least have some chance to fight back. To face a whizzing cluster of machine gun bullets, while unarmed, made me feel sick. The big shells had not bothered me, but just the sound of that machine gun burst made me feel pale and sick to my stomach, all night.

The next morning, at Cravanche, the driver of the wireless truck was proudly exhibiting it, to show where the night flying Boche had dotted the "I" in "Signal" with one of his bullets. That Heine must have scoured those roads all night. I'll have to hand it to him, he had guts to fly a plane the way he did, and as close to the ground, on these foggy, dark nights. The flying in the moonlight above might have been easy but it was no cinch to go hedge-hopping along in the mist, close to the ground.

Our first billet in Cravanche was a haymow, but later we had to change to the attic over the infirmary. It was drier but had little ventilation. I always did prefer a haymow for solid comfort.

I remember Cravanche for three things; first, that standing in town, on a high hill above Belfort, we could see with field glasses into Switzerland on one side, and into Alsace on the other. Down below, against the face of

above *The Lion can be seen faintly in the upper left of the photo of Belfort.*
below *The Lion of Belfort carved in 1871 by Bartholdi*

a cliff, on the opposite side of the city, we could see the Lion of Belfort. It is carved from solid stone right in the face of the cliff, done by Bartholdi. The same man who carved the blocks making the Statue of Liberty. When I learned that, to me, the Lion seemed like a bit from home.

The second memory of Cravanche was because Louie got piffed one night, and as the captain's orderly, had to go to the captain's room for something. Rather than let him go as drunk as he was, I walked him for an hour, till he was sober enough to only stagger a bit. I got a fair cussing from him, for my trouble. That was only because he was drunk, in reality, Louie and I were pretty good pals, usually.

The third memory was of a little French girl near us, who was dressed week days in drab clothes with wooden shoes. On Sunday, going to church, she was as well-dressed as any American girl, with a neat hat, and polished, black shoes. She was a treat for sore eyes

Cravanche, on Main street, with woman washing clothing at public fountain in foreground, right. The wheelbarrow has bundles of clothes in it.

Early in the morning of the 23rd of September, we were rolled out and marched way down the hill, to a waiting line of box cars, down in Belfort. It was a dreary, rainy morning, and we were all pretty damp when we were finally loaded in, packed as tight as usual. Woods and I landed in one place, together. We were sitting with our backs against the side of the car, only to find that the blamed car leaked. There was nothing for us to do but pull on our slickers and sit on our packs to keep our seats out of the water. All thru the long day and night we rode that way, with a drizzly, mean rain, falling steadily outside, and a ceaseless stream over us inside. We were by no means the only ones to get wet inside, but Woods, indisposed as he was with a bad cold when we started, he was soon in far worse shape, and with a fever.

FIRST TASTE OF SHELLING 151

above *Two other town views Note that but for the stone buildings, with the caps on the chimneys, this might be America.*

below *The names on the restaurant of identify it as a French scene, if the wooden shoes and cap on the man didn't already make it evident.*

I reported his case to Sergeant Wester, but he could do nothing until the train stopped. So poor Woods had to sit there and suffer in silence. Part of the time he leaned against me, for the car was as usual too crowded to lie down in and the floor too wet anyway.

Doughy was lucky that trip, being assigned to a string of trucks, as first aid man for them on the long trip to wherever we were headed. He was the only lucky one, for the rest of us felt like ducks. The train finally stopped early in the morning of the 24th, at a station named Nettancourt.

Our rations, in cans as usual, with a few loaves of bread for good measure, were piled in the center of the car, and there were six full cans of jam still in the pile when the "ALL OUT" yell came down the line. Maybe it was because I was peeved, or maybe I was just lucky, but when the jam of soldiers grabbing those cans was finally untangled, I was holding two cans of jam in my hands! I didn't need to look at them to know what they were. I had been about ten feet from the can pile but for once I had been at the bottom of it, and when about thirty others pulled themselves off of me. I knew damn well that they might have been beans or tomatoes but this time they weren't.

Poor Woods had to be taken off the train on a litter. After the captain had been found, he detailed me to find a phone, call in an ambulance, and see that Woods was sent to a hospital. I spent two good hours finding a phone, and when I finally located one, in a small barrack a quarter mile out of town, I had one hell of a time trying to tell a French Captain that I wanted an ambulance from an American hospital. Either he was dumb, or my French was punk, likely the latter. Perhaps, as I later thought, he feared that I was a spy, trying to give information as to the division's movements over the phone to some confederate. Anyway, finally a Lieutenant appeared, who acted as interpreter, and after another hour's work on the phone, at last I got some American on the phone, and related my message. It was three p.m. before Woods was finally dispatched to the hospital for the ambulance had twice lost the road route.

I had been up all day on the 23rd, all that night, and twisted in a small spot in the box car. Now nearly all day of the 24th, as a nurse to Woods, I sure was tired. Just before he left, I did give him the only think I could as a present. I slipped one of my two cans of jam under his blanket. I told him to hang on to it, and they were big cans too. Woods had been out of his head, part of the day, but he smiled a thanks, as he finally was lifted into the ambulance for the long ride toward a warm, dry bed.

That was the last of Woods. I never did hear whether he died or recovered. Such is life in the army. Radano, another of our detachment, had left for a hospital a few days before for a minor operation. Woods, then, was the second. Neither ever returned.

I was tired as hell, and got to the billet, down the road a half mile, just in time for mess. After which I got a bare hour's rest, before we were called out to start on an all-night hike, toward the big front at last.

16

TO THE FRONT

Nettancourt, as I found it on my map, was southwest of Verdun, and just above and west of Bar-Le-Duc and Revigny. That long night march was toward the east, where, against the dark sky, we could see the intermittent flashes of heavy guns, a full sixty miles away. We could hear the low, dull thunder of heavy shells crashing somewhere up on the front. I might be tired but that sort of skyline ever ahead, kept me pepped up way into the wee hours. We plodded steadily on, by marching fifty minutes, then resting ten minutes each hour.

I had my two souvenir 75mm shell casing art in my pack. Just before starting, Lane picked it up, staggered under its weight, and called me a damn mule to cart such a load. I had three blankets, plus those shells, as part of my load. Heavy as it might be, I kept pace with Lane, all thru the night, and he had a light pack, with only one blanket.

Plop, plop, plop all thru the night, as the heavy trench shoes ate up mile after mile. Our only music being those guns somewhere ahead, and sometimes our own whistling or singing, to keep us cheerful. Our tin hats were too heavy to wear, and most of the boys had their light caps on, with their tin hats clank, clank, clanking on their packs behind. Usually, soldiers slipped some cord thru the chin strap, and let the hat swing from side to side, as they walked. The noise bothered me, and the swing of even that bit on my back was annoying. I had soon hit on a harness snap, which I wired to the hat, tight up under one side, so that when the snap was clipped into an eyelet or around some cord on my pack. In this way, the hat laid flat, and did not bounce or roll about.

All night long we marched on, with no one else on the road. It seemed that we never were going to reach our destination. A ten-mile hike is long enough, fifteen is plenty, twenty is plain hell, but it was nearly thirty for us that night. The road behind us was fairly dotted for miles with cursing, sweating boys who could not keep up. Poor Cliff dropped out early, with his short legs doing their best. Even I was a hundred yards behind, as we finally came into Conde. We had gone thru Laheycourt, and then our guide had taken us north, thru L'Isle-en-Barrois, instead of on the direct route to Conde. We even had to about-face, and march about a mile or two back, having started on the wrong road.

I slept all day on the 25th, and part of the 26th, but about evening that day we were marched out of Conde, to a field about a mile or two north, where we lay all night, waiting all night with unopened packs. Next to us was a long line of French trucks with their Chinese Coolie drivers, ready to load us and leap into action, at a moment's notice. Apparently, we were a division in reserve, and were being held ready for movement, and thus we were under strict orders not to open our packs. This allowed us to load and being moving is less than five minutes.

Trust a soldier to make himself comfortable, if possible. At first, we stood around and slushed in the mud and rain for a bare half hour, waiting for an invitation to spend the night in the dry trucks. The fields around us began to look like a deserted hay field, for only long rows of dead, dry grass could be seen. But rather, it was wet grass, or weeds, because it was raining steadily. A damp, chilly drizzle.

The field had been an old potato field, and the weeds and vines had been left where they had fallen. Being unable to open our packs, and use our dry shelter halves, we had only our overcoats and those damned, cheap, slickers, which were soaked through. We put one under us, either, it didn't matter which, and the other over us, and our heads on our packs. Then one volunteer would cover us with weeds. All thru the night, whenever I stood up, all that I could see was odd humps of weeds with an occasional soldier moving about.

Morning came with a little sunshine, for a few minutes. It was chilly, and damp. We were given the same orders as the prior day, do not open our packs for either shelter, nor dry clothing. Our shelter halves or half tents, were always used as an outer wrapper for our blankets. We dared not remove them for they'd get soaked. Besides making an awfully heavy load, they would then be wet and useless for whenever we did get a chance to rest.

Some of us got up and walked about, while others lay just as they had all night. We hated to turn over because each move brought new, cold, wet spots that played against our bodies. It's miserable enough to have to stay in one little field for a night and a day without having it rain also. We had to lie there thinking about the nice tents our shelter halves would make. Also, how nice and dry those Chink driven trucks must be. For some obscure reason, none of us, not even the officers entered those trucks. We, the enlisted men, had our orders not to, but it surprised me that the officers didn't preempt them for their own use. They did, however, commandeer our litters. Each officer used one of the litters as a bed, keeping their bodies off the ground.

That morning, during dry spells between showers, I could see far away across the hills, and was surprised to see far to one side, several other snake-like lines of trucks. Each line marking the route of some other road. Apparently, the entire division was lined up along those hills, ready to move at once. Thus, we weren't the only ones being soaked. Perhaps we were even luckier than many others, for we did have those dried weeds to help keep the rain off.

Toward noon the sky cleared, and the everlasting drizzle stopped. We could plainly see at least three other lines of trucks and there were probably many others out of sight. Those French Camions, with their Chink drivers, were certainly an exposition on the scarcity of males of serviceable age in France. Just along here, in our own areas, there must have been way over a thousand trucks, each with its Chinese driver, and a few extra men and mechanics with each truck company. Probably a few old or wounded Frenchmen as company commanders also. It seemed strange, at first, that the French should have gone to the expense and trouble of hiring and training these Chinese to drive trucks, for the Chinese were notoriously the least modern of races. The expense item was undoubtedly the reason why the Chinks were used. With wages of only a few cents a day, it couldn't amount to much compared to the cost for using that number of American drivers. That could be prohibitively expensive.

One blessing might be that the Chinks would undoubtedly have a broader outlook, and a better understanding of the rest of the world when they finally returned home. The war was a great leveler of all classes and creeds, and in its way, would probably aid the cause of world democracy for hundreds of years. The ties and friendships formed by soldiers from all over the world, fighting side-by-side, would encourage travel and communication between nations, once the war was over. It'd allow each nation to better understand the troubles of others.

Our last warm meal had been served early in the afternoon on the 26th, and the 27th seemed doomed to go by without any mess call. Funny too, how hungry one gets, just waiting and waiting, without a thing to do. So, we did the only thing possible, and wandered about our tiny field. We inspected every visible thing that may seem strange or queer. From the far corner of the field, I saw what appeared to be a wooden pump, or well, far down in the valley below.

Our orders were to be ready to move in five minutes time, and that pump couldn't be much more than a five-minute walk from us, so off I went, with little Reigle along. Down in the valley, what had appeared to be a deserted field, proved to be a partly tilled field. It had a few rows of carrots, and potatoes still remaining. Reigle went on with our canteens to the water pump, while I hurried back to my pack where I had an old style, long bladed mess knife. Using that knife, we each dung up enough potatoes to fill our pockets. The carrots we used raw, just wiping the dirt off, and peeling the outer skin, we ate them raw.

Raw potatoes are no gift to a hungry man, but the battalion had several small bonfires going now, and over one of these I proceeded to cook my potatoes in water. I had to wipe the dirt off first, on the wet grass and then peel them in a towel, for my water was precious. At that, they were fairly clean, and when I finally got them peeled and sliced, and cooking in a bit of water in my mess kit.

The boys kidded me as I worked and laughed at the idea of frying potatoes in water over a bonfire, but say, how they did crowd around when the hot steam started rising. The sweet smell of piping hot potatoes began to float around on the breeze. It has stopped raining altogether now, and everyone was walking about. The few slants of sunshine began to break thru the clouds, and pretty soon half of the battalion was grouped about my fire.

"Damn, but those spuds smell good!" someone said.

"Where'd you them, Sanitary?" asked others, and when I pointed to the field below, a few of the more venturesome hiked off in that direction. Most, however, were afraid to leave the field, fearing that they would be called down for disobeying orders. The Sanitary bunch, however, were more venturesome, and Louie and Knorr were soon down after a mess for themselves.

The crowd got thicker and thicker around me, and when the spuds began to brown, some could stand it no longer.

"Say, Pill Roller, I'll give yuh two francs for that mess kit of spuds." Offered someone.

"I'll make it five, here," said someone who was up close and the wafts of cooking spuds was stronger.

"Five, hell, I'll give six." Was another bid.

From six, the bidding got hot, for it was then that I turned my spuds over, and stirred them up, letting the top ones get to the bottom, cooking and preventing burning. The sight of those beautiful brown, bubbling spuds was plenty. Those boys had the bidding skyrocketing clear to twenty francs for that one mess kit full! I should have taken that bid certainly, but what good would money be to me, up there at the front? I needed hot food. I ate every bit of the blamed potatoes in that mess kit all by myself. I was not full, so then I made another batch, but this time I sold half of them for six francs. By that time, several other chaps had been out digging and many other mess kits were sizzling when I finished my second mess.

According to the rumors thru the battalion, the old solid range mess had been checked in, and we were to get a rolling kitchen, but as usual, it was slow in being delivered. It should have been delivered to our cooks the evening before, and when it did finally arrive, it was late on the 27th. By that time, I wasn't so very hungry.

That night we were allowed to sleep in the Chink driven, French trucks, but it was a damn poor place to sleep. True enough, we were dry, for the incessant drizzle that had started again at nightfall was not affecting us in the trucks, but it was impossible to rest in them. The side boards came only to my shoulders, and from there up the rounded, loaf-like canvas top began, that was stretched over framework. That interfered with my head. If I sat with my back against the sideboards, I had to bend my head forward and that soon got tiresome. If I tried to slouch down, the narrow seat was not wide enough to slide out on. Also, the trucks were narrow enough that the two rows of feet covered the floor so completely that there was no room to lie there. Half of the time, I tried to sit up, and the other half I sat with my elbows on my knees, and my chin in my hands. Just trying to rest....

All night long the continuous thunder and roar of guns far in front of us could be heard. Pleasant dreams, for certain not.

The 28th was a repetition of the 27th, only that we did have something to eat. At that, we raided the potato field once more, on general principles. We kept a small pile of spuds handy on the ground, in case of need. About 3p.m., an official looking Colonel came strutting up, looking for our C.O., who happened to now be Captain Tom Armstrong, a tall, older chap, Company Commander of "C" Company, and also the Battalion head, in place of Major Heidt, who had been promoted again.

After a short talk, the Colonel left, and Captain Tom ordered us to fall in, in a hollow square formation, where he could then talk to us. Practically half of the battalion was now on duty with the various Infantry companies in the division, keeping a liaison system intact, and so it was a fairly small square that was formed. The three companies, on three sides, and the H.Q., then the Sanitary Detachments, and the other Officers on the fourth side behind Captain Tom.

"Now boys," roared the old Captain, when we were lined up, "A Colonel from headquarters just came by with a complaint that some of the division soldiers have been stealing potatoes from the nearby fields. Those fields are worked mostly by poor women, for the men are gone. It's a mean trick to steal from them, what little crop they raise. Of course, I know that none of our boys would do such a thing, but the Colonel asked me to have you call in, and tell you about it. In this manner, you'll think twice before doing any such thing. Now that poor woman has complained to headquarters, and will likely be well-paid for the potatoes that she's lost. Perhaps some other fields have been raided, and the poor owners may not know of it till too late to report it to our H.Q. They will suffer the losses. A few potatoes to these poor folks may represent a fortune, right now."

As we well knew, many a peasant reported damages to his fields and possessions, just in order to receive payment for them. If the owner of the potato field claimed damages, she would get paid for ten bushels for every one really taken. It was a shame, if she didn't for that was about the scale on which others based their claims.

While the Captain was talking, Captain McNenney, trim and neat, standing at ease, in front of the detachment, had noticed a litter, still open. It stood out to one side, a little in the way of the assembly, and just behind Captain Tom. For some reason, he decided to move it. He reached down to pull it back out of the road, and we all gasped. We had been right near the Colonel when he gave his message to Captain Tom, and Louie had at once pulled that litter over our stash of potatoes.

The captain pulled the litter back without seeing what he had exposed to view. He straightened up, brushed his hands off.

Captain Tom was just finishing his lecture, with the same compliment to the men, "Of course, I know that none of our men have been doing such a thing as robbing a poor widow's field, and I am only telling you this so that you'll not start stealing," and so on… The captain's voice trailed off, as the snickers grew and grew. Discipline was alright, but even these vets could not stand too much. Captain Tom glanced about, then his eyes followed the pointing hands of a dozen men, and he took one startled look at the pile of potatoes, right behind his heels. He looked at them a second, while the whole Battalion roared with laughter. Finally, he kicked one aside, as if to see if it was real, and then turned to face the laughing battalion. "SO, BATTALION DISMISSED!" he roared and turned with a smile on his face. It might be a joke on him, but he could appreciate a good trick. I suppose he knew how hungry his troops were; cold, wet, no hot food, and let it pass.

All the rest of the time that we were in that field, however, those potatoes lay there, in a space all to themselves. Not a single soldier claimed them, nor even touched them. They had become strictly, absolutely taboo! Even Captain McNenney took it as a joke, and never called us down.

That night, still awaiting deployment, we were allowed to open our packs, and we slept under our shelter tents for once. The rain drizzled all night again, but with small ditches around our pup tents, we were dry and comfortable inside. We sure appreciated that night's rest, after the way we had spent the two previous nights.

The push up at the front must have been successful, and the guns had even quieted down that night. Apparently, we were not apt to be needed in a hurry, for the French camions with the Chink drivers moved on, and all was peaceful.

About 8:30p.m., on the night of September 29th, we finally moved forward, on foot. We hiked thru the rain will about 1a.m., landing in a small village, Mondrecourt, I think it was. I was too tired to find out just what the name was, for I had tried wrapping my puttees or leggings wrap from the top, down. They felt easier on my legs, at that, but the inevitable rain coursed down my legs, and ran right into the folds of the leggings and into my shoes. After that trip, I wrapped those puttees only from the bottom up, letting each fold cover that top of the one below, and that kept out the water.

Our billet that morning was a haymow. In the rush of trying to change into dry underclothes, get out for morning mess, and watch my belongings, I lost my flashlight, one pair of shoes, and a suit of underwear. Mess call had come just when I was undressed, changing in to dry underwear. We had pulled into town about 1a.m., but stood around in the rain for two hours before being assigned to billets. After someone found a barn door open, we assigned ourselves. By the time I was undressed, mess was called. After mess, I slept till 5p.m. and was up just in time for evening mess, after which we hiked on again, toward the front.

That was the night of Sept 30th, and on that hike, we passed several little grave markers, along the road. In one place, two dead horses, not yet buried. Certainly, from the looks, and from the incessant gunfire all night, we must be getting near the front. Always we seemed to be marching forward. That shellfire was always about so far beyond us, but this night it seemed to have widened, and swept in the half circle about us. Many of us wondered if the Boche had not broken through on our flanks, and we wondered if we were marching right up into some giant trap. We must be in the center of some great curve, for the sky was lighted up in a full half circle, in front and to each side of us, yet the center seemed to be as far away as before.

Biercourt, nestled in a valley, was our landing place that night, and here we won barracks again. We got hot coffee right after pulling in. I went back for more, and even got thirds that night. Biercourt, or any other place where I could get thirds at the mess tent, was all right by me. It did prove to be a fairly nice place, at that. We stayed there till the 5th of October, saw a Y.M.C.A. entertainment, got hot chocolate at a Red Cross stand, run by some woman. We also got free socks and a knitted cap, distributed by a Red Cross outfit at some nearby hospital.

Our medical Caducea were good at that hospital for stuff distributed there. Queer, isn't it how outfits stick together? If we Pill Rollers were at any time near a hospital, we could get many items there, free, just because we were in a Sanitary Detachment. A wounded or sick Pill Roller, in a hospital, received the same treatment as an officer of any other outfit. Quite often, the attendants would steal some Major's ice cream and chicken, only to pass it along to some poor wounded buck private hearing the magic medical Caducea. Perhaps because they, like us, were often the butt for many jokes from the boys in the regular infantry or artillery outfits.

All our movements were made at night so that we would not be observed by the Boche planes, many of which were to be seen during the day, but usually high in the air. During our stay in Biercourt, one day I noticed two smoke columns rising from the woods, down the valley. The boys said that at least one was caused by a fallen Boche place, crashed and burning there. No one was sure just what caused the other. Late that afternoon I suddenly heard the roar of aircraft in full flight. All at once, a Bouche came flashing over the hilltops, flying low and going like mad! Right behind him came four or five Allied planes, tying on his tail in wonderful shape. That Boche was in for plenty from the looks, and the way he swung about showed that he knew it. The whole group of ships were biplanes, and pretty evenly matched for speed. The Boche cut down our valley, hedgehopping over the trees, and swung in a steep, sharp turn, just as the leading place behind him got in gun range, and opened up. To me, it looked like damn dangerous flying for boys behind to keep from piling into one another, but they swung over on his tail as if they were all connected with one piece of string.

CHAPTER 16

"Rat-a-tat-tat-tat" sounded from the guns with the lead ship. As he drew down on the Boche again, and the shells from his machine gun ripped past my ears, I was right in range below, on a high mound of ground. I made myself scarce, diving down for shelter, only to find by the time I turned around, the planes had all departed. Undoubtedly, that Boche must have been on his last flight, but I never knew for certain whether he escaped or not. It was another one of those flashes seen during war, tremendously exciting, while it lasted, but completely unfinished. It was one more unfinished incident to record in my journal, and dream on the resolution. My smokey dreams that night, were of Park Field, and my unfinished flying application.

17

VERDUN

On the 5th, about 8p.m., we started out over fine roads, on an easy hike to Verdun. It was a nice, dry night, with only the flashes from the guns up in front to light our road. There were not so busy tonight either. About midnight, we pulled into Verdun, and going over some bridge, we turned back down a street which doubled back and forth. It ultimately led under the bridge, and into a cut thru the hill, where we were billeted in some big building, on the ground floor. One queer thing that attracted my attention, was the heavy logs braced, slanting over the doorways. This shut off any direct rays of light that might gleam out and also acted as shields from stray shell shrapnel.

Everything was quiet when we entered Verdun, but about a half-hour afterward, a spiteful "Plap" sounded overhead. Pieces of shrapnel tinkled down on the tile rooftops. About every half hour during the night, we heard the same sound repeated. That shrapnel was our first taste of the big front, and it surprised me, for I had thought that Verdun was well behind the active lines. Come to find out, it had been right in the active front, for four long years. The town was heavily damaged and was still receiving its hourly quota of shells. The current shelling was probably to discourage troop movements around Verdun, not targeting a specific site.

Verdun, historic Verdun, with all its mystery and glory. It had been famous for years and now we were in it. We got plenty of evidence of the mystery, for the next day, Doughy and I made a queer trip. He took me over to a big building beside ours, both of which seemed to set in a big cut right thru this hill. We went in and climbed up to the fourth or fifth story, and walked thru a door, to find that we were on the roof of another house — our own billet. From there we walked right out into the street, up on the hilltop, which was level with the roof of our billet. Down the street a few blocks, we turned into a yard, skirted a house, and stood up looking over a stone wall in the rear. From there, further down the street, way below us, we could see one of the city gates. We were level with the top of that wall. Behind us, there was a long flight of steps, coming out on a balcony facing the street below, stopping about half-way down the wall. Thru the streets, alongside our hill, Doughy led me till he finally entered a side street, running up into the hill itself. This street was lined along both sides by rooms; some soldier's billets, other store rooms, and one was a large recreation room. We were in the famous "Underground city" of Verdun. One city built over the old one in many areas.

The whole interior of the hill over which we had traveled seemed to be hollowed out for store rooms, warehouses, etc. I wished that I might inspect them all but our trip ended with an endless seeming climb up a flight of circular stairs that led to the street above. From there, we went back over the bridge and down into our billet again.

Undoubtedly, there were other places of interest to see in Verdun, but we were not allowed to go on any sightseeing trips. Orders came out that afternoon for us to keep off the streets in daylight, and that the shelling and shrapnel kept us off them at night.

On the night of Sept 7th, we started up again, this time, as we head, to actual front itself. We all wrote last day letters, last minute memos filled with notes. We were divided into two Sanitary squads, Sergeant Wester in charge of one, and Sergeant Fitz over the other, then we moved up. I was in Fitz's squad, and we drew a truck in which to ride thru the dark night for about seven or eight miles. It seemed more like twenty as we went crawling slowly along, without a single light. It was very dark, and we had orders to not even light cigarettes. Finally, the truck spilled us out, with our equipment, and we shuffled thru the mud, along a winding road, that was piled along its sides with strange discarded articles of wars. In the morning those piles turned out to be hastily dumped heaps of hand grenades, trench mortar shells, and other trench fighting paraphernalia. On down the road, and down into a trench we filed, and finally found lodging in a scooped dugout, in the trench wall. This was where the entire party spent the night, piled atop one another. There was room for five men in that dugout, but there were ten or twelve of us, jammed into it in the dark.

How close to the lines we were, where we were, and a lot of other questions took our interest for the test of the night. Sleep was out of the question. Shells drifted over occasionally, but mostly they were little "whizz bangs", similar to the French 75mm shells, with a very few four or six-inch shells mixed in. Not that I ever measured any, but old salts described them

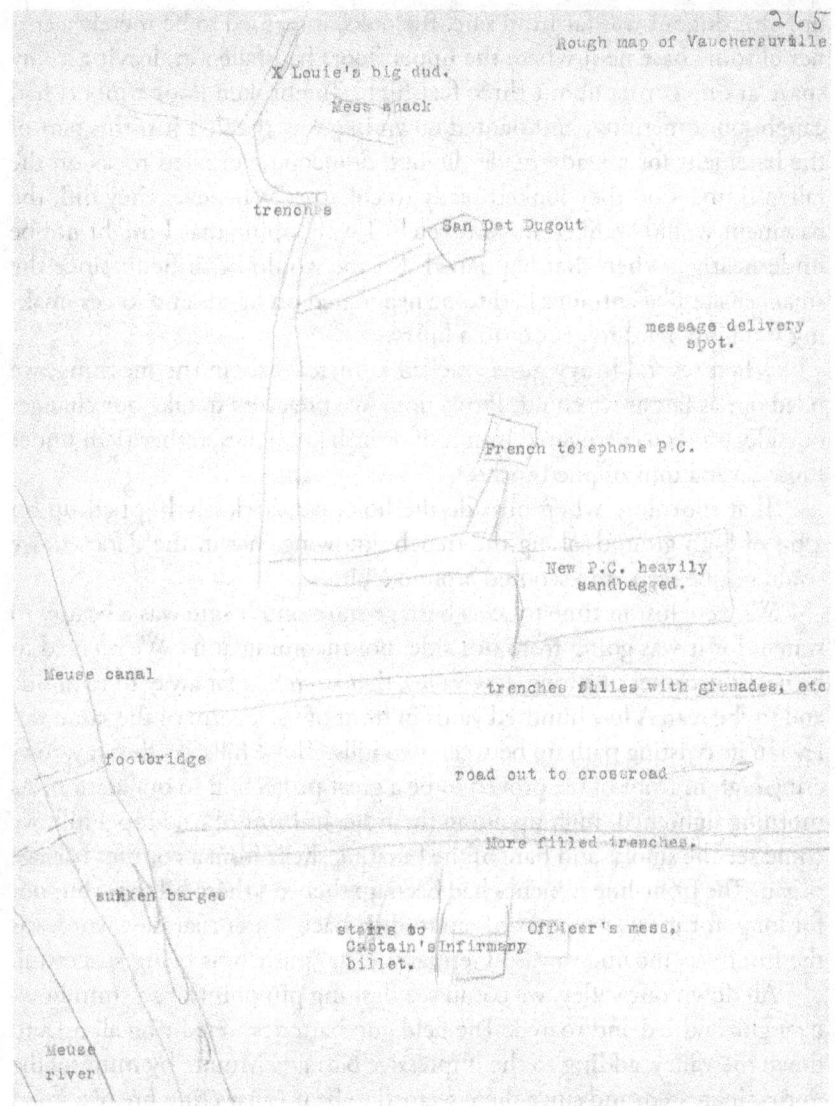

as such. The "whizz bangs" were so called because that was the sounds they made. They came at high speed, and at low angles. The only warning one had of their arrival was the almost instantaneous "whizz", just preceding the sharp "Bang!" as the shell exploded. They were mean babies, for they gave almost no warning. One had to dive flat the moment you heard the "whizz".

It was quiet indeed our first night seemed, after the incessant roar we had heard for hours at a time on various nights while we were marching up. Our dugout was far from safe. By looks, it seemed to be merely a corner of some basement where the upper floors had fallen in, leaving a tiny space at one corner about three feet high. The broken floor timbers had caught on something, and slanted down in a way that left just this part of the basement for a ready-made dugout. Someone had piled rocks on the fallen timbers till they looked ready to collapse. Whenever they did, the basement would be filled in completely. I was hoping that I might not be underneath it when that happened. Escape would be difficult since the small, snake-like entrance had to be negotiated on hands and knees, making it mighty hard to get out in a hurry.

When several heavy guns cracked at once, early in the morning, we piled out as fast as we could. Protection? We preferred to take our changes outside, under a corrugated iron roof over the trenches, rather than under those several tons of piled rocks.

That morning, when outside the hole, we carelessly hopped up on a bit of high ground, along the trench, knowing that in the darkness we could not be seen, and scouted around a bit.

We were just in time to see a barrage start, and it sure was a beauty to watch, for it was going from our side, not incoming at us. We seemed to be near the center of a long, low valley, that stretched far away to each side and to the rear. A few hundred yards in front of us, an arm of the same valley ran its twisting path up between two hills. Those hills, by the way, towering high in front of us, proved to be a great protection to our station. As morning lightened, high up along the ridge in front of us, atop a hill, we could see the smoke and flare of the bursting shells from a counter barrage began. The front-line trenches had been up there on those hilltops, but not for long, for meager reports began to drift back. Later that day, word was the front was moving toward Germany. Our "push" was being successful.

All down our valley, we could see flashing pin points, as 75mm howitzer guns rattled and roared. The field gun batteries were firing all up and down the valley, adding to the impressive barrage. Minute by minute, the uproar increased, and since there seemed to be no answering fire, we stood and watched. The continuous roar seemed to shake the morning mists away, and nearby trees and ruins began to take definite shape out of the shadow beyond. It seemed like only seconds, though it must have been long minutes till daylight began flooding our valley. Back across our valley, far behind us, came the spiteful crack of the big naval guns, mounted somewhere along the base of a hill behind us. They were firing over our heads, shells arching toward their targets in the next valley.

As daylight came, I managed to find the place we were at on my map, Vacherauville. Sergeant Wester said the name was, and on my map, it showed up along the Meuse River, about seven miles north of Verdun. Behind us, across the river and canal, was a fairly wide valley, the Meuse valley. It contains the famous "Mort Homme", or Dead Man's Hill, as the skyline. It was from a railroad track, along the base of this hill, that the heavy naval rifles were firing. They were probably regular naval guns, but mounted on railroad trucks, like the one we had seen in Montreux Vieux.

Vacherauville was on the outside edge of a bend in the valley, where the river and canal came north, and then bent back to the west. South of us lay the town of Bras-sur-Meuse, and farther on, across the river is Charny-sur-Meuse. Vacherauville was but a name for ruins from all the shelling. In some places the ground was torn out level with the former basements and cellars. In other areas, ground was piled high on a level with what had formerly been the second floors of destroyed houses. Even the trees nearby were stripped, as done by a cyclone. Most trees were bare, with only broken limbs remaining, where any trees were left standing. Along the canal lay the remains of a bridge, which had once provided a crossing. The canal was lined in spots with barges, drawn up years before, and now filled with shell holes, most lying on the bottom with decks barely showing.

That was the place in which we found ourselves. We were interested just then in watching that shell barrage go over. The roar was awful, but we felt secure in knowing that it was not aimed at us. Daylight came on apace, and as it grew lighter, gun after gun cut off below us, as the guns were moved to new positions. Doubtless many of these guns had moved up in the night, and by day, they now saw how poor their concealment was, so were moved as soon as possible.

One lone howitzer battery, about a quarter of a mile north of us, kept up a regular firing program for most of the day. I soon learned to look out ahead of the burst of flame, as it fired, and see the shell, looking like a tiny pointed piece of lead, as it shot up into the sky on its long arc over to the Boche. I'd hate to be on the receiving end of such fire. The shell was traveling at incredible speed, but I got so I could catch sight of it every time, and follow it up till it disappeared in the distance.

We did not stand up above the ground all the while, for soon after daybreak, tiny whispers passed over our heads too often, causing us to drop into the trenches. Boche maxim bullets, chasing like steel birds, were a good motivation for us to drop back into our trenches. Soon afterward, from another high vantage point, partly covered, I saw evidence that the Boche guns were replying with at least a few shells.

Down north of us, a string of horses pulling a gun, broke out of a clump of trees, and raced south to a larger clump. It was a field battery changing position and moments later, after the first gun was clear, a second one came across with a rush. This time, a few spouts of black dirt arose just behind it, as it raced across the open space, revealing that some Boche battery had it located. Fortunately, it got thru safely. A third section of horses towing an artillery piece, raced out on the same path and started on a dead run. This time the black spots arose closer, just ahead of them, and then finally, alongside. Thru the cloud of dirt, I could see the horses swing around and stop. I saw no other movement from that battery. I continued to watch off and on all morning, and I do not know when the other horses were cut loose. I could not tell whether the driver was hit or not, for it was too far away for me to make out individual actions. I could see that only a few of the horses seemed to be standing, and presumed that dead horses were anchoring the gun there, held by their harnesses to the live ones. That afternoon, when I looked again, the horses were gone. Someone had moved them, or maybe they all had dropped out of view in the tall grass.

It was mid-morning that the captain established our infirmary and under a corrugated iron roof, on a mound hear his dugout. Two men were detailed there to be on duty at all hours with a regular shift schedule. They served as gas guard and first aid men for the P.C., Post of Command, and the headquarters in Vacherauville. There was already a small telephone P.C., in a tiny dugout, with Frenchmen at its switchboard. Now a larger P.C. with a switchboard operated mostly by our men, was put into operation across from our infirmary in a heavily sandbagged dugout.

To enter the captain's dugout, one had to go from our infirmary, around part of a still standing wall, down two flights of steps. The dugout was in what had originally been the basement of some house. Our infirmary, apparently on solid ground, was up where some second story had been. One week later on a loose board in the dirt, under our tin roof, interested me. I tried to pull it out, only to find that it was part of a floor. Thru a crack I saw a dark void below, which was apparently some lower level. We were right over a part of some house which had been nearly buried by shellfire. I would have liked to explore that lower floor but to do so was a job that was too big for me. The packed dirt was like stone, and I had no tools with which to work. The untold stories hidden below would remain so.

Our mess schedule in Vacherauville started at 7:30a.m. with a cold lunch, a hot meal at 10:30a.m., and another at 3:30p.m. That filled out the day. No fires were allowed during the night, so the mess shacks had to work during the daylight only.

The first day, when not on duty, Doughy and I hiked down to the crossroads, where the Vacherauville street ran into the main road. A French 75mm gun was set up, and we'd watch it operate. That gun crew, all

Frenchmen, operated that damn thing like a machine gun. They could fire it over thirty shots per minute, for a short stretch, laying off to rest when the gun became too hot to operate.

About noon, a thin stream of French Algerians, or Frog coons, as we called them, came by. Big, husky fellows, each with some type of wound, were walking to their hospital. They had formed the first wave that morning, when the barrage lifted, and the troops went over the top in the trenches. The 29th was not in the American sector, but just adjoining it, under command of French General Claudel, commanding the 17th Army Corps.

Vacherauville was extremely fortunate in its geographic location. The heights above it protected it from shell fire in all directions but one. An Austrian "whizz-bang" had a line on us from that direction. To reach us, they must have been firing at an angle across the front line about every hour or so. Mostly during the day, and more often at night, they would drop a shrapnel shell or two on us. Apparently, he was just "strafing" us and not aiming at a particular target.

Our kitchen was located in an iron roofed dugout, across a bend in the trenches from our dugout. Often, we skipped over across the top to get there, rather than follow the winding trenches. That was all right the first day or so, then one morning, just as we were getting ready to go over, when "Whizz-bang!" We hit the ground just as a shrapnel shell burst over us. From then on, we went around, following the trenches!

During the night, the shelling always was heavier. The cooks, and anyone not on duty, stayed in the iron-covered, trenches. It was quiet, so we of the Sanitary Detachment raided the kitchen and were rewarded with a nice can of syrup. We took some bread too, and enjoyed a nice treat. Better still, the can would last several days, so we made a couple of quick raids over the next few days. Even war at the front had a few advantages, or compelled us to exploit minor opportunities. Our blown-up town was a P.C., Post of Command, and also a sort of message center where planes would drop messages to be phoned back from the P.C. About noon, the first day a plane came over quite low, and circled above us. It appeared to locate partially cleared space designated as the delivery spot. It then descended, tossed out a tube, with a long ribbon attached. The first man reaching the tube took it to the P.C., and there was always a race to see who could get it first. Those initial planes were rotten shots, for their drops never seemed to even come close to that cleared space, often missing by 100 feet or more.

We soon got used to receiving messages, and would wave at the aviators as they went by, and pointed to the target spot, if they could not seem to locate it. Several times we stood out on top, waved and pointed. One afternoon some dumb bell flew over, and seemed unable to locate the drop area. Our boys were dancing around, pointing, waving caps and handkerchiefs. He finally dropped it but without the tube. Only a ribbon flittered down! He had fooled around too long, and just as he started off across the lines, a group of pursuit aircraft dropped down in his path. We later heard that his suspicious actions had caused some officer in the P.C. to phone back to the aviation H.Q., and found out no plane was due over us. It was really a Boche in a captured plane doing reconnaissance! The pursuit group brought him down unharmed and found a nice collection of hand-made maps and notes. If he'd gotten back, it would likely have resulted in hell dropping on Vacherauville if he had once gotten back to his lines. He had mapped our entire town, the P.C.'s and all, while fooling around above us. We were damn lucky that he didn't escape. We would have received ten Montraux Chateau shellings rolled into one!

We got one fine lesson a few days afterward, just at mess time. We had been getting our mess kits filled at the cookshack, which sat low down in fairly level space. As usual we then sat eating in any nearby spot that suited us. A can with hot water was always kept near the kitchen in which we could wash our dirty kits. Rather than go to our dugouts to eat, travel back to wash, we ate there. So, we had lined up on a low dirt shelf in a trench when a "Whizz-bang" cracked just above us. Boy, what a white-faced bunch that was! As the pieces of steel whistled around us, at the kitchen doorway, those pieces found several targets. It must have burst right above the kitchen for one cook, Bill O'Donnel, got a shrapnel piece down thru his right shoulder. It ripped clear down, thru his right arm, exiting by his elbow. Another cook got a scratch over one eye, and Sergeant Billington, who had been wearing his chin strap of his tin helmet under his nose, had his tin hat blown down right across the side of his head. In such a manner, it drew the strap up tight on his throat, and he nearly choked before someone cut him loose. I was well off to one side, and some of the other boys took care of the cooks, then hustled Bill off to hospital. After that we no longer stayed at the mess shack than we had to…for a short while.

A few days later we were getting careless again, bunching up for mess, when another shell dropped over at almost the same time of day. It came over just beyond the mess shack, on the edge of a trench, "Thud!", then rolled into the trench. It rolled to a stop alongside a 12-inch dud that had been lying there. Louie happened to be right in the mess shack door, when the sharp "Whizz!" sounded. He dropped his mess kit in a flash, and dove into the nearest trench. He had such a start that he couldn't stop, and went over the edge into the trench. That shell hit there then too, so both of them ended almost together. Louie saw the dirt and dust flying around, looked down and saw that big 12-inch shell, and fairly tore out of there! He came spinning like a cat, feet and hands on the ground, digging and clawing his way forward, till he spun in beside us, gasping in terror. He must have spun clear around five or six times, flying across that fifteen-foot gap! Though death had just passed us by, we roared with laughter at Louie's antics. He was pale white for hours, and never got in the trench with that big dud again! In fact, we all avoided that trench with the dud in it.

Vacherauville seemed to get but few shells in comparison with the nearby towns of Charny-sur-Meuse and Bras-sur-Meuse. They seemed to be visible from across the lines, while we were so close to the foot of the fills in front that we were partly hidden. Charny-sur-Meuse and Bras-sur-Meuse got our share and more, for the Germans could probably see the activity in those towns.

Vacherauville had at some time gotten its share, for one giant crater was fully twenty feet across, and nearly as deep. As if a joke, in the very bottom of that crater, someone had placed a tiny one-pound dud. At that, I even heard one dumbbell seriously ask if that small shell caused such a hole. I'll bet he learned better after a while.

After the first day, scores of prisoners came thru town. Out at the crossroads, several husky Frenchmen amused themselves by taking souvenirs off of them, to be sold later to those crazy souvenir hunting Americans. In fact, some of the boys stood there and offered francs to those Frogs, just for them to pick off the souvenirs they desired. And all this time, the prisoners were under American guards, those Yanks could have taken their souvenirs for nothing. At first the prisoners went right by, but later on, several groups of them were brought to our P.C. for questioning.

One afternoon, when Doughy and I were nearby, one large prisoner group was brought in, and an Intelligence Lieutenant took charge. We especially noticed one arrogant looking Boche, who was smoking a cigarette, pacing. When the Lieutenant said, "Attention!" in German, "Achtung!", he snapped into it like a steel spring, and that cigarette disappeared in a flash! Not even a trace of smoke remained. A few minutes later the Lieutenant gave "At rest", and the cigarette reappeared, having been somewhere in his hand. By accident, that stunt was repeated in a moment, and we could not even see the cigarette go. That Boche sure was disciplined, and we had no desires to be in any army in which he had soldiered! Part of the time that damn cigarette must have been burning his hand, but from habit, he held on to it. It didn't even smoke or at least he had a method of controlling it.

Days at Vacherauville flew by, as on wings, and several incidents happened that were not dated in my memo. There were fewer aerial battles here than there had been in Alsace, but those few were usually deadly. Up here they fought to a finish, and did it in a hurry. The first day I saw one observation plane making its loop back and forth across the lines. Located up on the hillside east of Bras-sur-Meuse, I could see an artillery signal unit laying out white signal spares on the ground, allowing the aerial observer to read them on each return trip. Somewhere, perhaps miles away, the guns they were controlling were spitting their leaden messages to an unseen target, controlled only by the directions relayed to them from the aircraft observer.

Everywhere I looked, I could see more evidence of the results of the signal units. They strung and maintained telephone lines. To keep even one line going was an effort, but here they kept hundreds operating. Shells might cut some wires, but others were immediately strung to replace them. If I had made friends with the boys in the Battalion, or at least with those stationed in the P.C., I might have heard many queer stories. Instead, I was a Pill Roller, and belonged to the Sanitary Detachment, so the friends I made in Battalion, were few. I had no method of interaction to them.

One afternoon a quiet, limping file of French Algerians passed thru Vacherauville, passing down our main street and across the foot bridge. They used that bridge, instead of going down to the camouflaged bridge at Charny-sur-Meuse. They were all husky chaps, but unlike the free-swinging boys I had seen on the first day up front, these poor chaps limped along. They walked with heads down, wincing at every step. Some wiser bird than I, told me what the trouble was in one short word. "Trench foot". I then noticed that they either had their shoes all cut up, to relief their swollen, aching feet, or had their shoes entirely off, relying only on rags over their stockings. Most were a slovenly looking bunch, just the type to leave wet shoes on day after day, without attempting to dry or clean their feet, unless ordered to. Could be though, that the conditions up front completely prevented any condition to get dry stockings and shoes. They sure were paying for the mistake or carelessness, for the trench foot disease was plenty of punishment. At least half these boys that had it, were likely to lose their feet entirely. "Trenchfoot" was easy to prevent, but mighty hard to cure, according to our medical bulletins.

On clear days, a few observation balloons were usually in view. On cloudy days they stayed down for then it was too easy for enemy plane to slip up on them, and attack with flaming tracer bullets. I'm told that Boche balloons were filled with hydrogen, which ignited pretty easily! We saw one fine example of the use of tracer bullets during the last days of September when two balloons were hanging in the air on our side. Some

Boche slipped up unawares popped the smoky tracers rounds into each balloon, and escaped before the anti-aircraft guns got fairly started. Someone must have been asleep to let him come up as easy as he did. He sure did some flying to get back, for every gun in range opened up on him! This continued over the hills, and we heard continued rolling drum fire from machine guns, as he hustled back to safety.

One afternoon I had just about decided that both armies must be shy on planes. I had seen but very few, when suddenly Stoehr call my attention several "V" formation wedges flying across the sky, far above us. In a few minutes, more came past, all heading directly over the lines. The sky seemed to turn black with the number of planes passing over. Wedge after wedge went flying by, all aimed in the same direction. Many were still passing east, when the first ones reappeared, heading back west. It was a beautiful sight, for it was a great demonstration of the air supremacy that the Allies had at that time. Yet, for all its beauty and impressiveness, death rode on high. For as Doughy and I lay there watching, the sun peeked forth through the clouds, and high above the other planes, I saw the sunlight glisten on a tiny, wasp-like pursuit plane as it banked downward.

Apparently, the lower planes were all bombing and observation planes. The pursuit squadrons were keeping guard above from foes. They were beautiful to behold, where we could barely make them out, till the sun caught them and they glinted reflections. That made us more vigilant, and suddenly, from far across the lines, near that invisible point where they seemed to be turning back, I saw the sunlight glisten on the slowly spinning wings of a diving plane. From the size, I knew it must be one of the bombers, going down, out-of-control. The spinning stopped and it headed straight for the ground. I saw two more crashing down, in their death dives and could only guess how many more dropped that I could not see. Later in the day, we heard that a large German supply depot had been discovered, and that the Allies had devoted every available aircraft to bomb it.

One peculiar thing about the front lines, was that there were few, if any, really big shells directed at the front-line trenches. Big shells were used to break down heavy barriers, blow up bridges, buildings and gun emplacements. Up on the front, the shrapnel shells and whizz bangs vied with the maxim and light guns for effectiveness. There must have been several six and eight-inch guns used on the front trenches, in our sector but they were the exception rather than the rule.

One night a doughboy came walking in with a slight wound, on his way back to a base hospital.

He dropped in with us for the night. Since the shells usually came over pretty heavy in the darkness, he was far safer with us, than all alone, going back in the daylight.

The Boche knew that most troop movements were made at night, and so all night long, they shelled our crossroads and prominent roads, on unpredictable intervals. Quite often, the small Sanitary Detachment that had been stationed near the crossroads had plenty of work to do, while we were loafing.

This lone doughboy, though, used as he was to the incessant shell fire up front, seemed to be nervous as the night wore on, and the larger shells passed over.

"Say, do they shell youse guys dis way every night?" he finally asked.

"Sure, about the same every night, only once in a while they get going a little heavier." Answered someone.

"My GOD," the doughboy groaned, "I thought we was catching hell up front, but a guy can sleep a little, even when them damn whizz bangs are popping, but these ash cans get on my nerves. Believed me, I'm pullin outa here as soon's it's daylight."

All the rest of the night, he sat bolt upright, in his corner, shaking and shivering whenever an especially large shell came over.

As the front lines moved forward, day-by-day, the shells near us at night grew larger and larger, by their sounds. They began to resemble the giants we had heard at Montreux Chateau. Even the boldest of us shivered when one of those screaming "ash cans" came groaning over, thru the night, and roared down near us. We were extremely lucky, for of the eleven dugouts in Vacherauville, not one was hit during our stay there.

The front lines seemed to be going back to the west, though, and not on the right. The town of Metz lay to the east about 50 miles, and the lines seemed to be holding stronger in that direction. From that direction, every night some "whizz-bang" saluted us at half hour intervals.

One night, Mase Kirwan and I were on duty, for the midnight to four a.m. shift, and a bunch of peculiar sounding shells had lit just north of us a bit earlier. They broke with a glass-like sounding "plop!" and me, being in charge of the shift, had trotted out to see if it was mustard gas. If it was, and near enough to any of our dugouts, I'd have to sound the gas alarm. I figured it as my duty to take responsibility to check, not order Mase to go. He'd likely think me afraid to go myself. I really did many heroic seeming stunts more from fear of being thought a coward, than from any real heroism. I wonder if others operated in a similar manner in dangerous situations. So, after trotting down way past the last dugout, and finding no smell of gas, I hurried back, anxious for the shift to be over.

Those many night hours were the loneliest, of any I'd had. With the shells coming over with their deadly monotonous sound, a peppy, happy feeling was impossible.

As a rule, our shifts were just so many more hours to while away. The only difference being that we must stay out on top, under our iron roof, in the little roofed corner of what had once been some building wall. Tonight, the gas shells had worried me a bit, but otherwise all was serene. We were relieved at 4a.m., and then we were glad to head for our dugout. More shells screaming over in the dark were not easy on our nerves, and four long dark hours on duty up in that little corner hadn't helped our feelings either.

We were just coming down the rise of ground, leading down to what we called the main road, when some dispatch rider came chugging up on his motorcycle, and hopped off about twenty feet up the road. Maybe he was looking for the P.C., in the sandbagged dugout across the road. Perhaps he was just dropping in to spend the rest of the night, after delivering messages elsewhere. Anyway, just as he stepped away from his cycle, he saw us coming down the incline, and yelled to us.

"Say, buddy," he yelled, "can you—"

"Whizz-bang!" and our regular half hour visitor roared in, too quick for even us to drop. It hit the corner of the dugout, just opposite us, and pieces of shell and shrapnel went hissing! "Wheeee-ing", away thru the darkness. The flash of the shell, a mere twenty feet in front of us, showed everything plain as day for a second. We could see the dispatch rider coming toward us, one hand upraised, as if to wave.

"Oh, oh, ohhhh" he groaned, staggering toward us, falling, as we ran at once to him.

"Hit you buddy?" I asked, snapping a belt pocket open to have bandages ready, as I came up to him.

He felt about in front of himself, and then sheepishly said, "No...I guess not, but a piece must have struck my gas mask, and knocked the wind out of me. Scared me pretty bad, at first, with that damned shell busting right in my face, but I'm all right now."

I bent close to him, and snapped the flashlight I carried on his gas mask for a brief instant. A deep scratch showed how close to him death had traveled just brief moments before.

"You're lucky," I said, "And I guess we all are! Better get out of here in a hurry, though, for that damn Austrian whizz-bang has been sending quite a few over tonight. And say, better get that gas mask out, and if it looks like it's damaged, throw it away and get a good one. So long!"

Mase had stopped with me, but when he found that the boy was

O.K., he hurried on, and I went right on his heels. During the day time, Vacherauville, was not a bad place, but at night it was getting too hot for any fun. The next day I saw an example of just how close a big gun could come to hitting a mark. Down past the crossroads, and out to the left, the road forked. One road leading up along the Meuse River toward Samogneux, and the other road up the other valley toward the front. My map showed some town called Louvemont there, but I could see no trace of it. Down the Samogneux road a truck train was coming, and suddenly a burst of dirt erupted high into the air along the road. Then another, and several more! The truck train stopped, and as I watched, a series of shell bursts tore up the roadside, for perhaps a quarter mile. It must have been some perfect working battery of four or six-inch guns, and boy, what a row of black spouts of dirt did they launch upward! They couldn't have missed the road by more than four or five feet, but they did seem to miss it, for every one of that string of shells tore up dirt. A direct hit on a truck or the road, would have had dust and fire with secondary gasoline explosions. It was a surreal, pretty sight at that, though it lasted not more than two minutes at most. All that remained was a dirt cloud hanging in the air for ten minutes afterward. When the trucks started again, they all seems to be moving, so I figured that there were no casualties. If there were any, the first aid station at the crossroads would have handled them.

18

SPECIAL MAIL

That day, not marked in my memo, about the 25th of October, I got two letters. It surprised me to get mail at the front, or as near as we were to it. One was from home, and I was glad to get news from home at any time. The other was an official looking envelope from the War Department, so I left that for later.

Mother's letter told me the regular news, among other things, that they had moved back to Freeport again, and both she and Heiny were working. Eve's mother had phoned her to say that she had read in the papers that I was overseas, and that she wanted to know what I was doing and where I was, if Mother knew. Later she sent a poem, copied by Eve from some paper that she liked. Mother enclosed the poem in her letter, and it was one of the finest war poems I ever saw.

<u>The War Bulletin</u> by Mary Carolyn Davies

Each word of it is printed on some face;
And even time can never quite erase
The news again. Not ink, but blood—so they,
The bulletins, are made – each word, each line,
Each letter in the lists – One sudden day
Last week, of which I do not like to think,
It was my neighbor's heart's blood make the ink.
Today—God keep me silent! It was mine.

Other letters there were also, for the Woolworth organization had printed my name in their lists, in a paper they had been getting out in the Chicago

District, and a Miss Schultz wrote me from Coal City, Illinois. Also, I received a nice letter from Miss Goddard, a teacher in Indianapolis, who had been my English teacher at the Freeport High School.

Finally, I turned to the official looking government envelope, bulging with bulky contents. What had I won or lost, or what was I in for?! To me, a government envelope seemed like bad news, and that was why I had left it till last. In a way, that envelope did contain bad news. As I opened it, out fell a bunch of telegrams, examination papers, and copy after copy of army communications, from one camp to another. It took me a full hour to go through them all, only to find that my examination papers for a flying Pilot's commission had been passed, with a grade of C-, or fair minus. I had been ordered to report to the Aviation Examination Board in Little Rock, Arkansas, and later at Payne Field, Atlanta, Georgia, for final examination and assignment as a flight cadet.

There were 68 sheets of paper in that envelope, all concerning my application. One of them also noted that some other chap in the 29th had passed his examinations. He was R.E. Fielding, but where he was, I didn't know. I couldn't even remember who he was, if ever I had even known him at Park Field, outside Memphis. Only 68 pieces of paper, making a fine example of Army "Red Tape"!

Here for months, I had forgotten that dream of ever becoming a pilot. If I had stayed in the states, by this time, I would probably have had my commission, and wearing those silver Army wings on my breast. Once again, I had passed up a chance for promotion in the army, though this time I had gotten to France so much the sooner. As an aviator, perhaps I would have gotten into action anyway, even if it would have been months after the 29th sailed for France. I had but few doubts about passing the final examination. If called, I had considered it as unlikely that my first examination papers would be passed. The final examination, as I understood it, was mostly physical, and if my marriage had not held me back during my first examination. I did not fear any physical exam for keeping me off the list during the second tests. Spilled milk is nothing to cry about, so I packed those papers inside my souvenir shells, and watched planes fly over for the rest of the day.

Some observation plane, apparently from an American unit, was dropping messages to us regularly during the last week. We kind of got to know him. I sure had to hand it to that flyer and his observer. The pilot would swing down in a banking turn, then go hedgehopping through the town, with his wheels only a few feet off the ground. On his final hop, he would barely clear the one-story pile of stones, located at one corner of the flat space where messages were dropped. Just as he roared past, the observer would toss out the message and ribbon. Seldom, if ever, did he miss that cleared space. Other planes often missed by two or three hundred feet. But he usually hit within fifteen or twenty feet of dead center. We followed his efforts since his plane was marked by three playing cards on the side. I often wished I hand known his name. He sure was one sweet flyer!

Kirwan and I usually landed on the same duty shift, and each evening we tried to find something to do. The officers had a mess established right behind our infirmary, in a little shack that once had been one room of some building. Kirwan and I, by exploring, found a way to get in, and we sampled some of the jam we found. After a rather heavy sampling for a few nights, the cook took to hiding all the best items on the menu. What with the shrapnel, no one cared to stand guard at either of the mess shacks, so while Stoehr supplied the syrup from the regular mess kitchen, we tried to find the candy from the Officers mess.

Yep, there were chocolates somewhere, for the headquarters down toward the crossroads, was issued chocolates at each meal. We knew that the Officers must be playing hog with our supply. Try as we might, we could not locate it. One of our favorite night seats got to be in the signal supply truck, which sat tight against a wall, just below us. We sure were surprised on the 29th to see the Officer's cook, who was packing up to leave, walk down to that truck, and open one of the covered seats. From under it, he removed two armloads of the blue chocolate candy boxes. Here he had hidden them, where we sat on them every night! Even if they had been locked, we would've busted the lock and taken the supply, but we didn't know they were there.

Shells came over each day. It seemed to us that they were a little larger each day. On the 27th of October, I rushed out of our dugout twice in the afternoon, each time because some large shell had landed near enough to make the weak roof shiver and groan. I certainly didn't want to be under it when a shell hit close to us. Those rocks stacked, forming our roof, were not the things to give one a pleasant dream!

October 28th, some shell lit just south of the old bridge, and only a few feet from the edge of the canal. It must have hit an extremely hard piece of ground, for it left but a small hole. While exploding, the point of the shell whirled a full quarter of a mile away, barely clearing a low stone wall. It slid across the small yard beyond, finally landing right under a makeshift table where four boys had just been playing cards. They had heard it coming, and were all lying on the ground, or it would have certainly cut off a few legs, and maybe more.

The morning of the 29th, Wester, in charge of half of the detachment, moved them back to Verdun. The next day, the 30th, under Sergeant Fitz moved the rest of us back in a truck. We had spent a few hours short of 23 days in Vacherauville, with only one seriously wounded man, thank God. The front, if Vacherauville could be called that, had been "easy pickings" for us. True, we had had plenty of shells come near us. The last two days, several big "ash cans", like used in Montreux Chateau, had been dropped on us. That single night in Alsace had been far worse for us than the whole three weeks in this sector.

Back in Verdun, we felt as if we were a hundred miles from the front. Chocolate bars were issued that evening, and that night we slept in the first-floor rooms of the Cathedral. Besides us was a nun's college, called St Marguerite's. Both were on the side of the hill, and while we were on the first floor, when we stepped to the windows, we found that we still were above the house tops of the city, in the valley below us.

It seems queer, for we had entered the Cathedral from the street on top of the hill. We went down two flights of stairs to our floor, and stepping outside, in a narrow garden there, we could see that the Cathedral was built into the hillside.

Shells kept coming over all day, and through most of the night. In the early morning, when I awoke, just before sunrise, and stepped to the window to view the city, I found the shell fire had ceased. Everything was quiet. Funny, too, there seemed to be smoke rising from the chimneys still below me. I thought at first, that other soldiers must be billeted in those houses below us, but then I realized that smoke seemed to be coming from every chimney.

I was but half awake, and I stopped looking long enough to wipe the sleep from my eyes. When I looked again, it appeared that even more smoke was rising, in little wispy streamers, like someone had started a small fire in each fireplace in the city. I rubbed my eyes more. Couldn't it be possible that the civilians were already moving back into this ruined city? Perhaps I was dreaming, and I pinched myself to see if it hurt. It sure did, and I was awake. As I looked forth again, about to awaken one of the other boys for his opinion, I suddenly saw a pin point of flame leap up toward the sky, far across the lower valley.

"PHOOWHAMMM!", and the whole city shook and trembled, at this giant explosion. Instantly I recognized it as a giant naval rifle, probably a sixteen-inch gun, firing from some railroad mounting far across the valley. I had noted the flash, as the gun fired, and suddenly the morning mists dropped away, and where the misty flash had been, I could see a familiar hump backed railroad car, just like the rifles we had seen back on the tracks below Mort Homme. That gun had fired over our heads, while we were in Vacherauville.

above Verdun

below Verdun Cathedral on hillside

above Verdun Cathedral on hillside
below Verdun Cathedral

That one explosion shook the morning mists entirely away, the chimney smoke vaporized too. In reality, what I had seen was all morning mist, not chimney smoke. Now in the full light of day, a minute later, I could see that each house was an empty, cold shell. Most of the roofs below had gaping holes in them. Moments ago, it was a misty dream city, filled with life. Now its cold realism was that of a skeleton city of death. That one naval rifle shot had shaken all dreams from my mind, and it also roused all the sleeping boys in the room behind me. Try as I might, when I attempted to explain how the mists had made it seem like a live city, I could not express my words to them that sounded convincing. That bare, empty city of wrecked homes was lying, plainly before us.

Before we left Verdun, we managed to secure souvenirs of "Le Grand Theatre", the famous old theatre of Verdun. Somewhere in the ruins, Knorr had found programs for the play, "La Passion a Nancy", given sometime before the war. The programs were not dated, but they did show various advertisements. They also showed the location of the seats in the theater and prices. From 12 francs for a "Premiere Centrale" seat, to 2 francs for a "Cinquiemes" seat. On the back of the program was a small map, showing the location of "Le Grand Theatre" or the "Theatre de la Passion", as it was variously called on the Rue Jeanne d'Arc. Knorr also found old seat ticket stubs, and we split up such spoils. My souvenir collection was growing, but I kept finding room for more.

The afternoon of October 31st, we rode in the back-breaking Chinese driven camions, back through Bar-Le-Duc, to a little town west of there, called Robert-Espagne. There, as usual, after three changes of billets, we landed a little room to ourselves on the main street, while the rest of the battalion billeted in barracks, east of town. And Lord, what a battalion it was. There had been few combat casualties, that I'd heard of, but the whole battalion was suffering from mustard gas.

Their intestines were lacerated and irritated from the gas, and they were suffering intensely from the attendant diarrhea. The pill rollers caught Hail Columbia, as usual, because our remedy for the gas cases was castor oil, and then Bismuth. More castor oil, and more bismuth. The soldiers could not seem to understand that the oil was the best thing that we had for soothing the irritated membrane in their digestive organs. We were the despised "Pill Rollers" once more! They cordially hated us because we could not cure them, and do it immediately; it would take time.

In Robert-Espagne, I saw Red Jenkins once again, but this time his smiling face was haggard, and his once red hair was streaked heavily with gray.

"S'matter, Red?" I asked him. "Did you get so scared your head tried to turn white on you?"

"It damn near did," he muttered, and then he related why.

"We were in a little wooded area, right near the bottom of a valley. The Lieutenant leading us, wanted to establish a new P.C. in the basement of an old house in the edge of the trees just across the open space in front of us. A barrage was shortly due to open up on the Germans dug in on the hill above. We crossed the field, and followed under cover of the house, he wanted me and my buddy to put our phone in the basement. So, when the barrage started, and the first wave went over, headed uphill, he'd coordinate cover fire. We trotted along and set up our phone in the cellar, as ordered. When we finished our hookup, and had a clear wire, we looked out to find our whole damn line had dropped back across to their old position. The woods near us had gotten too hot, and our boys had skipped back without letting us know. Our damned shells were making so much noise, we hadn't noticed their retreating. Before we could pull out, the Heinies opened up with a counter barrage, and we were in a hell of a place! The barrage lifted for a minute, and we started back, only to have barrages from both sides open up to beat hell! We dropped in a place between two trees, or rather, a tree and a stump, and there we sat all day, wearing our gas masks till I thought I'd choke to death! Those damn masks are worse than the gas itself, if you got to wear one for very long! Those barrages were falling, one about ten feet in front of us, and another just behind. Some shells trimmed branches from our tree, and yet we didn't get hit. I'd almost sooner get hit, than have to go through a whole day of hell like that again! Somehow, they slowed up about dark, and we managed to get back. I'll tell you we were all in, from squatting down, cramped like toads behind those trees all day. Hardly daring to move an eyelash, for fear of getting a piece of shell through us. I ain't sorry I left the aviation corps, back at Park Field, but I'm damned if I'd do it over again, given the chance."

That was Red's story, his drawn face, and gray streaked hair, spoke better than the meager words he used ever would. Red had been a telephone lineman back in New Hampshire, and a daredevil at Park Field. Now he was a gray-haired old man, though only twenty-one or twenty-two years old. He'd lived a lifetime in a day.

19

WAR'S END AND WAITING

November 4th, the French started to celebrate the false Armistice. The shelling and fighting reduced to almost nil. It was quiet. The 29th, with many of our boys suffering from mustard gas, was ordered back up to the front. On the 11th, just after we had rolled our packs, ready to move up to the front again, this time toward Metz, we received the tidings that the war was over! The Armistice was signed on November 11th, the war was over. Simple as that. One wonders, why had it taken the Germans so long to surrender? So much death and destruction. Way back in Freeport at the Five and Ten, maybe Mr. Heilmann had been correct? The only winners in war were investors, the Wall St. crowd. The dead and maimed soldiers on both sides, certainly were not.

A few weeks later, the letters from home told of the celebrations that the folks back home had staged. When the glad news arrived, how whistles had blown for hours, and days, and how everyone went wild. To us in Robert-Espagne, the news was too good to be true. The Sanitary Detachment had been but little affected by the mustard gas, but the battalion itself was still in awful shape. We hated to see our boys head back toward the Metz front in the shape they were in. So, the news was but a respite to us, and too good to be permanently true, but great for our boys.

When we finally did believe it, we went quietly about our work, viewing interestedly the little parade the French inhabitants staged, with their queer masquerade costumes, dragged forth after fours-years in hiding. They even had Chinese lanterns, hung on long twenty-foot poles, in the same manner that the Chinese used them in their parades. Our chief interest right then was in finding out when we would be going home.

186 CHAPTER 19

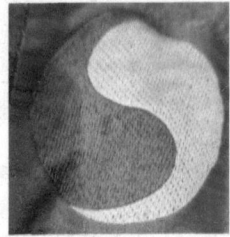

In Robert-Espagne, we were issued the little blue and gray circles that we sewed to our shoulders (left), denoting us as member of the 29th, the Blue and Gray Division. We had noticed the shoulder insignia on soldiers in other divisions, but we had never been issued them until now. I sewed mine on that day.

We got a new man, James, a minister's son, though he never acted the part. Also, Sergeant Fitz was shipped off to O.C.S., Officer's Candidate School. He was a good soldier, but not one very well liked, at least by the members of our detachment, because he was too self-satisfied. He seemed to think a Sergeant had priority rights on everything, much the same as an officer. Perhaps the authority over others being so similar, induced that attitude, but it is one I never appreciated either in a Sergeant, or an Officer.

The 29th Division, being in reserve at that time, was lucky, or unlucky, whichever way you may like it. Lucky enough to be quartered for the winter in France, instead of being one of the Divisions sent into Germany.

On the 17th of November, the 104th Battalion hiked 12 miles south to Montplonne, where we were billeted for once in an old schoolhouse, formerly a Catholic priest's or "Abbe's" room. James and Stoehr soon found an old chest that had easy locks, so we raided it for souvenirs. I got several cards, a cute little metal letter seal. It was a statue of Christ on a column pedestal casting as a wax seal, bearing the Abbe's seal. Also, I found an old envelope, with two films, which I later had developed. One picture showing a group of girls playing some game like "Ring around the Rosie", in

a courtyard, and the other showing boys playing leapfrog in front of the school. I saved that one especially, since it showed our billet. The big windows in the picture were just over the cabinet from which the film came. It was the only picture I secured in France, besides the postcards. The school picture had been taken years before the war.

On November 21st, we hiked on southeast, over the hills and down into a beautiful valley, the Valley of the Marne, I believe it's called. We marched across the valley to Tronville-en-Barreis, and then over to Nancois-Tronville, where we were loaded onto the familiar box cars once again.

The funny part of that trip was that we traveled right up through Bar-Le-Duc, the Revigny, and then turned south, through Robert-Espagne, where we had been billeted, on our way to Voisey, down in the southeastern part of the Haute Marne district. We arrived in Voisey about 4a.m. on the 22nd, and then had an 18-kilometer hike to Bourbonne-les-Bains, just north of there. I never could understand why we did not load on the train at Robert-Espagne in the first place, and ride right through to Bourbonne-les-Bains, as the track ran to there, but it is just one more example of army inefficiency. Maybe they wanted us busy, and slowed down. Perhaps the red tape wasn't long enough in this case to get us there, so we had to hike a bit.

We did hope to get into a town where American soldiers hadn't been too popular, or billeted very long. In the Bains, we found a squadron of the 3rd Cavalry, that had been there for 14 months. They had been one of the first U.S. outfits into France, only to wait and wait, and never got into action. It just was that cavalry was not used, not in this war. With the trenches, horses weren't much use up in the front lines unless one got too hungry. With the trenches, barb-wire, tanks, horses hauled guns and caissons, that was about it. So, the 3rd stayed in Bourbonne-les-Bains and learned the French language till they talked like natives.

Our billet in the Bains was on the top floor of No. 32, Rue de L'Hotel Dieu. It was a peach of a place, with cusheas and even a fireplace.

Thanksgiving went by, with a pretty nice feed for once. The only thing of interest after that was "When do we leave?" Rumor had it that we were to move on the 11th of December, and sail on the 16th, but rumor was wrong. We did not.

On the 2nd of December, we saw a peach of a show, "Snap it Up," given by the artist of the division. There were some boys in that show, dressed as girls, that could make one's heart go flip flop. They were the next best thing to the real article, and many a chap secretly believed he was being kidded, when told that they were boys. At the final curtain, they pulled off their wigs, and thus proved they were boys indeed.

Bourbonne-les-Bains was just one long agony of waiting for the orders to go home. My little memo filled up with minor events, crap games everywhere, pinochle and checker games with Louie. We held wine parties when we had money, and onion and bread sandwiches when we were broke. Onions and bread were the only extra things we could get out of the mess kitchen, so they had to make sandwiches.

I met Iverson down at the "Y" one night, and found that Red Smith, my old buddy from Park Field was in the ammunition train, and had been in a training camp in southern France, while were in Alsace, and went up north of Verdun.

After Fitz left, we had no Sergeant, and since Stoehr had the education to take the medical examination necessary. I was right in line, but the captain didn't want to pass out a sergeant rate to a "Cowboy from Illinois", as I was called because of my bow legs. He made Kirwan first Private First class, and then jumped him over all our heads, and gave him Sergeant's stripes. Both Stoehr, the rest of the boys, and myself. We all felt like we had been cheated. We would rather have gone home with no Sergeant at all, than have Kirwan appointed. He had been shoved over all our heads, but he seemed to realize it, and was not too bullying in his manner. He seemed to take it as a lucky gift, and kept to himself, as usual.

My spare time I occupied myself at the infirmary, copying down our commendation from General Claudel, and other souvenir papers, for the rest of the boys. I was the only one who could use a typewriter with any speed at all. I had to make copies of everything, to give each of the Sanitary bunch a souvenir copy. Boy, going through the office copies of all orders,

298

31st October, 1918

From: General Claudel, Commanding the 17th Army Corps.
To: General Charles G. Morton, commanding the 29th I.D.U.S.
Subject: Commendation.

My dear General:

At the time when the 29th I.D. U.S. leaves the sector of the 17th A.C., I wish to let you know how much I was honored to have it temporarily under my command, and I wish to express to you all the satisfaction it gave me.

On October 8th, one of its brigades stormed with splendid dash the difficult height of Marlbrouch and the powerful defenses of the Bois De Consenvoye.

On the 10th, the other brigade advanced beyond the heights of Ormont to capture the Bois de La Reims.

Since then, the whole division was employed, with splendid perseverance and unfailing energy, to carry off the fortified Clairiere de Molleville, and the Grand Montagne and Bois D'Etrayes areas.

The combat and weather conditions were hard most of the time. The 29th I.D.U.S. dauntlessly overcame them, took a total of about 2,000 prisoners, guns, machine guns and important material.

Will you kindly express to your splendid troops, to your General Staff, to your services, all the thanks of the General commanding the 17th A.C. and of their French Comrades for their effective and zealous cooperation.

I am sure that under your command the 29th I.D.U.S. will soon win new laurels.

Please believe, my dear General, in the expression of my most grateful and devoted sentiments.

(signed)   H. Claudel

Redacted items: 29th, Verdun, and Morton.

And also, Major General Morton's commendation.

General Orders,
No. 59.

HEADQUARTERS ~~XX~~ DIVISION,
American E.F.,
1 Nov. 18.

Now that its part in the action north of ~~[redacted]~~ is finished, the Division Commander wishes to take occasion to express his deep appreciation of the skill, endurance and courage shown by the officers and men of the division, including both staff and line, in a most difficult and prolonged fight.

Everything was opposed to our success. We had a most determined enemy in our front and one skilled by four years of warfare, whereas this was the first real fight of our division. On most days the weather was bad and the ground difficult, added to the fact that the fighting was largely in woods. On account of the woods, ravines and dampness, gassing of our troops was easily accomplished and full advantage of this fact was taken by the enemy to whom the use of gas was an old story.

Without exception the organizations of the division and their commanders responded heroically to every call upon them and at the end of the fight we had not only gained our objectives, but we held them and turned them over to our successors. We advanced some eight kilometers through the enemy's trenches, and captured over 2,100 prisoners, 7 cannon, about 200 machine guns and a large quantity of miscellaneous military property. We had the pleasure of seeing two hostile divisions withdrawn from our front, one of which was composed of some of the best troops of the German Army. On many occasions captured prisoners stated that our attack was so rapid and our fire so effective that they were overwhelmed and had nothing to do but to retire or surrender.

In this brief summing up the results of its first fight the Division Commander feels that every officer and man participating, whether in planning or in executing, should feel a just pride in what has been accomplished. This is but repeating the praise that has been bestowed upon the division by both American and French superior commanders.

By command of Major General ~~[redacted]~~

S. A. Cloman,
Colonel of Infantry,
Chief of Staff.

Official:

Harry Coope,
Adjutant General.
Adjutant.

Copy of commendation from Morton

31st October, 1918

From: General Claudel, Commanding the 17th Army Corps.
To: General Charles G. Morton, commanding the 29th I.D.U.S.
Subject: Commendation.

My dear General:

At the time when the 29th I.D. U.S. leaves the sector of the 17th A.C., I wish to let you know how much I was honored to have it temporarily under my command, and I wish to express to you all the satisfaction it gave me.

On October 8th, one of its brigades stormed with splendid dash the difficult height of Marlbrough and the powerful defenses of the Bois De Consenvoye.

On the 10th, the other brigade advanced beyond the heights of Ormont to capture the Bois de La Reine.

Since then, the whole division was employed, with splendid perseverance and unfailing energy, to carry off the fortified Clairiere de Molleville, and the Grand Montagne and Bois D'Etrayes areas.

The combat and weather conditions were hard most of the time. The 29th I.D.U.S. dauntlessly overcame them, took a total of about 2,000 prisoners, guns, machine guns and important material.

Will you kindly express to your splendid troops, to your General Staff, to your services, all the thanks of the General commanding the 17th A.C. and of their French Comrades for their effective and zealous cooperation.

I am sure that under your command the 29th I.D.U.S. will soon win new laurels.

Please believe, my dear General, in the expression of my most grateful and devoted sentiments.

(signed)   H. Claudel

Copy of commendation from Morton

I got a lot of nice document copies as souvenirs myself. One of them was the commendation from General Claudel.

Then too, among the other papers from home, the November copy of the Chicago District Woolworth paper had a poem, that many of the boy's wanted copies of, as a souvenir of me.

"Over There" *by Milton Weil*

There are lots of "Woolworth Sons"
 Over There.
They have gone to fight the Huns
 Over There.
They have steamed away to France,
Mighty proud to have a chance
For to help the "Yanks" advance
 Over There.

There is a duty to be done
 Over There.
There are battles to be won
 Over There.
When the fight starts, Woolworth men
Will be on the job, and then
May each one kill "FIVE OR TEN"
 Over There.

May the Lord protect the right
 Over There.
May the "Yanks" win every fight
 "Over There.
When they've killed Germans galore,
And the final fight is o'er,
Each can start a Ten Cent Store
 Over There.

For that time, my memo book showed mostly the results of crap games, for a long stretch, such as on December 14. Kelly won 104 francs from the Truck Co., and Louie who was with him, lost 105 francs. That was bad business. Usually we won, that is, the money usually was coming our way. Even Lane won, but his money went right home. The boys got to calling him "Two Francs" because after winning fifty dollars in francs, he'd send 48 dollars of it home, and lived the rest of the month on the remaining

2 dollars in francs. For cigars, Lane would stand near the cigar counter at the "Y", watch some soldier purchase cigars. He'd then follow him into the street, run around the block, so as to pass that soldier oppositely. Then when the cigar purchaser was passing, Lane would gravely fumble in his pockets, hesitate, then say, "Say buddy, haven't got a match on you, have you?" Meanwhile fumbling around in his pockets, as if he had a cigar. Then, as the match was or was not produced, he would exclaim, "By God, I must have lost my cigar, and it was the last one I had. Ain't that hell! Broke, no money till payday, and I lose my last cigar." When the genial soldier would fork one over, Lane would smile a "Thanks", and pass on, cigar in hand! He even pulled one on the detachment one afternoon. Six of us, up in our billet on the Rue d'Hotel Diee, were playing poker for I.O.U.s for payday was but a few days way, and we were broke.

That is, all of us, but Louie. Lane sat opposite Louie, and Louie had two cigars in one breast pocket. Knorr, knowing Louie was not quite broke, asked, "Say, Louie, lend me a couple francs, till payday, will ya?"

"Well, let's see," said Louie, drawing forth the few francs in his pocket. "I got eight francs, but the captain's wash will come to about three, or maybe four francs, an I gotta get it. He'll pay me back after a while. Only I gotta save that much out, and two more francs for my wash. Sure, I can let ya have two francs, all right." And he passed two over to Knorr.

"Say, Louie," said Lane, a moment later, "can you let me have two francs till payday too?"

"Nope", answered Louie. "I lent my last two to Knorr. I need the rest."

"But dammit, I'll pay you back." said Lane "You know I'd never cheat you out of two francs. You had a lot more left in your pocket, and I should think you'd be willing to lend a friend like me some, if you do lend to others, like Knorr."

"Yeah," said Louie, "but them other francs I gotta have for the captain's laundry. He'll raise hell if it ain't back in a coupla days, and I need that money for it. If he pays me right back, then I can let you have two francs."

"But you lent Knorr two francs. Seems to me I've always TRIED to be a good friend to all you boys, haven't I?" and Lane looked around beseechingly at us. "You know, Louie, I'd do most anything I could to help you out, and I haven't got a damn franc to buy even smokes with. I don't call that a fair way to treat your friends, do you boys? Here Louis lends Knorr money, and won't me. I'm sure sorry you don't like me Louie, but I always have tried to treat you fair."

Lane was a damn liar, and knew it, but knew also that Louis wouldn't tell him so right out.

"You might, at least, let me have one of those cigars you have there," Lane went on, pointing to the two cigars in Louie's pocket.

"All right," said Louie, passing one over, and glad to settle such an absurd argument that easily.

"Thanks!" said Lane, lighting his cigar.

Then, leaning back in his chair, he puffed out his chest, and blew smoke rings for a moment. "Damn good cigar, Louis," Lane finally said, "And it cost me only a minute's conversation."

"Say boys," he finally explained, after blowing more smoke rings, "you sure gotta hand it to Old Man Lane. You boys oughta give me a vote of thanks, for the things about human nature that I keep teaching you. Sure, I know you call me a damn grafter, and maybe I am, but when it comes to knowing human nature, you sure gotta hand it to me. Now look here, (as he wafted more smoke rings) this cigar cost me a one minute of conversation. If I had asked right out for it, Louie would have refused me, but by kidding him into thinking I really wanted him to lend me money, he was glad to give me the cigar instead of the francs. I knew I wouldn't get two francs from him.

YOU GOTTA HAND IT TO OLD MAN LANE, If Louie remembers this, it may save him from a grafter someday."

Louie was peeved, and could have bit chunks out of Lane right then, had we not been in the army.

To tell you the truth, Lane did teach us plenty at that.

On December 17th, we received three new men in the detachment. Hamilton Murdock, a tall, dark haired, quiet chap. Fred Missel, also tall, tanned, but stooped over from working as a machinist on a lathe before the army. And last, Charles Freed, a short, heavy-set chap with fair hair and a short moustache. To us, the funny thing was that they had been on board ship in New York harbor, when the Armistice was signed. Yet they had been shipped over. Nice trip, eh what?

On December 18th, Doughy and James, the minister's son and new soldier, were up in their billet on the hill. They found that by going up on a shed roof near their room, they could access a storeroom. There they found a French postal uniform, and several caps. Doughy brought me one of the caps, and wore the postal uniform down after dark to our billet. Part of the spoils were two French watches, both of which were non-functioning.

On the 19th, an old man in their building found that they had been in the storeroom, and there was a great how-de-do. Stoehr had replaced the postal uniform, and came rushing down to us to make me burn the cap, which I did. On the way back, he threw the two old watches into the creek, thinking they were the last pieces of evidence that we held in our possession. They were, and any searchers would have found nothing to connect us with the rifling of the storeroom, but the two watches were expensive, for they cost Stoehr's bunch two hundred francs. They were the only things that the old man missed, and the tracks inside the window, plus the marks made in prying it open, were too easily followed and traced to someone in the billet. Poor Doughy and his bunch were crestfallen, but they paid like gentlemen. The hard part of it was the loss of that nice souvenir uniform and the caps we disposed of.

Tuesday, December 24th, we went out for a Christmas tree, and incidentally got about $75 worth of mistletoe, at New York prices. Some of the boys had a fit, figuring what that mistletoe, so abundant here, would bring if sold in New York. It did our pockets no good here.

Then, Christmas day, Wednesday, the old man living below us, was found dead. It appeared natural, so we were quiet for a while.

Our Christmas dinner, 1918, included two kegs of beer, mashed potatoes with gravy, stewed corn, baked rice pudding with syrup, cake with blackberry jam, and choice of roast turkey or goose! Also, everyone was given a pack of Piedmont cigarettes, 1 pound of chocolate candy, white grapes, and bread. All served as a 2 o'clock dinner. So, who wanted supper? All this was served in a stable. It was cleaned out, and we all laughed because it was still smelling like horses—! That place was in comparison with the nice clean hospital that I'd been in a year ago at Park Field. I was lighter too. Here my stripped-down weight was 190 lbs. I'd gained more than 60 lbs. in a year. I might cuss the army cooks, but they sure got results.

December 27th, I was released from all drill duty, for my only pair of shoes had holes in the soles almost big enough to put my feet through! The trick I used in Montsaugoen of keeping my barrack shoes in place of one pair of trench shoes, nearly got me in "Dutch". The barrack shoes could not stand heavy marching, and soon gave out, and now my other trench shoes went ditto, just at a time when the supply department had only up to size 6½ in stock. Thus, for some time, I did no drilling. I did my turn on duty in the infirmary, wearing my shoes down there, and changing to carpet slippers that I had placed in my barrack bag, while in Montsaugoen, and which now came in handy. At mess time, I did the same thing, always changing to dry stockings, as soon as I was back in the billet.

January 10th, "Vendredi" or Friday, I was on a delousing detail, examining underwear belonging to men in the battalion, while they were taking forced baths. That night I found "cooties" in my own underwear, they spread too easily! I promptly got a pail, soaked all my underwear in a boiling mixture of every disinfectant I could find in the infirmary. I then bathed in an antiseptic creosote solution. I got results, for that was the only time I had "cooties". That bunch I had were prizes at that, each nearly a quarter inch long, but they looked larger, like an inch.

Monday, or "Lundi" was January 13th. Knorr and Louie had a scrap, if such might be called. It really consisted of a comedy, with big Knorr trying to hit Louie. Louie, that little flash of lightning, was using his hands to hold each of Knorr's sleeves. Bill could not hit him. Louie was almost double-jointed, a natural acrobat, and quick as a flash, though he looked awkward as Sam Hill. It was over nothing, so when they saw how useless it was, Knorr stopped while the bunch just laughed at their antics.

Time was passing. Friday, February 14th, was the next important date in my memo. Knorr and I left for a ten day leave in the Isere District. The first night, I slept in a bed, once more. Between sheet for the first time in about a year. We stopped in Lyon about 10p.m. and I was foolish enough to pay five francs for a bed for a night. Early in the morning, we left for Grenoble, arriving about 11a.m. and found we were billeted in a nice place, the Hotel Bordeaux, in room 65. Knorr was my buddy, and we sure appreciated that hotel with its dining room, wine room and all!

Grenoble was in a new leave area, and the Americans had been using it for only two weeks when we arrived. Thus, to civilians, we were still new. M.P.s and French police were on constant duty, to see that our "Beaucoup Francs" did not corrupt nice working girls. A permit was even necessary to appear on the streets with a French girl. At that, I couldn't blame the French for their restrictions. Here, we Americans thought nothing of spending twenty francs in one day. I, with a bare 100 francs for the 10-day trip, thought I was nearly broke. To these working girls, used to receiving but six or eight francs a week, the opportunity to earn a fortune, to them, in a few nights was too good to be true.

Really, it was the same thing that would have happened in any war torn country. It even happened near our own war camps, right in the states. After four years of war in France, with men as scarce as they were, half of the girls of marriageable age could not expect husbands, and morals ran correspondingly low. A girl, in such circumstances, will use all her feminine weapons to make herself popular, or desired. They will do things at such times that she would not dream of otherwise. Any man, let alone the "wealthy" Americans, might be a possible husband, and so those bans suffered. The M.P.s might guard the main streets, but boy, what a reception we got when we slipped away on side streets!

Many of these same boys, now enjoying themselves, would later go back home and tell weird tales of these "wild" French girls. They did not dream that their sweeties back home, might have done similar "wild" stunts in their old home towns.

A chap from the Signal Battalion named Wolfron, Knorr, and myself made a date for a trip to Sassenage, with three nice French girls. We met them on the street car going out. The Conductor tried to overcharge me a franc, but my companion, a dressmaker named Suzanne, talked right up, and he refunded the money in a hurry. Those three girls were of nice families, and not gold digging. In any circumstances they would have done the same, and I wondered how many American girls, in a similar situation, would have been so careful of an escort's expenses. I could have easily afforded the loss of that franc, but it was the idea of my companion fighting to save my money that appealed to me. Her language to that Conductor was nothing if not forceful, as I could tell from her tone of voice, though I could not understand half of what she said.

Getting off at Sassenage, I made a fool of myself. With Suzanne directing us, we got off on the off side of the car, and as it rolled on, we walked up the road. I was in the lead, setting a good example by throwing one arm about Suzanne's shoulders. The other two boys did likewise, and in a moment, we heard a roar of laughter behind us. There, on the platform, where we would have seen them, had we stepped off the correct side of the car, was a sightseeing bunch of soldiers. That group was joined by some American Nurses. Not sure why, but they were roaring with laughter, but as no M.P.s were in the group, we trotted serenely along on our sightseeing trip.

Grenoble, situated in the French Alps, is in a beautiful spot, and Sassenage, nearby, is one of the points of interest to sightseers. There, with snow-capped mountains rimming the green valley. There scattered about were ancient Chateaus peeking forth from vantage points on the mountainside. There were interesting caves and cascading falls along a mountain stream to visit. We did trips to various other interesting scenes, and with a dinner in a small inn to top it off, we spent a truly enjoyable day.

A few days later, we also made a short trip south to visit two bridges at Claix. There, a high, centuries old Roman bridge, was now used by sightseeing pedestrians only. It overshadows the modern bridge below and beside it. Both the old and new bridges are built using the same arch principle, and the new one shows but little better workmanship than its ancient neighbor.

CHAPTER 19

Claix by Grenoble—left Roman bridge & the newer bridge

Too much cake spoils the party, and I was sick for three days on my leave. Perhaps I visited the wine room too much. I never did drink enough to get intoxicated, but maybe it was I could never seem to get enough wine to become intoxicated. Either way you say it, the results were the same.

One evening, Knorr and I blew into the hotel about nine p.m., and peeked into the wine room just for a look. We then decided that one drink would go fine. It did. At a nearby table sat Wolfron, and "Shorty". I had at some time done Shorty a favor, back in Bourbonne-les-Bains, and now he happened to remember it.

"Come on over, Pill Roller," he invited, "both of you!" and he waved us into seats facing him.

"Me and my buddy been trying to drink up a hundred francs tonight, but we're going too slowly. You guys gotta help." With that explanation, he forked out the roll of bills from one pocket, and sorted them out before himself, and called for service. He got it.

Knorr and I were nearly broke, and Shorty was insistent. He had plenty of cash, and it was his treat. One round of drinks came after another. I favored brandy.

Ten o'clock and then eleven, rolled past, and shortly after eleven, a peculiar looking couple came in and sat down. Wolfron and Shorty were facing us, and behind them, at another table, sat this couple. A tall, graceful blonde in a trim, tailored suit, and her companion, a beefy looking young Frenchman, or Italian possibly, dressed in a sloppy business suit. He had apparently been visiting too many bars that night, but the fair blonde was wide awake. Too much so, for his good. She must have been a pianist, for between slow sips at her drink, she would run her marble white fingers over the stone topped table, like it was a piano.

"Tat-tat-tat-tit-ta-ta-tit," they would sound. Like little hammers pounding a melody on the stone. Her companion would try it, but where her last action was a sort of bump, with her wrist and elbow, he would crack his elbow against the edge of the table. Instead of getting it on top, the blow would rock the heavy table. Not only that, but it evidently hurt him, and we all watched and laughed at his comical, drunken expression. He tenderly rubbed that elbow, and then, like a fool, he tried it again.

The blonde enjoyed making a fool of him for our benefit, and Shorty, sitting nearest to her, turned clear away from our table to watch. Not only did he watch but he saw something. The blonde, snappily dressed in her short skirt, crossed her knees, below the table and the swing of her silken clad limb was only too evident to our unified gaze. We could see quite a bit. Shorty enjoyed the display, blinking his eyes at seeing so much hosiery all at once. The blonde smiled on, in the same manner. Shorty, not to be out done in nerve by even her, brushed his head, then scratched his dome reflectively. Next, he picked up his cap, fitted it on his head, re-arranged it, and "accidentally" knocked it off. When he stooped to pick it up, he kicked it under their table. His eyes must have hurt him when he was so close to that hosiery but he was a gentleman. He didn't pinch it to see if it was real. I think I would have, maybe I was not a gentleman.

The blonde smiled even more, if that were possible, and swung her silken hose about even more. She repeated her "Rat-tat-tat" trick for our benefit, and her escort hurt himself again, as usual. Shorty, to keep things moving, tried his hat on again. This time he was nearsighted, and couldn't seem to locate—the cap. Anyway, it was the cap he was supposed to be looking for, and it sure took him a long time to find it, right under his hand, as he rested it there under the table, on his hands and knees.

Everyone in the room was laughing by now, except the escort. He couldn't seem to see any humor, and couldn't even see what Shorty was doing. He gave his blonde a befuddled look, and seemed satisfied with her angelic smile, for he took another taste of his drink, then tried to break his elbow again! Shorty was blinking his eyes, after that second trip on the floor, and was just preparing for a third exploit, when the blonde left. She took her sponge of a boyfriend with her. It was too bad, and had spoiled a good show!

Before the café, or wine room closed, we had to carry Shorty up to his room. One of the others was not much worse, or better, but as usual, I felt fine…Very fine.

Maybe that was what made me sick for three days. I made up for lost time when I got well. On February 24th, I packed Grenoble in my memo book with the other dreams of bygone days for that night we landed back in Bourbonne-les-Bains. Our leave days were over, and we still waited to go home.

The first time that I knew the 29th Division had a football team was when we went over to Bar-sur-Aube to see them play on March 3rd. I was slightly peeved, for only a few days before Lane had brought in a stray copy of the New York Police Gazette, showing a picture of the Great Lakes Naval Training Station football team. It was supposed to be a picture of the best, or first team, chosen from ninety some football teams at the station. And, as tackle, it showed Chet Langenstein, of Freeport, Illinois. Chet, had been one of the all-state men on our high school team. That made me want to play football, but I wanted too late I suppose.

On March 21st, I went back to Bar-Sur-Aube, to see more football games, and incidentally, to catch a glimpse of the King and Queen of Belgium, who were the guests of honor.

Monday, March 24th, was another memory day for me. That day, after much serious cleaning up of our billets, we marched out 8 kilometers to be inspected by General Pershing. After standing for half a day anticipating him, he finally marched quickly past us, at the head of his staff of Officers. It was called an inspection, but he went by almost too quickly to even see us.

The inspection was held in a small valley, but the smaller detachments, not having room with the infantry below, lined up along the roads on the hillsides. We were near one end of the valley, and far down below us, I could barely see the troops as they swung about when passing in review. For some reason, we did not march. The sun peeked forth just as the review started, and as I watched a long column of men below me swing about, I suddenly saw the glisten of sunlight, reflected from hundreds, even thousands of tiny grass-like blades of steel, their bayonets. Those waving bayonets, polished like mirrors, swinging in rhythm below us, sent a shiver of dread down my spine. True, the war was over, and I never expected to face a bayonet charge, but just to see the sun light reflected so, from over twenty thousand shining steel blades was chilling. At last, I knew what a "field of steel" really was, and why a bayonet charge is so deadly. Looks alone count for plenty.

Thursday, April 10th, and we finally got our orders to leave Bourbon-les-Bains. Sorry to leave? Not much. According to my memory, during the winter season we had been there, it had rained or snowed, every day but five, in almost five months. The town was probably a peach of a place in summer time, but it was no gift in winter.

Going home, though, wasn't as easy as it looked, for we headed for the Le Mans area first, in the Sarthe District. After leaving Bourbonne-les-Bains on the 14th, we arrived in Beaumont on the 16th, and hiked over to the town of Saint-Mars-sous-Ballon.

On the 17th of April, we got acquainted with the town, and saw the remains of a castle that had been built in 894. Nearly 1100 years old! Some house, but only one corner was standing. Apparently, it had contained buildings, on the four inside corners. With their connecting walls, enclosed a spacious courtyard. It was situated high on its hilltop, overlooking miles of country below. I appreciated how old the "old country" was, after that.

By now I could make myself understood in French, fairly well. Each evening I took long walks through the country. On one walk, I met a little boy, five or six-years, who spoke English like a native. US soldiers had been in that area about a year before, and he had learned it from them. Through him I met his sister, dad and mother. I got into visiting nightly sometimes taking Wolfron along.

Bouillon cubes were given away at the "Y" stand in Ballon. They were competing with the Red Cross stand that gave away candy and sugar cubes. Armed with a pocket full of these sweets, I was always welcome at the local farmhouses. One evening at the little boy's home, Wolfron and I shared a bouillon cube drink, placed in water, very salty, with his dad, Messr. Letterte. He thought he had been poisoned, and drank a full quart of "cider" or white wine! We didn't call on him after that!

A couple of miles further out, we met the Mairie (mayor) of St. Mars, and his family. After teaching him how to shoot craps and treating his family to sugar cubes nightly, they would open up with a bottle of cognac, and black "Coffee". They fooled me the first time. They had a late supper, as usual, and Wolfron and I refused to sit with them, pleading we'd had a full mess call. After supper, when coffee was served, we showed our amicability by sitting in. The Madame filled our tiny cups with the bitter black coffee. I figured I could stand that small amount, in the name of hospitality. Before the cup was half gone Madame reached over and refilled it. This time from a bottle looking like a water carafe, but boy, that stuff surely wasn't water. Not much! Pure cognac, really good. That's what! For

Sanitary Detachment of 104th Field Signal Battalion, 29th Division at Saint-Mars-sous-Ballon

Top row: Lane, Missel, Murdock, Knorr, Gray, Price, and Long. **Bottom row:** James, Schneider, Sergeant Kirwan, Stoehr, and Kelly (Reigle and Freed were absent, on leave)

a solid hour she kept that cup from going empty, and after that I came to like French coffee when served that way!

On our last trip on the 28th of April, the Mairie stayed up till 2a.m., and celebrated with a special bottle of aged "Ceeder", as he called it. It was SOME cider, too! It took all three of us to open it, the cork that came out of its inch wide mouth swelled up to over three inches, once we got it out. My head resembled that cork! On the way home, that night, it was the only time I ever saw two moons! Honest to goodness, there were two all the way home!

With my brassard on, if an M.P. caught me I could always say I was visiting a sick man. It never happened though. We "Pill Rollers" took life easy, usually, and certainly here in Saint-Mars-sous-Ballon. My special souvenir at Saint Mars was a picture of the Sanitary Detachment as it was then.

20

BACK TO THE USA

Finally, on April 29th, we left Saint Mars, going by truck to Beaumont, and that night, we had our last box car ride in France. Those cars we won there were American made, but Lord how we were packed in. It was a tortured place, all night long, and the worst night I ever put in, by far. Well, maybe not as bad as the wet train ride I'd had with poor Woods.

The Iowan—converted sugar freighter

CHAPTER 19

At 8 a.m. we arrived in Saint Nazaire, and a few days later, on May 8th, we were loaded on a converted sugar freighter, the Iowan, and set sail for home.

The trip back wasn't much like the brisk rush over. The Great Northern, the ship that had brought us to France, on one trip after the war, broke the Atlantic crossing record. We could proudly say that we came over on the fastest passenger ship afloat. The Iowan was the opposite, no record breaker at all!

Most of my memos of the trip back are of crap games. I had 3 dollars, the evening we were paid off at Saint Nazaire, after I had paid my I.O.U.s. On board ship, shooting craps on steel decks, I remembered the stunt the coon at Park Field had used. I spent about five dollars in those. Had I been a better crapshooter, I would have won hundreds, in some of the big crap games aboard. I never got more than a start in those games. The boys playing them were too good for me!

On the 20th of May we slowly steamed up the Hudson River again, and this time I was out on deck. The 104th Field Signal Battalion claimed Jersey City as it home city. That day I was surprised to see two pleasure tugs, the Squantum, with the war camp committee, and some sightseeing tug, with the mayor's welcoming committee sign posted. They came swishing down past giant liners going in with their loads of boys coming home. Finally, one each came up alongside of our little freighter. The big transports didn't matter, when, their boys, the Jersey City boys were coming home.

The Squantum

Jersey City Mayor's Welcome boat

Apples, oranges, candy and packs of cigarettes were ammunition for them to bombard us with, showing their good will. One boy got hit in the eye, from one good missile. Of all the welcome, the one thing that pleased me most, was to see, high on the top deck of the mayor's committee boat, a lone figure in khaki. Waving one arm in welcome, one arm still hung limp, was Bill O'Donnel, the cook who had been wounded by the whizz-bang shell in Vacherauville. He had been our lone serious casualty there, besides the mustard gas victims. Here he was, wounded, but still living.

I appreciated how lucky we were in Vacherauville, when I saw him, and remember what a 79th Division boy had told me in Grenoble that during the 11 days they occupied Vacherauville, the Boche scored hits on seven of the eleven dugouts there. In our 23 days there, not one dugout was hit.

Suddenly during the quiet din, I heard a familiar "PWHAAP!" high in the air, and saw an anti-aircraft shell burst high above us. Some gun on the top of the Colgate building, was saluting us. It was meant well, but sent a shiver down my spine. Here, months since I had heard that ever familiar "PHWAAP" almost daily, I heard it again. It gave me cold chills for hours. Months before it was part of the daily noise. Perhaps one would have accompanied the parting of my earthly ties. Now, forgotten almost, it was a ghostly reminder of day gone by.

CHAPTER 19

For a little while, the boys on board tried to recognize friends on the two tugs, and several found members of their families. Finally, everything quieted down, till we slowly warped into our dock. There, just as we were being snubbed in, a bond trotted out on the space at the end of the dock. They began playing a welcome home piece, and behind them several women, in uniforms, one carrying a white flag with the Red Cross.

That sort of welcome was too stereotyped, too blatant, but I did not expect the boys on board to welcome it the way they did.

"YEEAAAAAAH!" "YOU DAMN SLACKERS!"

"BLOW YOUR DAMN HORNS, YYUH X—X—X, YUH MAMA'S BOYS, YUH XXX—X— FIGHT DODGERS!"

"DAMN YOUR FLAGS, GIVE US SOMETHING TO EAT!"

And many more epithets, strictly unprintable, were thrown at the bunch on the dock below. Really, after all, I shared their distaste for such a welcome, only too evidently put on as a "paid for" program by politicians. It seemed like a "hired" exhibition. The welcome we wanted was to be in our homes again. It was still necessary to wait for discharges, and army red tape must slowly unwind, to release us.

At the docks, after marching off the ship, we were herded out to hear a bunch of dry speeches, by politicians, for an hour or so. Finally, we came back on the pier for our packs, and headed out to board a train for Camp Dix.

Just then, entering the pier again, I saw the saddest sight of the whole war. An ambulance was being slowly backed in to where a silent, flag covered stretcher lay awaiting it. We stopped in our tracks while it was loaded, and then pulled out. Every man uncovered, but others pushing behind, not knowing what was happening, yelled, "matter in front? Move on dammit, Lemme see too. Who's sick? Whassa ambulance for?"

Then they saw the silent stretcher, hidden under an American flag. They quieted, stopped and uncovered.

During our crap shooting on board ship, some poor soldier had died, and now with folks at home sadly waiting. Probably they had already been notified. He was leaving the army forever, without the formality of an official discharge. It was sad to think of those folks silently awaiting his return, who had prayed for months for his safe return. Now only to see him nearly in their arms, and then to lose him.

Everybody was anxious to get home. In a few days most of the Sanitary Detachment had left Camp Dix. The 104th was mustered out on the 26th of May with a mess of red tape. I signed up for a two week turn as an office clerk. In return for which service, I was discharged at Camp Dix, received travel pay of 5 cents a mile, clear to Freeport, Illinois. In so doing,

I was but one or two days later in getting home than I would have been, through the regular routine. My greatest gain was that I managed to hide all my souvenirs. Being discharged at Camp Dix, I carried home souvenirs that I otherwise might have lost.

On the 12th of June, I was discharged, receiving more than $129 in pay, and on the 14th, I arrived home. I had refrained from writing during the last two weeks, intending to surprise Mother, so no one met me at the train. I had been gone from November 7th 1917, until June 14th, 1919 without one furlough home. Freeport certainly looked good to me. As I walked up Main St, I glanced about for familiar faces and saw a few. Even to these few, I was just "another soldier". Hero days were over, over six months prior. The home town boys had been discharged a week or so before, and a uniform was now a familiar sight. Also, my 190 lbs of tanned, dark person must have made me nearly a stranger to even those who knew me.

Home again, June 1919 — My brother Henry, a friend, and myself.

21

POST-WAR AND WORKING

Heiny, my stepfather, was the first person that I met in Freeport, that knew me. He was working at the Riverside lunch room, right across the street from the train depot. I dropped in there to see him. He was so proud of me, as any father might have been. After talking to him a few minutes, I phoned to Mother, and though she said but few words over the phone, the break in her voice told me of the tears in her eyes. I talked to her only a few minutes, and then I started walking on up town, leaving my barrack bag at the Riverside. My brother would pick it up later in his taxi.

I passed no one that knew me, and when I got to Chicago Street, I had just missed the Home street car. I decided to walk on out, rather than wait another twenty minutes for the next car. Mother, though, had expected me on that car, and walked part way to meet me, when she saw that I had missed it. We met in the middle, and I kissed her, right there in the street, and then silently we walked back home, together.

That was my homecoming. After those long months of waiting in France, after the war was over, almost 8 months earlier. During the last days I spent in Camp Dix, I had decorated my uniform with fancy service bars, and even the two service stripes, denoting a year overseas. I really rated but one stripe, for we had been over about two weeks less than a year, I had even had my army trousers fitted by a tailor in Camp Dix. I wanted to look neat when I got home. After all that preparation, I ripped that uniform off in one day. It took me that long to find civvies to fit me.

My black broadcloth suit, my best suit in 1917 could still be used, but my brother had worn out the trousers and a new pair cost me $11.50. Odd since the whole suit had cost only five dollars at a special half-price sale in the spring before war was declared.

Mother and the family asked me but few questions about the war. I tried to tell them of various anecdotes, and describe the actual front lines to them. I didn't since I had never been to the front trenches, and life at Vacherauville had been easy. I told them stories about the fun we'd had, about Alsace, Montreux Chateau, and other places.

The next week I hurried on to Minnesota to see my first born, my little daughter. There, as elsewhere, when my wife saw me in civilian clothes, she wanted little of me. She had no use for the hard-boiled "bum" that I was. I, with little money, could only offer to take her and baby Norma Jean with me, whenever I secured a job, if she cared to come. She didn't, and made it plain when she said so.

22

VISITING EVE

Back in Freeport, Mrs. Williams, and Eve called on us one evening, for the express purpose of hearing all about the war. How was I to entertain them with the stories they wanted? I could tell them about Park Field, and Kelly Field, even Jefferson Barracks, other places in America. But they wanted stories of France, stories of war, fighting, and danger. Stories of heroism, and suffering, and things like that. I could tell them little that was interesting, along active lines. True, I had been in an active division, and did have one commendation, for the work at Montreux Chateau. That was perhaps the only anecdote that they liked amongst all I related that evening.

I was not talkative, dared not to be, for I had become accustomed to saying "Damn", "Hell" and other things even worse at every breath. How was I to tell even one good story with such language? I held my tongue, as much as I could. I did try to tell funny anecdotes of happenings in various places but they seemed to fall flat. It was tough to tell stories in the jerky, odd language I was forced to use, and keeping the cuss words off my tongue. Then too, I was dressed in ill-fitting civvies, and knew it. I didn't realize how much my tanned, dark face, hard-boiled attitude and language, needed the backing of neat fitting uniform to set them off.

Before entering the service, my clothes had always been neat, though not expensive. I could wear "ready-made" easily, and so never had a tailored suit. My civvies were for a 140 lb. boy, while now I was a two-hundred-pound, hard-boiled egg. My shirts were too tight, but through some freak of nature, my neck had diminished in size. My old size 15-½" collars were a full size too large. My loose, flabby suit did not feel right. After twenty months in a tight-fitting uniform. Also, my garters felt queer, and my legs seemed to be bare now, after using those snugly wrapped puttees for so long.

I knew full well that I was ill at ease, but I dared not spend much of my precious money for clothes, till I had a job and could pay my way. The ill-fitting suits, shirts, and collars had to do till better times came my way.

I was no war hero, and knew it. I wanted to drop my uniform and be like other men, but I should have worn it for a while longer. As it was, sitting there trying to tell Eve and her mother interesting story of the war, I acted like a caged wild man or half-dazed bum. If only I had known enough to wear my neat fitting uniform, it would have made a suitable background for my hard-boiled attitude and cuss words. My hesitation at telling stories of bravery might have been put down to modesty. One story especially spoiled that night, it was the tale of the pair of corsets.

I had shown my decorated 75mm shells, my pictures and all my little souvenirs, but the only real souvenir of the bunch, was the seal of L'Abbe Willaume of Montplonne. The shells were my pets, but in those long days of waiting after the armistice, many similar ones had lost their value, and now were just decorations. I had thought they would be odd, showing the queer, artistic workmanship of a French soldier whiling away dreary hours in a dugout. With so many imitations out, the shells were doubtful material of interest. They were pretty, and even interesting but not half so wonderful as they might have been, had they been more unusual.

I had some doubts, when I produced those corsets and tried to tell of my mistake in thinking that I was stealing oranges when I picked them from the box. I had more doubts as I saw the unbelieving looks on Mrs. William's and Eve's faces. Those corsets, after being stored for months in my bag, and then suffering the long trip home, looked positively shopworn. It was hard to think of them as coming out of a neat, new container. That story was a dud. In fact, most of my stories were.

I had been in one hot place, Montreux Chateau, but who cares to hear of helpless wounded men, lying there in the night, and dying as they were turned over? Who cares to hear tales of raids on the kitchen, up in the front lines, or stories of the chocolates that we missed, and other such things? I had killed no Germans, been in no hand-to-hand fights, and though I had been at the front, I had not been in the true front lines. Our casualty list in Vacherauville was too small to call it a dangerous place. From my stories of the front, it was a picnic spot, where one loafed away the days telling stories, and stole cans of syrup and jam. I could not tell, in my halting, jerky language, of the sleepless nights, in the small dugout, under that roof of loose rock. Nor of the dreaded shrapnel tinkling down day-after-day, nor the long hours of waiting in dread for the shells that never came. I could have described the dreaded hours of waiting, listening to shells go over, waiting for the one that might get us, but never did. I could have described the hardships of long marches, poor billets, and irregular, poorly cooked food, but would I have done it?

Certainly not, for why play myself as an exception, when thousands upon thousands of other chaps had suffered far more than I. They had marched farther, stood in the rain longer, gone on a canned "corned bill" diet more often, and stayed at the front days to my hours? True, I had been "Over There", but after all, thousands upon thousands of other boys had also seen service.

Yes, there were a lot of things I wished to tell, but dared not, lest I tell them wrong. And, bitterly, I knew when Eve nodded a short goodbye, that the hero in her heart was not me. For long hours in France had I dreamed of her welcome, if and when I might be single again. And now, knowing that someday I probably would be, I wanted to ask her to wait for me. My months of service I had thought would be my penance. Perhaps, marching home at last, I might be once more in her favor,

But now, in a short, hour talk, I had ruined my chance.

Dumbly I knew it then, and knew it better a few months later, when Eve married the farmer in Indiana but it was three full years before I entirely realized where and how I had made my mistakes.

23

BACK TO WORK AND THE FIVE AND TEN

I worked a few weeks in Freeport, at the Stephen's plant, where the Saliant Six automobile was built. I was an ordinary laborer. Finally, an old friend Sprague, in the Chicago office of the Woolworth Company, found me an opening as stockman in a Rock Island store. So, there I went, back once more in the Five and Ten. I lasted as stockman but a few short weeks and then got my chance as a floorman, or assistant manager, as it was called. That really began my education.

I had never had money to spend on girls, and so never had many feminine friends. While associating with girls in the Five and Ten cent ought to educate a boy, the stockman in dirty, ragged clothes is no gift, so the girls had passed me by. Also, as a stockman, I took orders from the girls, and had to fetch and carry almost as they desired. As a floorman, I bossed the bunch, so they looked up to me. By daily contact, I began to "wise up" on many points of feminine human nature. Slow-minded I might be and was, I always had my eyes open, and tried to figure out a reason for everything that happened. Where girls had been a thing of dread, after I came home, they now began to be a thing of interest. Sometimes.

My weekly pay was only $15, and when my board, laundry, and other bills were paid, I had but little left to spend. That usually went to some pool hall. Weeks rolled by and as my pool and billiard playing grew better and better, those games cost me less. I won instead of losing. In addition to my skills there, I won at dice so that by Christmas time, I usually carried a five-dollar box of candy to some girl every week. It seldom cost me more than a dollar, but it was an impressive gift, and at one or two homes, I was popular. I had to be reserved, for I was still a married man, and did not hide that fact. The girls who coveted my candy boxes were usually gold diggers. There were nice girls too, in many ways, but often, gold diggers in others.

No wise girl gets infatuated over, or with a fifteen dollar a week clerk, so I was safe. The kind of girls that might have thought me a prize didn't get a chance to say so, for they were the kind I avoided.

There was little Cleo, for instance, engaged to a chap in Chicago. She was glad to receive my candy gift, and moaning about her neighbors, she related, "In Chicago, my fellow used to bring me lots of things, but if he did it here, the neighbors would have a fit. Why Charley used to buy me stockings and silk underwear, way before we were engaged. The neighbors didn't think a thing of it, either, but out here, they'd call for the police."

Yes, Cleo hinted, pretty strongly, for "Other presents" but my $15 a week, didn't reach that far. Cleo was a nice girl, too, as girls go, but an absolute gold digger, and independent too. One night Charley came out from Chicago, and she spent two solid hours riding around the Loop, on the street car, just by herself, and only for the purpose of kidding the motorman. Then she went home to Charley, and made him take her to a show. The next night, when he was gone, she told me all about it, laughing it off as a good joke on Charley.

"I gotta teach him that he don't own me, yet, just because I'm wearing a five hundred dollar diamond of his," she said, and I figured that poor Charley would always have to wait, now and later, if she ever married him. She had him trained.

Then there was Bella, another extra girl, whom I dated a while, until she went to work at another store. Bella, short and piquant, yet so extremely modest that she wouldn't dare kiss me goodnight. She avoided dark corners, smutty suggestions or jokes like the plague. Yes, she was modest, very, very modest, in fact, too damned modest to be sure. A girl in this day and age, going with a man separated from his wife, and someday expecting a divorce. Bella's folks went on a trip one weekend, and when I phoned, she wasn't home. Later, the neighbors told how she had kept house, that weekend, with a well-known gangster. Someone peeked in, under drawn shades and saw them. So that ended the too modest girl, Bella.

All-in-all, I learned a lot in a year in Rock Island, and once more began to walk the streets with head up, able to talk to anyone, without being tongue-tied. The fear of making a mistake, or cursing at an inappropriate time, was gone. I learned not to fear the girls, for they liked to be bossed, a bit, and I learned to watch them, at odd times, and see their reactions to certain situations.

The busy, bustling life in a Five and Ten store, is an education to any person, man or woman. To me, a man in years, but a bashful boy in experience, it was an education indeed. I was a good worker, learned readily, and from Mother, I had the gift for tasty arrangement of articles in trimming the window bays, or counters. I progressed quite satisfactorily, till that day in August, when I disagreed with the manager, and after a trip to the Chicago offices, was transferred to Store 4, right downtown at 219 South State Street, in the busy Loop itself.

Those first days there, in charge of the basement sales floor, were filled to the brim with excitement, but I soon fell in with their busy, bustling, hurried ways, and so accommodated myself to their stride. I readily learned my duties, and did them well, but most of all I learned that there are different classes and kinds of girls. The bunch in Rock Island had given me a primary education. These mostly hard-boiled eggs topped that rural education off.

Not all these girls were hard-boiled, for our regular crew were, as a rule, pretty good, the extra girls were fierce. They could swear like a sailor, steal anything, and the sky was the limit, though they would go even further, if asked to. I forgot how to blush, there in the Loop store, for many a sweet looking angel, would mouth words that left even me with a bad taste in my mouth. One little queen, whose name I never learned, came in one morning, with a bunch of newly hired girls and she was dressed like a mannequin.

She was tiny and petite, an ashy blonde, with a well-formed face and body. Neat as a pin, with her clothes and wearing a dress of creamy satin, so heavy and expensive that it shimmered like silver.

Creamy silk hose, and jeweled pumps, completed her costume, and Lord how I wanted to slip my arm around that tiny bunch of sweetness! She looked like a millionaire's daughter, playing at a job. Two days later, she tore the satin skirt, a full ten inches, right down the front. All day long, she wore it that way, with white satin bloomers showing through the rip. She didn't even stop to pin it up! The next day, it was still gaping open, and the next day also. That night the floor lady fired her, without waiting for my permission. Why? Well, not because of the dress, but because she "stunk" so, that no other girl would work with her. Apparently, she wore her clothes till they fell off, and never took a bath. Appearances sure are deceitful, sometimes.

For some girls, the Five and Ten store was merely place to show off, to wear good clothes, and meet and "get" a fellow. And yet others worked there to earn a living. True, their pay is small, way small, but then, it is the old rule of supply and demand. I used to expect a clerk to be perfect, but for the $8 per week a girl receives, they are seldom or never are good. When she does learn the job, some other store offers her more, and she graduates on. The Five and Ten wanted girls from homes living under their parent's wing, girls wanting to work for fun, or extra money. They got just what they paid for. At first, I used to pity the girls, I still pity some, but not all. Some, through the luck of life, can earn but that small weekly wage, and must live on it. The bulk of the girls graduate on, either to better paid positions or to matrimony.

Even hard-boiled girls have good hearts, and I often found that the "good sport" was the kindest, most sensible girl, of any behind my counters. Usually you could trust her, with small work details and she seldom fought with other girls. If anything, she was a better, with her mind less on outside topics, and less interested in the good-looking men going by. And, for loyalty this type took the cake.

I received one shock in Chicago, and that was, one day, when a husky business-like chap pulled me aside. He read a court summons into my ear. I was being sued for divorce. I had just about forgotten it, except in unpleasant dreams, that I was still married. True, I made no secret of it, and all the store girls knew it. The deadening depression of dreaming about it, wondering what I could do, and how and when to process it, had gradually left me. I was just ignoring that problem, and now it jumped out at me. I could do nothing, and after finding out that the summons was an empty gesture, a mere notification, I dropped all ideas of doing anything. I had no money, and anyway, just what could, or would I have done, if I had been able? Eventually, I filed for divorce, since we'd been apart so long, and I was tired of the shadow of it over my head.

Day-by-day I learned, made mistakes, and then corrected them, whenever possible. Each day's observations broadened my outlook. My work went along fine, and someday I hoped to get a store to manage myself. I would have a good salary I thought. Just before I got my store, I found that whereas I was now getting $30 per week, a small store manager often got less. Of course, he was in line for promotion to better paid positions if he was successful.

My first store to manage was in Sturgeon Bay, Wisconsin in 1921. I proceeded to bust the records there that year. It was a large store, but in a small town, and did the smallest business of any store in the Chicago district. That is, until that year, for I boosted it by 16%, and put it past two other stores. My reward was $1800 for the year, and an added store in Antigo, Wisconsin.

Sturgeon Bay was a small city of 4,500 people, during the winter months. In summer, when the tourists came in, every house turned into a hotel. Overnight, it became a city of ten thousand, with trade drawing in clear from the north Eskimo village, across the famous "Death's Door", on down to Green Bay. Tourists and CHERRIES. Sturgeon Bay is famous for those two things. It has ringing it, Door County, on the peninsula, the world's largest cherry orchards. At picking time, trainload after trainload of pickers arrive, some from states far off. They spend a profitable vacation, picking cherries in the mornings, to pay expenses, then loafing, swimming, and fishing in the afternoon. On Saturday nights, they all come to town. Indeed, my Chicago experiences came in handy. My store was prepared for the mob, and we did a fine business!

Those cherry pickers were a mixture. Many were high school or college students with a few local Indians mixed in. There were also quite a few school teachers in the crowds, since they were off for the summer. The system of handling them was similar to that in the army. Each large orchard had its own barracks; one for girls and one for boys. Even meals are served right there, for a minimum price. It seemed funny that they kept these large barracks, all through the year, just for 2-3 weeks of picking. Then again, those cherries must be picked, and the barracks supported getting results.

I learned one thing from those cherry pickers, and that was that the rowdiest boys and girls here, were often the nicest at home. That applied especially to girls, for the boy who is a leader in devilry in his home town, generally is repeated here. Sometimes the nice girl, who was repressed or held down at home, celebrate their freedom when away. That is true especially in boarding houses, at school or college. Any place where young people gather without the guidance of nearby parents. Many incidents in the army illustrated that but this was the first time I had seen girls celebrating.

Sturgeon Bay with its beauties, gave way to Antigo, with no open water nearby, was remote, and I missed the Bay then. I broadened out in Antigo, for now, after a year's hard work in the Bay, I began to feel more secure of myself as a manager. I began to slack up a bit, enjoy time, and to observe things about me. One of the first things that I did was to learn to dance. Often, after trimming windows till nine or ten p.m., I would slip out to a dance hall, and dance till midnight.

I went to about two dances every week, but never took a girl. I was neatly dressed, feeling sure of myself, and with money in my pocket for once. I danced usually with anyone I fancied, who would take a chance on the floor with me. Not much chance, though, for I was a good waltzer, and a fair dancer at other steps. Those dances were another large part of my education.

All through Northern Wisconsin, dotted here and there, between all the summer resorts, there are dance halls. People come to regular weekly dances from all around. The crowd usually consisted of a few local town folks, and a bunch of tourists. The mystery, and attraction of it all is that one seldom knows whether a strange partner is a millionaire, or a mere clerk. I might dance once with some poor stenographer, having two weeks of vacation on a year's savings, and dressed to kill. The next dance, I'd pick some backward little girl, plainly dressed, like a local girl dressed up, only to find she might be a Governor's daughter. That type of mystery, and excitement, with the addition of very good music, is the chief attraction of these dance halls.

The railroad strike came in 1922. Just ahead of the strike, the city fathers of Antigo had planned on improvements, and had the main street torn up, ready for paving. Antigo is supported, in part, by the division point there on the Northwestern RR, and by its repair shop also located there. Rather than put a taxation burden to the workers, or strikers, the whole main street was left just as it was. Dug up its whole length, and a block each way for months, until the strike was settled. Naturally, that street being dug up and blocked off did not help my store sales any.

The office expected results, just the same, paved or not. Several times during the year I was called in to the Chicago office, along with other men whose stores were not doing so good. While we were assembled there, Billy Rand, the district chief, would ask us as a body, not to give excuses.

"Now understand men," he would say, "I don't want any excuses from you managers. What I do want is to hear constructive plans and promises to increase sales. We have assembled here to find out, if possible, of any way in which the superintendents, buyers, or any of the office men, can help you get out of the X column, and show a gain in sales. (Every one of the managers there, had a decrease in sales for that year, as compared to the corresponding period in the previous year. The decreases were prefaced by an "X" mark on the report.) Now, I am going to ask each one of you in turn to get up, and tell just why you haven't been getting results, and how you expect to change your methods in order to make a gain. Remember, no excuses."

Really, we poor fish there, ought to have mobbed him after such a speech. "No excuses accepted", and yet have the nerve the next minute to ask what the matter was. Another manager was in a similar fix to mine. A store was under construction next to his, shutting off the sidewalk there. When he tried to tell Rand of that shutoff, he was met with a storm about "no excuses."

It took me a few months to figure out any reason for that series of meeting being conducted so. The only real, constructive detail of these meetings was that an opportunity was given these managers to talk together and get ideas from each other. We did talk some, outside of the meetings, but usually we followed some chap who had discovered a speak easy that was handy. Prohibition started in 1920, bars did not exist, the speak easy did. One trip I remember was to a wide open speak easy, right in an alley, a bare half block off the busiest section of State Street. Certainly, that place had protection, to sell beer right over the counter, at two bits a stein or glass. They also had "tea", or diluted moonshine, at six bits for a tiny thimble-sized glass. The moonshine was carried in teapot, so the name "tea" was used.

However, the strike finally ended, and I had suffered along with a hostile Superintendent, till the year was up. I got my check for $2,000 for an entire year. My drawing allowance was $25 a week but that was charged up to me, and deducted at the end of the year. My pay was based on being 20% of the net profits, and net meant net. Even the pay of the office men was deducted before the net was taken. Each store was charged a percentage of the operating costs of the executive offices. Thus, in effect, after all the profits, the manager received one-fifth and the stockholders nearly four-fifths.

The next spring, 1923, I bought a cheap second-hand roadster, and managed to visit nearby managers at times. On one visit to a friend, Wilson. I mentioned salary, thinking that $2,000 a year was pretty good, but he laughed at me.

"Two thousand is pretty good for Woolworth, yes, but in Kresge's, the manager's percent is always fifty percent of the first six thousand dollars of net profit. So, any Kresge's manager gets half as much again. On top of the three thousand dollars, there is usually a twenty, fifteen or ten percent addition, out of all profit over six thousand. Even then, just figure out what you make a week, and average an hourly wage, then compare it with what a plumber or carpenter makes."

"Why that's easy," I said, and got busy. Two thousand a year makes about $38.50 a week. Let's see, I put in about ten to twelve hours a day, counting window trimming, for six days. That makes sixty or seventy hours a week. Yes, with Christmas work, all through December, I'll average easily seventy hours a week. That makes, —why, doggonit, that only makes fifty or fifty-one cents an hour!"

I was surprised, figuring it that way, to see how little I received. Of course, I had figured it often before, but always I had stopped at the weekly figure. Somehow, I had never figured it out by the hour.

"Sure, about fifty-cents an hour." Wilson chuckled. "There are but few white-collar jobs that pay really good wages. Here you spend four to six years, usually with the same long hours you are now working, to bet fifty-cents an hour. A plumber or carpenter, or almost any working man, engaged at a trade, spends only fifty hours a week, often less, at work. They get a starting wage of from twenty-five to fifty-cents an hour. After only a year or two as an apprentice, he can obtain a dollar an hour or more for his efforts. That makes his weekly wage about fifty dollars a week. Sometimes more, sometimes less, depending on the trade and hours worked."

"But, after all," I countered, "He may get that much year-after-year, but he has no chance for advancement, such as we have. Why, if I am lucky, and make a success at this game, I'll be earning five or six thousand dollars a year soon."

That observation made Wilson laugh. "Yeh, you think that a tradesman has but little chance for advancement, do you? How about starting his own business, or acting as foreman, or manager, for some other chap? A carpenter who cares to work, can soon start out as a contractor, and hire other men to work for him. Why many contractors, and poor ones at that, make ten thousand a year. And how many years do you think you will have to work to get that much? Also, figuring the number of managers in this company, each aiming high, how good are your chances to get to the top? I'll admit, I kick myself every time I think of the way I have worked to get as far as I am, while in a pair of overalls I might be making twice what I am today. Of course, if and when anything ever does happen to put me out of this business, I believe my experience will help me a lot in any other line. If I had started out as, say an apprentice carpenter, I might now be making twenty-thousand a year as a contractor. Yes, I believe that with the same attention and study that I have used in learning this business, I would be making that or more. I know it, I'm sure of it, but yet, I'm one of those dogs that have to be kicked into anything before I'll change my habits enough to start all over. I expect that unless I am kicked into other work, I'll still stay in the Five and Ten store for life. I'm too old now to start again."

Wilson's talk set me to thinking in a new line. I had been so wrapped up in my work, that I had paid but little attention to other trades, and did not know what other men earned. Now I began to keep my eyes and ears open, and soon found that Wilson was right. Other trades had doubled and tripled their wages. After the war, or during it, while the managers of the Five and Ten cent stores were on the whole getting the same, though the stores themselves were earning more.

And thus, my life continued, well after the war. Working for the Five and Ten, still convinced I was too old to begin anew with a different career. That did happen but it took years, after I trained as a CPA. I divorced Miss Marion by mail and court. She raised baby Norma Jean, and remarried, having another family.

I was in Sturgeon Bay, Wisconsin, and in early 1922, met Grace Chandler. We dated through that tourist season. Her father was a dentist there, and encouraged us to develop into a serious relation but maybe he was concerned his daughter was aging, and at ten years older than me, felt she'd be a spinster forever.

Together we enjoyed the summer, fishing, the lake shore, and the summer dances. On August 21, 1922, as a 25-year-old man, Grace and I married. I'd developed my inner-strength, call it what you will, nerve, fortitude, or self-confidence. All through my adult life, and I would need it in my married life, career and family. This is true for us all, develop it in youth and build on it for your future endeavors. Grace and I had two lovely children, Adah Jane born on March 26th, 1924, and a fine young man, Marion Leath, on July 13th in 1928. Adah became a pharmacist, and Marion served in the US Army in Korea.

Life was good; building and caring for a family demanded more nerve.

THE END

NOTES

The Meuse-Argonne Offensive was a part of the final Allied offensive of World War I. It was one of the attacks that brought an end to the War and was fought from September 26–November 11, 1918, when the Armistice was signed.

The M-Argonne Offensive was the largest operations of the American Expeditionary Forces (AEF) in World War I, with over a million American soldiers participating. It was also the deadliest campaign in American history, resulting in over 26,000 soldiers being killed in action (KIA) and over 120,000 total casualties. Indeed, the number of graves in the American military cemetery at Romagne is far larger than those in the more commonly known site at Omaha Beach in Normandy.

Verdun Cathedral now.

www.ingramcontent.com/pod-product-compliance
Lightning Source LLC
Chambersburg PA
CBHW011150290426
44109CB00025B/2553